ELUSIVE ADULTHOODS

ELUSIVE ADULTHOODS

THE ANTHROPOLOGY OF NEW MATURITIES

EDITED BY DEBORAH DURHAM
AND JACQUELINE SOLWAY

INDIANA UNIVERSITY PRESS

This book is a publication of

Indiana University Press
Office of Scholarly Publishing
Herman B Wells Library 350
1320 East 10th Street
Bloomington, Indiana 47405 USA

iupress.indiana.edu

The paper used in this publication meets the minimum requirements of
the American National Standard for Information Sciences—Permanence of
Paper for Printed Library Materials, ANSI Z39.48-1992.

Manufactured in the United States of America

Cataloging information is available from the Library of Congress.

ISBN 978-0-253-02973-7 (cloth)
ISBN 978-0-253-03000-9 (paperback)
ISBN 978-0-253-03019-1 (ebook)

1 2 3 4 5 22 21 20 19 18 17

CONTENTS

ACKNOWLEDGMENTS

THIS BOOK STARTED with a double session at the annual meeting of the American Anthropological Association in November 2013 in Chicago, Illinois. Although not all participants in that session could join in the edited publication, their papers at that session and our discussions of all our papers over meals and emails enriched our understanding of how anthropologists can approach the study of adulthood. We want to thank Jocelyn Chua, Jennifer Cole, Samuli Schielke, and Xia Sharon Zhang for their participation and conversation. The two discussants for the panel, Susan McKinnon and Brad Weiss, also gave us wonderful feedback and suggestions, and we gratefully thank them and audience members who asked stimulating questions. We are indebted to Susan Reynolds Whyte for her generous reading and review of the manuscript as a whole and her rich set of suggestions. Dennis Rogers provided thoughtful, detailed, and extensive discussion of an early version of the introduction that in revision helped guide all the authors. Gary Dunham and Janice Frisch of Indiana University Press offered encouragement and editorial support for which we are grateful. Judith K. Brown's work on women through the life cycle from childhood to seniority has been an inspiration to us. Keith Adams and Michael Lambek have been our most keen supporters and interlocutors through our fieldwork to the stages of this book. Finally but with deep gratitude, we want to thank our contributors, who put up with endless suggestions and requests from us, and offered us their rich ethnographic analyses and insights.

ELUSIVE ADULTHOODS

ELUSIVE ADULTHOODS

Introduction

Deborah Durham

THE TWENTY-FIRST CENTURY seems at its outset to be the century of elusive adulthoods.[1] We hear reports that young people cannot grow up, that they cannot attain adulthood. In urban Zambia, young people are "stuck in the compound" living with parents (Hansen 2005); in Rwanda they are stuck outside of the compound, unable to build the separate household in the family plot needed to move into adulthood (Sommers 2012). In North and Sub-Saharan Africa, youth are said to be caught in a period of "waithood" unable to attain social adulthood well into their thirties (Honwana 2012; Singerman 2013). More ominously, Henrik Vigh (2006) describes young men in Guinea-Bissau as in a state of "social death," a liminal social space with no exit. In India, middle-class young men are mired in "timepass," enrolling in advanced degree after advanced degree at second-rate universities, dabbling in campus politics or just sitting around drinking tea, unable to find the employment they seek (Jeffrey 2010); in Ethiopia, young men say they "live like chickens," just eating and sleeping, waiting but not progressing into adulthood (Mains 2007). In Japan, people worry about "parasite singles" enamored of the comforts of their parents' home and wary of an employment landscape that no longer promises stability, long after their ceremonial inauguration into adulthood at the age of twenty-one (Brinton 2011; Newman 2012). In China, young people have gone tribal: the "gnawing the elderly tribe" lives off their parents' and grandparents' dwindling resources (Zhang 2013), while an "ant tribe" is un- or under-employed in the cities (see Kipnis this volume) and a "moonlight clan" (Schott 2011) spends its entire income every month, instead of scrimping and saving as their parents did. In post-Soviet Georgia, young men hang around, "growing old without growing up," the path to a successful adulthood unclear in the temporal and spatial reorientations of the post-Soviet state (Frederiksen 2013).

In the United States, too, the elusiveness of adulthood is widely reported and studied, and the subject of many popular advice books and comedic films. Where college graduation is commonly held to be a threshold to adulthood, debt, inadequate jobs, instability in careers, and an increasingly late average age of marriage are said to make it difficult for people to cross the threshold and be considered truly adult (Settersten et al. 2008). These factors burden those who do not go to college as well as those who do, perhaps more so. Members of the working class may struggle without the family support that might help house them, support them in further education or training, or meet debt payments (Silva 2013). Whether the problem is structural, as statistics about jobs and debt suggest, or psychological, as blame is laid on a new generation of "narcissists" unable to resolve their "quarterlife crisis" (Robbins and Wilner 2001; Twenge and Campbell 2010), the American millennials are often depicted as a boomerang generation, stuck in their parents' basements, "failing to launch" and refusing responsibility. Jeffrey Arnett (2004) has detected in them a new psychological stage of life, between adolescence and adulthood proper. He labels their experience "emerging adulthood," a period shaped by ongoing fluidity and experimentation, an extension of the time of becoming, taking place before commitments are made to being a certain kind of person and self. Fortunately, for those struggling with the "transition to adulthood" in all its dimensions, there is a long and growing shelf of advice books at the bookshop. These range from the 2001 *Quarterlife Crisis* by Alexandra Robbins and Abby Wilner, describing the twenties in terms analogous to the already recognized mid-life crisis, to Kelly Williams Brown's more recent *Adulting: How to Become a Grown-up in 468 Easy(ish) Steps*, which both urges its readers to recognize that they are not "special snowflakes" and helps them understand and negotiate apartment rentals and vacuuming, call in a plumber, and get along with coworkers (Brown 2013; Robbins and Wilner 2001). Parents of this generation now have their own how-to manuals, with the publication of Julie Lythcott-Haims's *How to Raise an Adult* in 2015, responding to fears that this generation of Americans has been educated by overzealous parenting into perpetual childhood (Twenge 2006). The humor and self-deprecation often present in these books, however, belies the very real struggles and sense of social dislocation felt by many people in their twenties and thirties in America, even while laying considerable blame on individuals and their parents for not taking the responsibility themselves to grow up.

The distribution of these complaints and anxieties around the world raises the question of what adulthood means to those who feel they cannot attain it. Has adulthood changed, perhaps in the course of those processes known as globalization—a linked restructuring of economies, sharing of ideas through media and consumer practices, and the global spread of age-disciplinary institutions, including Western models of citizenship, education, and health that overtake local ones? At the very least, the scope of political and economic changes has disrupted the "traditional" life course everywhere, even as what is thought of as traditional can be either invented traditions (Hobsbawm 1983) or deeply rooted perduring practices. In the United States, the adulthood that is bemoaned emerged in its idealized and normative form in the 1950s, and unraveled soon after. Yet it is that limited form of adulthood that is often the index of proper adulthood in America and, some suggest, in other parts of the world.[2] In some parts of the world, it can seem that nostalgia for a lost path to adulthood is borrowed from the United States, as are other borrowed nostalgias that speak to very local concerns about ethnic difference or rural lifeways (e.g., Appadurai 1996: 29–31; Ferguson 2010), or as borrowed life stages are used to reimagine local difficulties (Weiss 2002). In other places, neoliberal changes have wrenched away the paths to a newly formulated adulthood that were built in the postcolonial era, which linked new middle-class lives to new kinds of maturation. In Madagascar, for one example, a weakened government led to diminishing white-collar opportunity, diminished educational systems, and the need for young people to seek other ways of developing their social maturity, including seeking it abroad (Cole 2010).

Sociologists and policy makers trace the achievement of adulthood through a set of measurable variables, which in a 1950s ideal happened in sync but are now out of sync: finishing schooling, securing a career-track job, marrying, establishing an independent household, and (sometimes) having children (see, e.g., Settersten et al. 2008). Among these variables, it is jobs that stand out most prominently in the many reports of elusive adulthood, because the income from jobs supports the new household, marriage, and children, and also because career-oriented jobs are thought to mark the end of the period of formal education. Settling into a career is important for more psychological models of attaining adulthood, too, as adulthood is reached through a consolidation of the ego-identity around a set of commitments, to vocation, to a sexual partner, and to an ideology, after a period of experimentation (see Erikson 1968). Many of the anxieties about adulthood reported from around the world focus primarily on jobs and income, from the ant tribes of Beijing, to the desperate African migrants crossing the Mediterranean to Europe, to the troglodyte Americans in their parents' basements. Yet is the predicament of a twenty-seven-year-old in the United States, burdened by college debt and living with parents, contemplating yet another new career path, feeling unprepared emotionally to take on the risk of family entanglements or even self-responsibility, the same as the predicament of a twenty-seven-year-old ex-combatant in urban Bissau unable to find any source of income to support a growing number of children as well as the siblings and parents he has left in their home in rural Guinea? Or the same as the predicament of their well-educated age-mate in Sri Lanka for whom only certain kinds of jobs can confer the status needed to marry an appropriate spouse? Or, indeed, the same as that of a female age-peer with a professional degree in Turkey, deferring marriage for the financial independence of a career, adult in one domain but not another (Önder Erol forthcoming)? And is it only the financial predicament faced by young people that constrains them, as media coverage so often implies, or is it more complicated in the way in which adulthood is configured, recognized, and questioned in the overlapping spaces of their local, national, and global environments? The connection between jobs and a meaningful adulthood is far more complex than simple income, as several of the chapters in this volume attest, even as that connection both persists and varies in form and content around the world.

Sociologists have been calling for an investigation of changing ideas of adulthood for over forty years, with major calls to action every five years or so (Blatterer 2007: 3). Sociological work focuses on young people, called either youth or young adults, on the threshold of what has become widely known as an increasingly problematic "transition to adulthood." A debate has emerged whether a "linear" transitions model, based on a life course assumed to be unchanging in general outline, should be replaced by a "generations" model that takes as its focus historical changes in what constitutes a life stage or an expected life course (Roberts 2007; Vandegrift 2015; Wyn and Woodman 2006). The phrase "social adulthood" is frequently used to indicate that it is a socially defined and recognized status, independent of age. At the same time sociological studies often do connect it with biological age, as the charts measuring age at which various things are accomplished in "transitions" approaches, and as historical generations identified by standard age brackets attest. Biological age is important to the biopolitics made famous by Michel Foucault. It is important when predicaments are bemoaned or policies are proposed to address too-young adulthoods, as when quite young people were asked to support financially weakened families in 1980s America (Newman 1988), or teenagers were heading impoverished households in Zimbabwe (Reynolds 1991), or young people were forced to participate in combat. Biological age also underlies anxieties about older not-yet-adults such as the American boomerang kids (Newman 2012), or the Africans in waithood (Honwana 2012). In both these cases (too-young, too-old adulthoods), age serves powerful normalizing functions when brought into conjunction with ideas of "social adulthood."

The recent Western phase of "emerging adulthood" has been introduced, it seems, to mediate between a biological idea of the life course, with adolescence understood as a critical psycho-biological phase, and an idea of the life course organized around socially constructed statuses. Two large-scale studies of the shifting nature and meaning of adulthood have recently been undertaken in the United States (see Settersten et al. 2008) and Britain (Thomson et al. 2004): both focus on the set of measurable variables (career, marriage, household, etc.), on chronological age, and also on how young people worry about, rethink, or do not think about adulthood. Looking at Western societies, Blatterer (2007) suggests that a true investigation into how people conceptualize and experience their adulthoods today must understand the increasing importance of individuation and of the individualization of the life course in the midst of multiplying options—in sum, the fragmented and creative ways in which people are developing ways of being adult in the here and now. With the proliferation of ways of being adult, he notes, a key aspect of adulthood—social recognition of adulthood—is now internalized, relocated from a set of external sources of age credential validation to a personal, interior, feeling.

Sociologists, psychologists, and historians have all taken up the cause of adulthood. But anthropologists have not. Robert LeVine (1980) once noted that even as anthropologists typically studied adults—or people they considered adults—and wrote about adult life, they did not study adulthood. Reacting to the fact that adults have been the focus of anthropological research, there is now a rich and growing literature not only on children or young people, but also on childhood, youth, and old age, and members of the American Anthropological Association have organized formal interest groups for these subjects. Edited books on age groups in anthropology look at children, youth, or the elderly, but do not include chapters on adulthood (see Cole and Durham 2007; Kertzer and Keith 1984; La Fontaine 1978). There may be good reasons for this—the frequently noted predominance of research on those we consider adults, against which these other groups are marked out, and the (less noted) lack of a concept of "adulthood" in other societies that is equivalent to the Western category. Yet there are also good reasons for anthropologists to raise questions about adulthood now in societies around the world.

In fact, anthropologists routinely invoke the terms "adulthood" and "adult" in their studies. This is especially the case in those studies of youth, many mentioned at the outset of this introduction, for whom adulthood is said to be elusive. Often the term is used casually to refer to people whose age would make them adults in the West. But the term can also arise in surprising ways.

For example, Marc Schloss (1988) wrote about an initiation ceremony in 1979 among Ehing people in Senegal that took place only every twenty-five years. Because of the interval, a five-year-old might be initiated (so as not to wait until he is thirty), and as a consequence be entitled to knowledge of sex and death, and given rights and responsibilities as an adult, which a forty-year-old, who might have been away when the Kombutsu ceremony was last held, is not. We might, of course, wonder how seriously such attributions are taken. Meru women in Tanzania working in urban jobs reinstituted female initiations, complete with circumcision, in order to be publicly recognized as adults at work and at home (Nypan 1991): to them, at least, it was quite a serious matter.

Why is adulthood now such a serious matter, showing up in scholarly and media reports from around the world? What is at stake in achieving adulthood that so many people seem so anxious to attain it, or to see their children attain it (as it is not always the young themselves who are complaining)? What other ways do people experience maturity, seek it, avoid it, or attempt to reformulate it? To approach such questions, we must think about adulthood (or other forms of recognized maturity) as an always emergent, meaningful experience in a social, historical context that spans local and global, home and world. Anthropology, a field that examines meaning making in these varied yet interrelated contexts, is especially suited to the task of studying adulthood, as the chapters in this volume show. What is more, the set of measurable variables to which sociologists have pinned adulthood are classic fields for anthropologists, who have long examined their differences and historically shifting meanings around the world. Marriage and the formation of households, parenthood, generational relationships, debt and obligation, rights to property and labor, the nature and experience of work, rites of passage, differentiated forms of personhood, and the sense of selfhood have long absorbed anthropologists. Core emerging anthropological topics, including citizenship, the state, modern schools, gender and intersectionality, work, and consumer practices in the new global economy, interconnect deeply with an emerging meaning of elusive adulthood. Studies of elusive adulthood have focused largely on the experiences of youth (see, e.g., Christiansen et al. 2006), and the constraints and problems they experience *as youth* yearning to move up. Much as in the old *Peanuts* cartoons, where adults are represented only as voice bubbles coming from outside the frame, adulthood is articulated in anthropology primarily in youth studies.

Chapters in this volume bring adulthood back into the frame, and examine a range of ways in which adulthood or other forms of maturity are experienced and questioned in changing circumstances. Because adulthood comes most into focus in local discourses when it is elusive, several of the chapters do focus on youth seeking adulthood. Others look at the difficulties people have in sustaining recognition as adults, or a feeling of being adult. Yet others ask how older people struggle to consolidate their adulthood as they seek to make further transitions in their lives, transitions that are their own but depend on relationships with others whose adulthood is unstable. For all, the stakes are high, but these stakes, if we stay with the metaphor, play out in different arenas. Not all are seeking an adulthood in terms that would be recognizable in the United States or Europe. For some, other terms for maturity—such as moral agency, the term used by Karen Sykes in her chapter—speak more accurately to local concerns. Yet at the same time, those seeking moral agency in Sykes's chapter counterpose their idea of a mature agency embedded in households to a recognized notion of adulthood mobilized by their own government, by international agencies, and by a preceding generation evaluating national maturity for their country. Each chapter deals with the dilemma of working with local concepts in its own way, yet much as anthropologists have puzzled over the various ways in which men and women link their lives, and call them all "marriage," these chapters do all address something that shares features with "adulthood."

In the rest of this introduction, I present some suggestions on ways to think about adulthood that take us beyond worrying whether people are attaining it or not. I talk about how the term has seemed the "unmarked normal" against which deviations are marked out, especially in Western thought. A quick look at the idea of adulthood in US history reveals the extent to which operations of exclusion and power were vested in the concept as it emerged in the nineteenth century, and as it became entangled with ideas of developmentalism and progressivism. There are many lenses through which to examine productively something like adulthood: in the following sections I draw attention to temporalities, to how discourses of adulthood index other fields of meaning and power, and to forms of recognition. But all of these, and other lenses that can be brought to bear, ultimately lead to two questions: what does adulthood mean to people in their lived lives, and why does it seem so important to many people today?

MARKING ADULTHOOD

If you ask people in the United States what adulthood is, they are often surprised to find that they cannot describe it to their satisfaction, although they readily recognize and use the term (Côté 2000: 1, 48). It is an "unmarked" category that has, until recently, encompassed a normalized condition, framed by various marked conditions, marked by their deviation from that normal and encompassing one.[3] The unmarked term "man" (as in "the family of man") both encompassed women and children, for example, and remained the general term against which the others were marked out in situations where that marking signaled lack, inequalities, and dominance. The concept of adulthood in the mid-twentieth-century West was a normalized condition, still predominantly male, that seemed general, and did not need scrutiny. We see this in medical research, which studied adult males to understand heart disease, obesity, or other conditions as they afflicted everyone, including women and children. Studies of heart disease still refer to a male-dominant adult population, while women's heart disease is a specialized field. Adulthood seems to refer to the entirety of the human life after adolescence, a generalized normality, and people in the West are continually marking segments of it that do not conform to its implication of dominant normality—young adults, the middle-aged, and third-agers as prominent cases in point. Today, adulthood as a normalized fully developed human condition is still a screen against which lack is noted (the complaints recorded around the world speak to that) and it is also a concept that itself is becoming marked by scrutiny, and often creative reshaping.

English is one of the few Western languages to have the word itself, "adulthood," or a word mapping neatly onto it (Côté 2000: 13). Cheryl Merser (1987) notes that the word "adulthood" appeared in the Oxford English Dictionary (OED) only in 1870. ("Adult" appeared in 1656, but probably came into use by the fifteenth century, along with the first appearance of "adolescent," of which it is the past participle of the Latin cognate.) And it can be argued that adulthood per se is a concept that emerged in the nineteenth century and flourished in the twentieth; some feel it reached its apogee as a very American concept in the immediate postwar era, with the help of a variety of government programs supporting college, marriage, and homeownership (Coontz 1992), as well as a postwar economy. (The sociological models locating ideal adulthood in concurrently ending schooling, settling on a career, marriage, and new household refer to this.) While we should expect very different ideas about adulthood, where they do occur, and somewhat different historical processes shaping them, histories of Western and American adulthood can alert us to how American adulthood was built upon excluding marked populations.

Philippe Ariès (1962) has argued that children were viewed as small adults in much of Western history: a more precise version might be that people were not distinguished by childhood or adulthood, but through a variety of other statuses.[4] One might be apprentice or master, daughter or wife, prince or king, and these statuses, while associated with a life chronology, were not tied primarily to specific age groups. A prince might become king before he reached his first birthday; a daughter could become a wife at the age of seven or become an apprentice at two (Brewer 2005). Nor did they unite larger groups under a shared rubric, although they drew parallels metaphorically. A master, prince, and husband were not all one sort of person, although the metaphor of prince and subject might be used to describe a master and apprentice. A set of historical shifts (changes associated with the development of modernity) began to coalesce in the seventeenth and eighteenth centuries to lay the groundwork for a developing notion of adulthood.

Holly Brewer (2005) has linked the emergence of new notions of childhood—and, by extension, adulthood—to changing ideas about political authority in the Anglo-American world. Older models had justified ideas about authority and seniority in patriarchal genealogical relationships: a child's obedience to his father, throughout their lives, was the paradigm for relationships between subjects and their king, servants and their master, and men and God. By the eighteenth century, a liberal political philosophy had proposed that political life be organized around reason and not on obedience. Childhood became marked by the lack of full reason, and children became excluded from various decision-making activities, including signing contracts and holding elective office. New ideas about an adulthood defined by the capacity to reason underwrote the great democratic movements to grant (at least theoretically) political power to all men. In many ways, the idea of adulthood is profoundly democratic and egalitarian—and as such, is also exclusive and privileged. The recognition of a universal capacity to self-govern, through the exercise of reason, and to participate equally in governing in the public sphere, is both critical to the idea of adulthood, and also important to the sense that its realization in various economic and political contexts is elusive to many around the world.

As Brewer noted, the move from obedience to reason served to mark out the very young as a distinct category, but they were not the only ones. The new democratic notion of reasoning citizens was organized around a whole series of exclusions of people marked out from being full adults. Not only children lacked the qualifications to participate in new public spheres of rational discourse—so, too, did women, who remained jural and political minors in the Anglo-American world into the twentieth century. Blacks, Native Americans, and other racialized populations were also often excluded from the category of full adults, as their capacity to reason was questioned, either on general racial grounds or through forms of individual testing (IQs, reading tests). Discriminating those without sufficient ability to reason did not simply mark off the boundaries of political and economic adulthood, it also created a desire and struggle to attain adult recognition by excluded groups (Field 2014). A democratic adulthood took shape in the Anglo-American world not only as a status to which, ostensibly, all men were entitled—it also took shape in its earliest forms as an elusive status desired by and fought for by the many excluded from it.[5]

In the economic world, as well, new configurations and ideas were forming and transforming relationships and statuses. The rationalities of adulthood, showing up in the political domain, were not unconnected to the economic sphere, whether in property, or in labor. In the early United States, debates about whether people were able to participate fully in the political realm sometimes turned on the question of property: those with property were assumed not only to have a vested interest in the nation and so share in its sovereignty, but also to have developed the forms of judgment and reason that came with caring for property, and for "developing" its profitability. Karl Marx famously argued that ideologies of the self-determining person, responsible for his welfare, emerged around the reorganization of productive activity around capital and industrialization. Instead of being tied to other people through complex relationships of dependency and patronage, the new person was "free" to offer, sell, and withdraw his labor in a "rationalized" labor market—or to hire, fire, and, of course, expropriate it through gimmicks of wage and worktime. Marx also noted that laborers became responsible for their own maintenance and reproduction, with the latter taking place primarily in a new domestic sphere (and, eventually, partially through state institutions). As laborers became independent agents responsible for themselves (and their families), they too pressed to distinguish their status through exclusions: labor unions worked to exclude younger people from the work force, arguing in tandem with child-saving movements that the young were both developmentally immature, and willing to work (irrationally?) for wages too little to fully support them.

A set of emerging concepts about developmental processes drawn from different fields also contributed, overlapping in intriguing ways with the economic and political sphere. The outlines of a theory of social evolution were solidly in place by the eighteenth century, in which social groups became organized in increasingly complex ways, led by technological advances and producing more intellectual and cultural sophistication (see, for one example, Condorcet [1795] 1955). By the same time, theories of individual development were also taking shape, visible especially in Romantic literature (Buckley 1974; Durham 2008). Carolyn Steedman (1994) describes how that literature depicted (and deplored) the lives of young people whose in-born developmental trajectory was stunted or deformed, leaving them disabled and immature in physical, spiritual, and social aspects—street denizens, perpetual children—if not dead. These two developmental fields—social and individual—converged in the writing of G. Stanley Hall, a leader in the new discipline of psychology. Hall (1904), who is credited with "inventing" the modern psychological notion of adolescence, placed it in a developmental life trajectory that moved from a "primitive" state of childhood, to the unruly barbarism of adolescence, to the civilized state of adulthood. (Freud [1955] also associates maturity with civilization, but in different ways.) The convergence between social evolution and personal development worked the other way, too: the fully mature "primitives" of the colonized world were seen as child-like, needing guidance to develop before joining a democratic community of civilized adults.

The developmental models have had many ramifications for ideas about adulthood. One that we will return to links maturation with upward mobility. Young people in nineteenth-century America often approached their birthdays, from their teens into their thirties, with trepidation. Their diaries each year reflected on their lack of progress toward adulthood, elusive to them, too, while society around them celebrated the go-ahead spirit of progressivism (Grinspan 2015). Complementing this, developmental models that emphasize on-going growth confound ideas that pin adulthood to a singular event, such as a birthday, ceremony, or certificate. One of the dominant structures to shape expectations of adulthood is the twentieth-century Western education system, which joined with medical and other fields to focus Americans on their chronological age (Chudacoff 1992; Field and Syrett 2015), and to measure successful progress by it. It was into that system that child-savers of the late nineteenth century hoped to place young people, protecting them from the adult world, and helping them climb the developmental ladder in proper steps—until they hit the age at which they were no longer children. One upshot of the conflicting relationship of developmentalism with event/date-based measures is the complicated set of ways that adulthood is recognized in the US legal system. By the later twentieth century, eighteen, typically the age at which one finished high school, had become the age at which one could make independent judgments and choices—at eighteen, one can vote, or enter the military. And yet one is not mature enough to buy alcohol (and, in some places, cigarettes), but long past the maturity needed to drive a car (at fifteen–seventeen, in different states), marry (as young as thirteen in some states at the beginning of the twenty-first century, with a judge's permission), or be morally and legally responsible for murder (a highly variable age, which can be as low as eleven). While developmentalism and exclusion can run hand-in-hand, they also run in different directions.

Adult Times

The connection of adulthood with progress and development, with a kind of "upward" and "forward" mobility in many dimensions, spiritual and material, individual and collective, undergirds anxieties about achieving adulthood in the United States and much of the West. This temporal framework in which to envision adulthood is present in many parts of the world, in part a legacy of colonialism and postcolonial reality infused with social evolutionary thought, and various assemblages associated with "modernity," including schooling, development projects, and biomedicine (see Ferguson 1999). Temporalities, such as but not restricted to this unilinear developmental one, are critically involved in many different notions of adulthood. A different but often concurrent temporality associated with adulthood is one of almost stasis: youth is often described as a time of "becoming," while adulthood is a time of "being," and adults are often thought to resist change and to be wedded to established ways of doing things. Anthropologists have long been interested in different ways in which temporality is experienced, organized, and expressed (see Dalsgård et al. 2014; Munn 1992). Not only are there different ways to organize time—such as the regimentation of an external clocktime in which time defines activities that should take place, as opposed to the flexible "cattle clock" of the Nuer in which activities defined the times at which they happened—but different models can coexist, be complementary, or at odds. Concurrent temporal frames in which to see one's life open up considerable conceptual space for anxiety, but also for a creative reimagination of ways of being adult.

The developmental, progressivist model of the Western life course is not only quite different from some models in other societies, it is also not the only one at work in Western societies. For example, the West also sustains a recursive kind of cyclical model of the life course, in which old age repeats some of the experiences of infancy, as in the Currier and Ives prints that hang in my house. In these, a person's life is set on a bridge, with the forties or fifties at the apex and the infant and nonagenarian both swaddled and spoon-fed at the bridge's two ends. On that bridge, life is not a steady ascent. Indeed, some ideas about the person in her life course consider it a moral downhill slope from a highly valued child's purity and innocence to a corrupted, decadent maturity. And the Western life course can be reversed, through drugs or surgery, and changeable from situation to situation, features of the temporality of life often remarked upon in other parts of the world. Finally, temporality everywhere also involves tempo, the "speed" or "slowness" of time passing as well as the sense of how "full" or "empty" that time might be.

What about a cyclical life in which the aging person does not return to infancy, so much as the infant retains the adult nature she once had? Several societies believe in reincarnation in some form or another; the newborn, in some of them, can retain the identity and even consciousness of the adult he was before. This can be problematic, of course—Beng of Ivory Coast must produce an infant willing to stay and live this new life out of the knowing, aged soul born to them (Gottlieb 2004). When a South Asian child cannot forget his preceding life, the experienced adult social expectations and knowledge the young child is born with must be accommodated, perhaps by allowing the child to live with his former wife (Gupta 2002). What, then, does adulthood mean in these societies—how is it recognized, how is it repressed and recovered, or a new one built on the old? How do these very young adults juxtapose their spiritual and even marital maturity with educational systems that presume ignorance, inexperience, and immaturity? What anxieties do they face? One might ask, too, about an accession to adulthood that is essentially about recovering a past—perhaps part of the bar and bat mitzvah, when thirteen-year-old Jewish children become moral adults by entering into the long historical traditions of their religion.

The developmental progressivist model is in its formal outlines nonreversible. Once you leave adolescence, or pass through emerging adulthood, you do not return. You might be inadequate as an adult in many ways, but you do not return to adolescence, or to your twenties. Stadialism, a theory of set stages, dominates Western models of the life course. Against this, Jennifer Johnson-Hanks has argued that lives do not, in fact, follow such neat trajectories, they are unstable, looping back and forth, and flexible, shaped by individual choices and by contextual (historical) ones, in what she calls "vital conjunctures" of lived lives and historical contexts (Johnson-Hanks 2002). She describes how, with motherhood, young Cameroonian women become adults, but then, putting their motherhood aside, return to girlhood to attend school and participate in schoolgirl life. I have also noted that age status is situational, more than chronological, shifting with the context (Durham 2004), a topic I return to in the next section. In the West, a flexible life course has been called "postmodern," especially when coupled with the idea of choice and self-fashioning. Tied to premises about consumerism, the postmodern life course is one in which age is a product—of plastic surgeries in which young girls make themselves into buxom women, older women strip off wrinkles and tighten vaginas, men consume Viagra to recapture the vigor of youth, and people wear clothes once marketed to specific age groups to create their own unique age, not fit into it (Edmonds 2014; Featherstone and Hepworth 1991).

There are different ways to experience a reversible life course. Ideas about a postmodern life celebrate the power of the individual to create his or her own age, even erasing the meaning of graded statuses. But reversible life courses need not overturn a stadial model. The stages may remain clear even as individuals move back and forth in age status, or as others attain recognized maturity at a very young age—or, by contrast, remain juniors into their chronologically old age without status, rights, or authority, buried with minors and not as accomplished elders.[6] George Meiu (2015), for example, has described how Samburu men participating in the tourist economy on beaches in Kenya disrupt but do not overturn the life stages of one of the most classic age-graded societies. Although Samburu carefully manage the progress of males from boys to warriors, and warriors to elders, through initiation ceremonies and marriage, entrepreneurs of the beachfronts amass the wealth to marry and build houses before becoming elders. Other Samburu working the beaches mismanage their wealth or fail to accumulate it, and are marginalized from the sources they might have drawn on in the village hinterlands, and never establish their elderhood. Instead of making the life course a postmodern mall in which age is individual and inventive, Samburu reconfigured elderhood to accommodate both "young big-men"—too young, yet established in marriage, patronage, and household—and "beachboy elders" who remain socially young even as they age. Much as with the Cameroonian women who move back and forth between girlhood and adulthood, or as with women using plastic surgery to look ever-young, the reversible life course can reaffirm the importance of staged statuses. Reversibility was, after all, a hallmark of the logic of structure in mythic thought (Lévi-Strauss 1963). At the same time, however, these life stages have gained new significance, and are understood in changing ways, as people engage with them in new historical conditions.

Tempo, a sense of how rapidly, slowly, smoothly, or unevenly time passes, and also a sense of anticipation, suspense, hope, surprise, or stability, is a sometimes overlooked feature of the life course, but one that has drawn attention in the studies of youth (see Frederiksen and Dalsgård 2014 for a critical discussion). Children and youth are often associated with futurity (Christiansen et al. 2006; Cole and Durham 2008), and youth with a sense of anticipation. A modernist chronicity, expecting a future that is both different from, and better than, the present, gives people hope for a future better than their present, and an expectation that their adulthood will be better than both their youth and the lives of their parents. In regions with high levels of governmentality, movement through the life course has been intensely monitored and regulated, most especially in the educational system with its annual promotions, and tests that affirm earned progress and betterment. Once out of that system, changes in status and progress "up a ladder" are less easily measured or evaluated. Unwilling to reproduce their parents' lives, or to live in significantly worse conditions of subordination or even abjection, many young people report feeling out of time/place—liminal—stuck or just waiting, caught in a temporality that is nonprogressive, even suspended. While their activities can be analyzed by anthropologists as productive and agentive, to them and to their society they often seem simply recurrent, mundane, and perhaps not even activity at all, drinking tea, doing nothing, living like chickens (Jeffrey 2010; Mains 2007; Masquelier 2013), unmarked by changes for the better.

If, as has been suggested (Blatterer 2007), youth is thought to be a time of "becoming" and adulthood of "being," or, as in some parts of the world, adulthood is a "finished" or "completed" time—what chronicities are associated with adulthood? Young people may see adulthood as a period of stability and regularity, a plateau structured around strict work schedules and neatly organized calendars, but the world militates against stability and predictability, today more than ever. Karl Mannheim ([1952] 1972) has become popular, lately, for his theories of "fresh contact," the encounter between people and circumstances that are new to them, the newness allowing them to interpret and shape those circumstances in new ways and mark off generational cohorts from each other. Mannheim focused on youth, but he noted that older people might also have fresh contact as well, if their life circumstances changed. Ideas of adults as completed beings or as those simply consolidating the "becoming" of their past ignore changing circumstances to which adults must respond, often creatively, with accumulated wisdom and experience empowering them, to invent new futures for themselves and others. Adulthood itself is unstable—in ways that provoke deep anxiety, but also in ways sought after and embraced by those seeking change, or for those able to be youth in one setting, mature in another, and elder in a third. And adults must anticipate expected futures, too—whether one filled with children and grandchildren, or with loneliness, poverty, and pain, or, as my university students sometimes imagine for themselves, a time (after retirement) when, freed from the burdens of "adulting," they can finally do everything they wanted to. Furthermore, the dichotomy between a youth of becoming and an adulthood of being focuses narrowly on the isolated individual. A more relational approach might recognize the ongoing work of becoming that adults engage in, as they continuously navigate and produce relationships across generations and with others in their lives.

INDICES OF ADULTHOOD

When writing about youth, I suggested that it was productive to consider it as a "social shifter" (Durham 2000, 2004). While I would still argue that youth is a particularly potent social shifter, adulthood, and other statuses, can also be considered through this analytic. A shifter, or a deictic, is a linguistic term referring to the indexical aspect of signification, in which an utterance derives meaning in part from the relationship between it, its context, and what it is referring to (Hanks 1990; Silverstein 1976). Instead of terms having meaning exclusively by standing in for something that exists "in the world," they also gain meaning pragmatically, through the relationship of speaker, audience, and a world constructed around them in the course of speaking. Classic deictics are words like "there" (a place that only has meaning with reference to the "here" of the speaker)—or a verb tense, in which a future exists only with reference to some other specified time, often that of the speaking moment. Roland Barthes (1983) argued that using shifters can also bring *metalinguistic* elements to the fore, revealing the structural underpinnings of meaning, such that, in his study, talking about fashion reveals the structural underpinnings of class. Shifters not only shift the contexts of meaning, they also refer to the metalinguistic, or metasocial, systems that underlie the production of meaningful terms. Talking about youth or adults/adulthood is also a way of talking about questions of authority, power, independence, knowledge, rights, and other elements that underlie claims to a social standing.

Thinking of the concept of "adult" or "adulthood" as a shifter offers us three intertwined analytical directions to follow. One is to foreground the relational and contextual elements of referring to adulthood. A second is to recognize the pragmatic dimensions of claims to adulthood, or discussions and discourses about it. And a third is to seek out the metasocial elements that are being indicated in discourses of adulthood and, in their indication, being held up for critical evaluation and modification.

That identities and subjectivities are relational is now well recognized in anthropology, and that point has been useful for understanding age statuses (Alber et al. 2008; Cole and Durham 2007). Such relationality is both structural and situational. Meyer Fortes (1984) has probably given the best account of how age statuses are constituted in structured relationships in a genealogical system, where genealogical relationships can make a chronologically young person senior to, "older than," someone chronologically much older. In Botswana, as Solway describes in her chapter in this volume, a woman's ability to move into full seniority depends on moving her own children into a more mature state, through their having children, getting married, or at least moving out of the house. Her age status is related to theirs. Structured relationships can allocate age status in systems that are not genealogical, as well: a college-educated supervisor or manager becomes senior to less educated older workers under him, for example. Such relational identities are often situational: a highly educated, salaried woman in her thirties in Botswana takes on the role—subjectively and formally—of an elder on weekends in the capital city, when and where family members living there meet in her house to present, discuss, and resolve family problems (such as a niece's pregnancy). But the same woman is reduced to low juniority—a youth sent on errands, and told to remit her income to her seniors—when she returns to her home village to discuss issues there (arranging a funeral, perhaps). Her age status is shaped by context, but it is also possibly contested, and the contexts reshaped, if she claims higher status in the village through her mannerisms (bodily and rhetorical performances), salary, and knowledge of process and procedure in the modern state (see other examples in Durham 2004). Relational, situated adulthood is pragmatic in the sense that, as people make claims to adulthood or to its lack, they not only situate themselves with relationship to others around them, and to a known age system, they remake what those ages mean to people.[7] It is performative, in the sense described by Judith Butler (1990) for gender. For people in Botswana, where subjectivities are understood to be profoundly relational and intertwined, these dynamics are par for the course (and potentially both empowering and disempowering, see Durham 2007). But while selfhood in places like the United States is also relational and shifting, the ideology of the self in America is one in which it should be constant, located within an integrated person, leaving some uncertain about their status overall.

This relational, situated, and performative element of age ought to be core to any anthropological approach to adulthood or maturity. So, too, should be a careful attention to the metasocial as it is indexed in discourses about adulthood. The woman in Botswana claiming seniority brings to bear metasocial indexing of forms of knowledge and authority, social and material resources, and of other social values. Karen Sykes, in her chapter in this book, examines how respecting obligations to one's closest social group is a primary index for moral maturity, and so understanding adulthood in Papua New Guinea requires understanding new kinds of extended households and the new obligations that come to organize and define the households. There are many such indexed elements that could—and should—be examined. Here, I want to focus on some of the most recurrent in contemporary discussion of adulthood: jobs, marriage, and household. These are often presented—as in the sociological studies mentioned above—as "things in themselves," the attainment of which grants adulthood. But they are not straightforward; they are enmeshed in structural meaning in specific social settings, and references to adulthood, elusive or not, are references to a structural setting that is both specific, problematic, and available for contemplation and for action through the metasocial indexing.

Perhaps the most consistent reference for elusive adulthoods is jobs. But jobs are not things in themselves, and having one is not necessarily a mark of adulthood nor a lack of one its failure. In colonial Africa, regular, salaried jobs often reduced men (and sometimes women) to social subordinates, mere "boys." (Anthropologists at the time noted such "boyhood" was situational [Mitchell 1956], and "boys" returning to their homes often claimed precocious seniority, as Carton [2000] described for South Africa.) Today, some men and women without jobs or with only marginal ones are recognized in many venues for their full maturity, as they are recognized as fonts of wisdom or for social management of complex households, or bring their rhetorical skills into church or public arenas. So what is it about jobs? Income, of course, and what that income allows that makes the earner more adult. While in the United States there is much talk about the need for "good jobs," what a good job is is not always clear. On the one hand, a good job brings good and steady income, which in the United States is especially important for highly valued independence, both from the burdens of debt to banks (which constrains further spending), and from the necessity of continuing to live with parents.[8] On the other, the jobs that signify adulthood are "career-track": a high-paying but short-term job may be considered a pre-adult occupation. A career-track job signals a resolution to the ego conflicts over identity and the experimentalism that are seen to characterize adolescence. Career-track jobs also offer the possibility of increasing rank, authority, and seniority over time. Income and career are different values, and refer to systems of value that sometimes overlap and also may contradict each other. In other parts of the world, while income remains one consideration, a greater one is that the job be of a specific kind, whether, as in Japan, one in which the employer (once) made a life-long commitment of security and steady but nonspectacular promotions, or, as in Sri Lanka, that it have the status of a government civil service job. As Dhana Hughes describes in her chapter on Sri Lanka, the highly contradictory set of values associated with civil service jobs—where people spend the day drinking tea, but have managed to get a coveted position of some security—outweighs the higher incomes available in the private sphere abetted by global capital. In Ethiopia, as in Sri Lanka, it may be better not to be known to be working (and earning), if the work is not in the white-collar sphere and evidence that with a new contemporary adulthood comes upward class mobility (Mains 2007). Yet in lower income neighborhoods in Cairo, people seek civil service positions for the stability of the fairly low paycheck, and also try to master a trade or skill, such as electrical or mechanical work, that might bring in more money (Ghannam 2013). For them, it really is the money that enables them to marry.[9]

For these Cairenes, marriage depends on income, and the furnished household provided to a bride is core to adulthood for herself and her provider husband. Studies of Egypt consistently note that people are finding it hard to move into adulthood because it is hard to come up with the material means to marry. Marriage is often a critical factor in assessing adulthood, and sociologists of the West frequently note later ages of marriage as important to delayed adulthoods. Yet what marriage means and how it is connected to a range of social structures and values is highly variable around the world, as anthro-pologists well know. In parts of India girls might be married very young, but they also entered their new households specifically as children, sleeping in the bed of a mother-in-law and under her care and tutelage for many years (Lamb 2000). Janice Boddy's chapter in this volume suggests that marriage is impor-tant in Sudan because it allows people to produce children who continue a name or lineage—some women there may be marrying and divorcing in order to have those children (sometimes through adoption), creating their adulthood through a household with a child, but not a husband. In parts of Brazil, marriage im-mediately catapults women into a new adult status, separated from her parents, even as the marriages themselves often dissolve rapidly. Upon marriage, women set up a home of their own, even though that house may be a simple shack built on the rooftop of their own mother's house and without facilities for cooking or bathing. Hollis Moore has studied Brazilian women who form relationships with men in prison in order to gain adulthood: the prison cells are elaborated as "houses," and women establish their adulthood through them (Moore 2015, citing McCallum and Bustamante 2012 on individuation through housing).

Marriage, having children, households: how these figure into adulthoods is clearly gendered in most places. Although gender has figured obliquely into this contribution, perhaps most prominent in the section on marking and exclusion, gender is clearly one of the underlying social principles most pro-foundly involved in assessing adulthood, for many reasons, and any indexing of these topics of household, marriage, or children invokes issues surrounding gender. Anthropologists have, indeed, written about adulthood through the lens of gender much more than adulthood itself. Women's studies have ob-served both how women become recognized as mature earlier than men, as they marry and have children at younger ages, but also how they are constrained to a junior status in several realms. Studies of masculinity note the threat to mas-culinity when men are unable to support a dependent wife and children—indeed, Dungey and Meinert's chapter in this book could as easily have been written about failures of masculinity as about the failures of men to support families as adults. Marriage, maintaining a household, or having children, may impact men and women in their status as adults quite differently. In Botswana, where most people have children before marriage, young women say that they have achieved new maturity when they have children, even when those children are raised by their parents while the mother is off at school or working in the city, or simply pursuing boyfriends. They must always be thinking of the child, they say, forgoing their own desires or needs to make sure the child is fed, clothed, and healthy—some say their parents force them to do this. Young men may strive to demonstrate their maturity by providing care for their children, but often fail to do so, whether because they fall out with the mother, their own families are unsupportive of the relationship, or their uneven finances make it impossible to consistently demonstrate care. For the men, recognition of their maturity can be harder to achieve or sustain.

Recognizing Adults

What initially interested me when I read news reports on transitions to adulthood in the United States was that many people in their mid-thirties who have attained the full set of accomplishments used to measure adulthood—job, marriage, end of formal schooling, house, children—still say in interviews that they do not feel adult. Brown's *Adulting* tells her readers that even though they "don't *feel* an adult they can still act like one"—distinguishing between public recognition, performed in an "interaction ritual" judged by others, and an internal sense judged by the self.[10] What are the differences between an adulthood that is acknowledged by externalities or forms of public recognition and one that is felt "inside" by individuals? When we talk about the Ehing ceremony in which males are initiated into adulthood, we talk about public recognition, a set of rights and privileges, some new dietary practices, but we have not asked how the five-year-old feels about being adult or not, or how the Maasai who has moved from being a warrior to an elder, through a ritual conducted in his thirties, feels about his new maturity. A contradiction between the two forms of recognition—having the credentials for adulthood but not feeling it, or feeling quite adult without being given its recognition—is sometimes held to be part of the "problem" of the transition to adulthood in the contemporary West (e.g., Thomson et al. 2004).

Structure and feeling have never been separated entirely by anthropologists, whether in the warm "joking" relationships between alternate generations (grandparent-grandchild, regardless of age differences), or the tensions manifest between (classificatory) fathers and sons, or, in matrilineal societies, uncles and nephews. The rituals that transform people from children into adults, or children into women, are never empty ceremony, and the status they produce is never encapsulated simply in a set of publicly recognized scars, or a paper certificate hung on a wall. They work directly on the subjectivities and emotions of participants, with fear, humor, anticipation, stoicism, and pride often foremost, experienced as elemental to the making of adults.[11] Many of these events also put people into a cohort, a community formed around their common experience (whether they are age-peers or not), with a powerful emotional impact in itself, as Victor Turner (1969) described in his many studies of "the ritual process." In anthropological accounts, emotions are not just personal responses to a standardized situation: they often speak directly to the *inter*subjectivity of emotion and selfhood, whether in building a necessary sense of communitas, or in affirming that emotion is generated as much by others as within the self (see Lutz and Abu-Lughod 1990).

Yet for those who refer to feeling adult (or not), the formal signs, rituals, and measures for recognition are *not* always effective, and the intersubjective and emotional dimensions have not worked their way into "feeling" adult.[12] These "feelings" are highly isolating, according to sociologists of adulthood, alienating individuals from their social institutions and norms, as well as other people. Performative theories tell us that embodying adulthood in performative acts should transform subjectivities and reshape the conceptual category itself. Instead, at least some people feel that their performances—recognized and appreciated in their worlds—leave them subjectively alienated. Readers of this contribution suggested to me that not feeling adult is a form of "imposter syndrome," a psychological condition (but not disorder) identified in the late 1970s, and associated especially with high-achieving people uncertain about their claims to a "higher" status. If this association bears out, we might note that imposter adulthood is connected in contradictory ways with upward mobility, a kind of doubt arising when that mobility seems to be attained.[13]

Some approaches to this emphasis on feeling associate the rise of the significance of feeling with aspects of late modernity. Discussions of the emergence of personal feeling as the primary location for the recognition of adulthood often cite a fragmentation and increasing incoherence of other, more formal, ways of recognizing adulthood (as in Blatterer 2007), a kind of identity anomie that leaves the individual to his own emotional and sometimes creative devices. How can one be a moral adult responsible for committing murder at thirteen, and yet unable to assume the moral maturity of voting? Old enough to wield the modern weaponry of a soldier, but not old enough to carry a concealed handgun? Still in college at twenty-eight, but working at a full-time job since sixteen? Classical anthropological understanding of rites of passage took place in societies where many fields of power and authority overlapped: the rites worked because those directing them had the authority and power to define others in many fields, and recharged that broad authority as they conducted rites of passage (La Fontaine 1977). From a somewhat different but parallel direction, the (new?) focus on individual feeling may, by some, be attributed to processes of neoliberalization. Since the 1970s individuals have been made more responsible for their own condition, as state-based forms of social reproduction have been weakened. As people take on the risks and responsibility for their own success and failure, they also take on responsibility for assessing their own status. This is also the implication if we borrow Foucault's (1979) insights into governmentality and biopolitics: as discourses of knowledge about people start measuring them in various ways, establishing norms and developing means to "improve" people with reference to those norms, people begin to self-monitor. The infamous panopticon of medicine, sociology, and other human sciences provides people with many means of constant self-evaluation, and many ways to fall short of normalized measurements. In all of these approaches, individuals' responsibility for recognizing their own adulthood seems to reflect a failure in the social domain.

One social domain with a set of contradictory relationships to adulthood, public recognition, and emotions is consumerism and the markets. James Côté (2000) thought that modernity could free individuals to shape their adulthoods in their own terms, but that younger generations have surrendered that freedom to profit-oriented markets, which offer them "ersatz identities" to satisfy their narcissism. His is a more pessimistic vision than the celebratory one of the "postmodern life course," in which people in a free-market world are liberated from age categories based on biology and calendars. Consumerism and markets are frequently linked with the paradoxical relationship, within them, of choice and constraint, of self-fashioning and fitting into fashions controlled by business interests. Prior to the twentieth century, younger people often had little access to (or were excluded from) the means of self-fashioning; instead they served as the "conspicuous" signs of parental identity, or were supporting their parents' families. By the end of the century, young people have gotten access to, and keep, their own money, the means to fashion identities through markets. (This access to money and its use is notable not only in the West, but in places like Botswana.) Choice, self-fashioning, mastery of fashion and market values, and self-responsibilization through that fashioning, are all sometimes elements of being or feeling adult. But, because choices can prove wrong, and debt can rob one of the freedom markets promise, markets can throw adulthood in the form of responsibility, independence, and knowledge into doubt. Such doubts fit a model of adulthood based on rationality, on the ability to assess choices, measure risk and debt—where having purchased a home, or assembling a complex household of dependents, affirms the ability to manage it like an adult. From the beginning of the advertising era, in the nineteenth century, markets have segregated customers into age categories. Markets distinguish between children, junior, and adult clothing; furnishing for tweens and for the college bound; books for "young adults" (aged twelve to eighteen) and for those younger and older. In advertisements, they have urged potential consumers to examine themselves for signs of proper age and aging, and to manage those forms. Do you have gray hair, wrinkles, aging teeth—are you man enough to need deodorant, enough of a family man to need life insurance (Chudacoff 1992)? Even as markets offer people age categories with which to identify themselves, or against which to measure themselves, they also offer them means for self-development.

Consumerism and the markets are built around emotion, as well as the rationality of exchange, measurement, and self-assessment, and they engage both the personal sensibility as well as the public materiality of recognizing adulthood. Many accounts of market-based consumerism associate it with pleasure and desire, with love and doubt, and with anxiety and disappointment, when the pleasure of a new item fails to materialize, wears off, or gives way to the promise of more pleasure, more improvement to be attained with new items (Campbell 1987; Illouz 2007). Self-development in the United States builds on the concerns of the nineteenth-century diarists who monitored their progress toward adulthood in a century obsessed with progress and development, with respect to moral and emotional disposition as well as more worldly accomplishment. Such self-development continues today, as people manage not only their physical appearance, but also engage in "skills" training workshops to be leaders or communicators (Urciuoli 2008), and to manage their emotional health and maturity with the aid of paid professionals or new products (Illouz 2008). Because becoming adult is also often associated with upward mobility as much as aging itself, both the material and emotional means, available through the market, present themselves as items of measurement and assessment, and marks of personal progress.

Consumers are not simple pawns of the market, of course. They have shaped the age-market through their own tastes and practices, creating, for example, a cultural category of "teenagers" out of bobby socks and rolled skirts (Schrum 2004), or creating the possibility of a "third age" with more active, healthy (and wealthy) aging. For some, markets provide the means both to make oneself over into an age of choice, as in the postmodern life course, or to devise personal and individual ways of aging, as surprising as giving birth long past menopause, joining the Peace Corps at sixty-five, or taking up sky-diving in one's nineties (as did George H. W. Bush). But some, too, move outside the markets to fashion new adulthoods, as young Indians do, organizing community-oriented village projects that do not promise the upward mobility associated with local expectations of adulthood's proper form (Jeffrey and Dyson 2014).

A twenty-three-year-old university student in Botswana regularly posts pictures of herself in various forms of dress acquired through the proliferation of cheap goods in stores there, each associated with a different life-course status—office worker with neat hair and a briefcase, university-aged partygoer in tight pants and sunglasses, sober and matronly church member in headscarf and long skirt. These self-fashionings, however, will only be successful if she both recognizes herself as mature in the costume, and—not independently of the first—if others do as well. Indeed, such playfulness locates her more in a kind of youth than in maturity, in Botswana as in many places—still experimenting, still unfinished, filled with the power of self-development realized through negotiating relations with others (see Durham 2005, 2008). Consumption, as a form of self-development, has all the hallmarks of youth, if one participates fully in its changing fashions and promises of pleasure. The young Indians forgoing income and consumerism to develop clean water sources for their villages may assert a more convincing maturity, even without the upward mobility associated with adulthood. Yet consuming new things and self-development through the market take place throughout the life course. Mark Liechty (2002) has argued that new forms of market and consumer practice in Nepal spearheaded both a middle class and the emergence of "youth" as a life stage. What, then, does the growth of a recognizable (though diverse) middle class, of "youth," and of high consumerism around the world signal for adulthood? As consumers, do people of all ages unsettle adulthood through consumerism and self-development, through emotional materialism and the rationalities of the market? According to the prevailing views of adulthood, young people attain some of its qualities as they gain income, make decisions concerning its use, demonstrate knowledge in a marketplace of choices, establish class claims, and shape their own identities independent of their parents. At the same time, those who might otherwise be considered adults display many characteristics that seem to make them youth, feeling personal failure (and romantic joy!) in the consumer markets, reinventing themselves with new products and practices, correcting their faults and self-developing, being playful with consumer experimentation, knowing that commitments can readily be tossed aside with old skis, shoe preferences, or a change in shampoo brand.

Conclusions

There are many reports that adulthood is elusive, and most reports attribute it to the lack of adequate jobs. And it is certainly the case that low income and lack of career-oriented employment constrain many people around the world as they seek to improve their lives and to attain recognition for a new age status, or simply to maintain themselves where they are. But the elusiveness of adulthood goes well beyond people being unable to attain it because of limited finances. Adulthood is also elusive because what it is, and how it is recognized, are often obscure to those people who seek it or live comfortably within it. It is not insignificant that, in sociological studies in the West, people both "know" what it means but are unable to come up with definitions that satisfy them. Ask a friend established in her profession, and she is likely to say, only a bit flippantly, "I'm not adult yet at the age of fifty" (after all, fifty is the new thirty, as she read in a newspaper) or "I became an adult when I got my own blender (or other kitchen device)." While people in their everyday lives may not have a simple definition of adulthood, scholars, especially sociologists, have fastened onto a set of discrete measurable accomplishments—marriage, independent household, and either income or career-track job. Yet we may be confusing these accomplishments with adulthood (or maturity in other, local terms) by not examining more closely what adulthood itself means. And this is truly the job for anthropologists.

When I ask people in the United States who finished school in the late 1950s how they came to feel adult, they usually tell me they did not think about it, although they married, worked, and set up households on meager incomes soon after finishing high school or college. They do not say these steps were easy—they were not, and most relied heavily on help from their parents and tell funny stories of their early missteps. But they say (in retrospect) that they did not worry about whether they were being adult or not. Those who came of age in the 1960s and 1970s grew up listening to The Who sing, "I hope I die before I get old" (in the song "My Generation"). Old meant thirty—that generation had been warned not to trust anyone over thirty, and were told to fear their thirtieth birthday when they would "become old." (Interestingly, The Who's Pete Townshend is reported to have said in 1989, then in his mid-forties, that "for him, when he wrote the lyrics, 'old' meant 'very rich.'")[14] Adulthood for that generation was to be avoided, for its association with bourgeois materialism and complacency. Not everyone today wants to be an adult—the Chinese youth in an industrial city written about by Andrew Kipnis are wary of its implications, and many young people in North America in the 2010s are seeking alternatives to stable careers and home-ownership, opting instead for purposefully unstable consulting work or simple income without commitment from "the gig economy." Yet for many in many parts of the world, it does seem that adulthood has gone from being a fairly unmarked condition of normal maturity to something worried about, now as marked as the statuses that used to be marked out from it. Surprising to me, and my generation, many young people now want to be adults. Which returns us to questions posed at the beginning of this introduction—what is at stake in being an adult that so many people seem to want to be one?

Of course, there is no single answer to this question, because there are too many different contexts and histories lying behind the answer. Yet the recurrence of the claim that adulthood is elusive does raise the question.

Before the millennium turned, the Comaroffs (1999) suggested that generational difference—the difference between youth and their seniors—was the new global fault line opened up by a millennial capitalism that pitted a postmodern "global" against a local site shaped by modernity. That fault line may have shifted over the ensuing years, but its effects may still make generational distinction—forged when youth become adults—more salient and fraught. I have suggested several other possible answers in this introduction, but any one must be examined in its local ramifications. One is the spread of development discourse around the world, the very visible emergence of middle classes—often a new category—around the world, and the association of attaining adulthood with upward class mobility. At the same time, many global economic factors make a middle-class life either inaccessible or highly unstable. The stakes for becoming adult are, in this perspective, the stakes of developmental and class mobility. Even for those who see adulthood to be a time of stability, in which their lives can match those of their parents and they can reproduce similar lives for their children, a global recession, the more rapid movement of capital into and out of communities, and the weakening of social support systems, makes adulthood unstable. A second answer looks at how adulthood, as a kind of normal maturity, has been associated with democratic liberalism and citizenship. Adults are those capable of exercising the qualities associated with citizenship, typically reason, morality, and a kind of cultural knowledge. Such notions of adulthood are inclusive, in that the global human rights discourse recognizes everyone as adult by virtue of biological age and their human nature. But it is also highly exclusive, in that many people feel excluded from domains where citizenal adulthood would be recognized. They may feel excluded from public decision making, or diminished in an encounter in the market, at a bank, in a government office, in a local law court, or in rejected negotiations for a marriage. Adulthood in its democratic, liberal form promises universal access, and yet, as people navigate the many communities and levels of social organization in which they are embedded, they encounter many exclusions. Insofar as the contexts and opportunities they navigate invoke the developmental, age-related idea of adulthood, people can also say that they will grow into those contexts, that they are not yet adult but working toward it. Finally, adulthood seems important and problematic today because the grounds of recognition are shifting. The ritual of a twenty-first birthday in Japan announcing adulthood, or the pronouncement at a college graduation ceremony that the girl has become an educated woman, might mean little to a prospective landlord, bank manager, check-out clerk, or supervisor for a low-paying job. And all of the signs of accomplishment might mean little to the fifty-year-old who feels a failure at adulting when bills escape his notice, or feels ever-young taking up new hobbies, or whose relatives fail to ask for or give help, or who has yet to have maturity confirmed by offspring deferring to or caring for her.

Whatever the context and history of a local search for adulthood, anthropology offers many analytical strategies to elucidate its meaning. In this introduction, I have drawn attention to three areas, but anthropology is an open-ended discipline and many more will occur to readers, or be evident in the chapters that follow. However, I think studies of adulthood ought to raise questions about temporalities, of the life course and of life in general. These temporalities include the directionality of time, its recursiveness, reversibility or linearity, its ability to anticipate a future or reinscribe a past as part of making the life course. Temporality also involves tempo, the sense of how time passes and whether it is full, empty, hurried, paced. And these terms—empty, full, hurried—steer us to thinking about time as emotionally shaped, as having an emotional dimension as well as simply directionality or measurements. The time of adulthood may be a time of satisfaction or of lost opportunity, of hopefulness or of anxiety, of patience or impatient busyness, of taking comfort in receiving the care of others cultivated over the years.

A second area I draw attention to is the way in which discourses of adulthood—the spoken and the practiced, the officializing and the inventive—index other things, on different levels. On one level, adulthood is relational, and claims to adulthood refer to sets of relationships with other people through which adulthood is realized (or not). On another, adulthood is situational and contextual, and being adult is a way of defining that context, but also is guided by it. And on a third, discourses of adulthood are also discourses of underlying structural values that allow adulthood to be a salient issue: who has knowledge, what knowledge is, how it should be displayed or put into action; the sources of power in any particular society, be they money, age, class, wisdom; notions of whether the mature self is independent and settled, or intersubjective and constantly shifting; and many other values that undergird everyday living. Complaints about adulthood, or satisfied discussions of it, are ways of talking about these underlying values.

And the third area I draw attention to is how adulthood is recognized and acknowledged. On the one hand, there are public forms of recognition, most obvious in certificates, initiation scars, changes in clothing, and rites and rituals, but also in the small everyday rituals of recognition, and misrecognition, at a bank, a licensing office, a family gathering, or streetside greetings. On the other, there is the field of "feelings," of subjectivity. Anthropologists have done considerable theoretical work to show how public demonstrations (of various sorts) and subjectivity are interconnected, each shaping the other.

And yet studies of adulthood often indicate that people sense a gap between performance and subjectivity, between public forms of acknowledgment and the way they feel about their status. This raises the interesting question for anthropology of how the two come to seem distinct to people. One possible arena for examining this, and for understanding how people come to seem adult in both fields of recognition, is in the ways in which consumerism and the market operate. Consumption provides both means for display and public acknowledgment, but is also an emotional experience; it is a field for the rationality and authority associated with adulthood, but also a field where distinctly nonrational sentiments are raised and dashed, and subjective qualities are sold.

Each chapter in this book raises its own set of questions about adulthood. Because they are anthropological, at the heart of each is the question, what does adulthood mean to people in this part of the world, and how is that meaning constructed, contested, and recreated in ever-changing terms and circumstances? The coverage is not complete, either geographically, or in ways to ask or answer that question. Instead, the set of contributions is intended both to provoke more research on what adulthood means to people, and to show the wide varieties of ways in which it is conceptualized, sought, and, for some, creatively reformulated to meet changing opportunity. And for some, how it remains an elusive goal, an ever-elusive horizon whose shape is not entirely clear. As happens in the best anthropology, each chapter is inspired by its fieldwork, by the problems posed by people in their own settings as they struggle to make sense of their lived lives. Indeed, the suggestions for ways to think about adulthood that I have presented in this chapter come out of thinking about my own field experiences in Botswana and Turkey, as well as thinking about the many ethnographies of youth I have read. It is this direct experience that shapes our contributors' ideas about and experiences of adulthood, as much as anything.

Jacqueline Solway, in her chapter on Botswana, describes how women and men seek to shape a respected and recognized maturity through their relationships with their children. At the same time, their children are also fashioning a maturity that both uses elements of the past and yet reveals new ways of accessing those elements, and new values attaching to them. Marriage, in particular, provides new ways of announcing seniority for younger people, in a venue that had always been a stage for seniority, where relatives of the married couple established their own maturity, rather than the couple itself. Solway's chapter draws into discussions of adulthood a long-standing concern in Botswana for the intersubjective and relational nature of all forms of self and status.

Dhana Hughes in her chapter writes about a young man, Saman, who, having survived the long civil war in Sri Lanka and having managed to get an education, has failed to achieve the adulthood he hoped for. Without connections, and with an education that is only second-rate, he finds himself working low-class and low-paid jobs in the city or farming, unable to get the valued government job that would give him the status to marry well in his home village and raise the status of his whole family. Even higher-paying jobs in the private sector would not serve the purpose, because of their precariousness, but also because of the high status government employment has there. For Saman, maturity can only be achieved with upward class mobility: without the status of the tea-drinking, unproductive civil servant, he is unable to move into adulthood. It is Saman, with his university education, who will move his entire family upward in status, but he must achieve this on his own—he lacks the social connections to promote his mobility.

Education is also a key issue for the Ugandan men featured in Claire Dungey and Lotte Meinert's chapter. While Saman in Sri Lanka, in Hughes's chapter, is wedded to an idea of a strictly progressive move to adulthood, irreversible, the young men in Uganda with whom Dungey and Meinert worked are fully aware that they will move into and out of adulthood, that it is unstable and easily lost and (less easily) regained. Dungey and Meinert describe a curious temporality that haunts these men: they are waiting. Unlike the frustrated waiting that others describe as part of youth "waithood," these young men have been trained to wait, and to see waiting as an active practice that might lead to advancement. In schools, in particular, waiting has been taught to them, in the form of waiting for transport, waiting for teachers to arrive or to teach, waiting for food or for promotions that come from inscrutable examination systems. While there is certainly a diversity of opinion on all this waiting, for many it is an activity, a busy-ness that fills their days and leaves them little time for things as mundane as housework. Taking the lesson in waiting to heart, for those whose adulthood has slipped into and out of view, waiting is one way to attain it.

Andrew Kipnis, in his chapter on young people in an industrial city in China, examines how they look forward not to an elusive adulthood, but one that is all too recognizable and accessible to most of them. Most of them anticipate eventually, even soon, taking a job in one of the factories that dominate the city; there they will be subject to extremes of discipline, physical and social, and will through those disciplines and the reliable income they bring be able to marry, set up a household, and begin to care for their parents. This adulthood is normal, at least in their view. And it is, for most, a satisfactory settling into a stable maturity. Kipnis finds, however, in the roller skating rink, that many young people seek out the uncontrollable and dizzying experiences that they know they cannot have while working at monotonous jobs under the close eye of supervisors. And some pursue that sense of instability, of unpredictability, by taking jobs that pay less, have few long-term guarantees or even promises, but which allow them a measure of independence and equality in working with others. Kipnis's chapter importantly reminds us of the dynamic interplay between an adulthood that promises little change from the past, but remains well within reach, in a "Fordist" factory town, and of the uncertain rewards and failures of a new economy.

Janice Boddy surprises many readers with her description of Sudanese women, more highly educated than their male peers, seeking out different ways to carve out a mature, adult life. For many families, their daughters' futures look precarious in an economy devastated by oil booms and busts and a long civil war: early arranged marriage, even as a second or third wife seems a better future than as an unmarried sister. Other women use the new technologies of the cell phone to make money, transacting cell phone time as currency, and to develop relationships, sometimes clandestine, outside the family or neighborly circle. And yet other women are experimenting with new possibilities. In a society where full adulthood is realized by reproducing a (male) family name and line, some women are establishing themselves as adults without husbands. New legal codes make it possible to adopt abandoned babies, and to give them a name, for women who have once, however briefly, been married. Of course, only those with education and other resources can pursue such an innovative path; others are simply married, at an early age, as second or even third wives, out of necessity.

In Papua New Guinea, an older generation that is credited with founding the nation confronts those born into it. While the older generation can define their adulthood through nation-making, their juniors are often dismissed as "raskols," unproductive if not destructive, still boys. As Karen Sykes argues in her chapter, this assessment is shared by those who can only see the generation in terms of national statistics and national measures of productivity. But for the men of that generation, their maturity is formed less through contributions to the nation, defined by national statistics, than by their ability to enter into and sustain sets of exchange with kin, forming households that span different villages and ethnic groups in the process. Their activities are often economically as well as socially productive, but because their moral maturity is realized more through these new households, their economic activities, unevenly performed throughout the year, escape tax or other records. Sykes contrasts the work of moral maturity in Papua New Guinea, which she describes as taking place while they "invent the rules" of moral living, with Žižek's claim that political maturity is reached in late capitalism by "breaking" the political rules one was born into.

For Russians coming of age in the era of perestroika, rules were being broken all around them, and the standard ways of achieving a respectable adulthood changed too rapidly to be grasped. Anna Kruglova writes about a generation, living in a Russian city, that feels old without ever having achieved adulthood. Things changed too fast, their plans were for a world they did not mature into, they married impulsively already knowing the relationship was failed. They look around them at the generation before, which managed to grasp onto the soon-to-disappear structures that led them to leadership, security, and real adulthood. They look at their juniors who seem to burst rudely into spaces they do not belong, act like "babies" but realize the things that would have granted the perestroika generation some measure of recognizable maturity. Even as they condemn these youngsters, however, they draw upon the idealized images of childhood and youth that were presented to them, full of innocent promise, that left them adults without that hopeful future, already old, squeezed out of the expected life course. Yet even as children, they had seen adulthood as a time of trauma, of unrealized hope.

In each of these chapters, if adulthood is elusive, it is because it is never what it was thought to be for those who seek to attain it. For some, as for Kruglova's Russians feeling too old now to really be adults proper, the rapidity of social, political, and economic change has made it hard for them to navigate new paths while still seeking the older statuses that have disappeared. For others, it is less that the world has changed, than that they themselves are changing it. In Botswana, Solway finds women seeking to advance their maturity in ways that are both recognizable from the past—through their changing relationship to their children—but also in ways that are inventing as they pressure children to move out, take on family responsibilities, and make their own claims to adulthood. Like Boddy's Sudanese, these women have resources they never would have had in the past, and are shaping adulthoods that are quite new, but out of resources, such as children, that are quite old. In each of the chapters, adulthood presents itself as elusive to people of all ages because it involves, as Sykes puts it, not breaking rules of behavior, or not being able to follow the rules in spite of trying, but inventing them, and in the process questioning some of the core values and structures of their social worlds.

Deborah Durham is Professor of Anthropology at Sweet Briar College. She is co-editor, with Jennifer Cole, of *Generations and Globalization: Youth, Age, and Family in the New World Economy* and *Figuring the Future: Globalization and the Temporalities of Children and Youth*.

NOTES

Some of the writing for this chapter was accomplished while I was supported by an NEH Summer Stipend, a Fulbright Senior Scholar grant, and the Sweet Briar College Faculty Fellowship, all of which I gratefully acknowledge. Early versions were presented at conferences, and the final version of the chapter has benefitted from feedback from discussants Brad Weiss, Susan McKinnon, Dennis Rogers, Jonathan Spencer, and Craig Jeffrey, and from suggestions from Susan Reynolds Whyte. Keith Adams, Adeline Masquelier, and Jennifer Cole, and my writing group at Sweet Briar College, Cheryl Mares, Heidi Samuelson, Marie-Thérèse Killiam, Lynn Laufenberg, Alessandra Chiriboga, and Kimberly Morse-Jones, helped me clarify, streamline, and think about issues in the paper. I want to especially thank Jackie Solway who has forced me to think at every step of the way in writing this.

1. This is a purposeful allusion to James and Prout (2015: 1), which opened with the line "The twentieth century is said to be 'the century of the child' and at no other time have children been so highly profiled." The 2015 book is a revised version of their edited volume published in 1990; those words open the 1990s volume, as well.

2. Americans aspired to the various elements that congealed as normative adulthood for a much longer time—households, education, marriage, vocation/career—prior to the 1950s, but it was in that time that it came within reach of a large segment of the population.

3. Markedness is a concept developed more specifically in linguistics, where it can be applied to a range of semiotic levels, from phonological to categorial (Trask 1999).

4. Ariès's argument has been subject to considerable dispute and discussion, especially for its reliance on artistic representations of elites, yet it opened up a field of historical inquiry into the social and historical construction of childhood. See Prout and James (2015).

5. It is worth noting that focusing on citizenship and voting rights narrows the terms of adulthood to one of rights. Women in the nineteenth century could claim more moral maturity, sometimes, than men, through motherhood and a domesticity uncorrupted by the business world. As discussed later, I have not foregrounded gender in this introduction.

6. Africanists will be very familiar with the numerous older men who never achieved recognized maturity, designated in English as "herdboys" or in local languages as just "boy." Meillassoux's (1981) classic Marxist work on the struggle for maturity in Africa clearly shows the challenges faced by juniors to marshal the means to recognized maturity in peasant society.

7. The situational logic of age status has parallels with the logic of "vital conjunctures" described by Johnson-Hanks (2002), in that both draw attention to the fluidity and recursiveness of the life course, and its openness to innovation and invention. But the two are also different, in that the situational example is more context-dependent, whereas the vital conjuncture is more keyed to transformative historical events, such as pregnancy or death.

8. Not too long ago, in the United States, the ability to assume debt was a mark of adulthood; and today living with the family is not seen to compromise it in many "minority" populations.

9. There is also a sense that people should marry "equally"—the educational levels and other forms of status should be relatively equal between bride and groom.

10. Brown tells her readers that many people don't "feel" adult, and says that acting like an adult, or adulting, is the key. Adulthood seems to rest on competence in basic daily activities, like paying bills on time, and not feeling adult happens when you sense yourself incompetent.

11. For an excellent example, see Corinne Kratz (1993), on girls' initiation among Okiek in Kenya. At the same time that we recognize the extent to which anthropologists have looked at the interlocking nature of structure and emotion, we should also note the extent to which

some emotional or subjective experiences of Africans have been ignored, including romantic love (Cole and Thomas 2009) and pain (Livingston 2012).

12. Hence Twenge and Campbell (2010) claim that colleges (as well as many other elements of society), instead of educating students into adulthood, ostensibly granted with the college degree, shape a more child-like emotional experience for them.

13. I would like to thank Heidi Samuelson and Cheryl Mares for suggesting "imposter syndrome." The idea that it is associated with class mobility brings to mind Pierre Bourdieu's (1984) discussion of class differences, where habitus, deeply engrained orientations to aesthetics, space, temporality, situate one in a class environment; outside of that environment, one's habitus can leave one uncomfortable. I find it interesting that adulthood is often, in the West at least, depicted as "ersatz," "impostured," unfelt, or unreal.

14. Wikipedia, "My Generation," en.wikipedia.org/wiki/My_Generation. Viewed August 17, 2016.

REFERENCES

Alber, Erdmute, Sjaak van der Geest, and Susan R. Whyte, eds. 2008. *Generations in Africa: Connections and Conflicts*. Berlin: Lit.

Appadurai, Arjun. 1996. *Modernity at Large: Cultural Dimensions of Globalization*. Minneapolis: University of Minnesota Press.

Ariès, Philippe. 1962. *Centuries of Childhood: A Social History of Family Life*. Trans. Robert Baldrick. New York: Knopf.

Arnett, Jeffrey. 2004. *Emerging Adulthood: The Winding Road from the Late Teens through the Twenties*. New York: Oxford University Press.

Barthes, Roland. 1983. *The Fashion System*. New York: Hill and Wang.

Blatterer, Harry. 2007. *Coming of Age in Times of Uncertainty*. New York: Berghahn Books.

Bourdieu, Pierre. 1984. *Distinction: A Social Critique of the Judgment of Taste*. Trans. Richard Nice. Cambridge: Harvard University Press.

Brewer, Holly. 2005. *By Birth or Consent: Children, Law, and the Anglo-American Revolution in Authority*. Chapel Hill: University of North Carolina Press.

Brinton, Mary. 2011. *Lost in Transition: Youth, Work, and Instability in Postindustrial Japan*. New York: Cambridge University Press.

Brown, Kelly Williams. 2013. *Adulting: How to Become a Grown-up in 468 Easy(ish) Steps*. New York: Grand Central.

Buckley, Jerome Hamilton. 1974. *Season of Youth: The Bildungsroman from Dickens to Golding*. Cambridge: Harvard University Press.

Butler, Judith. 1990. *Gender Trouble: Feminism and the Subversion of Identity*. New York: Routledge.

Campbell, Colin. 1987. *The Romantic Ethic and the Spirit of Modern Consumerism*. Oxford: Blackwell.

Carton, Benedict. 2000. *Blood from Your Children: The Colonial Origins of Generational Conflict in South Africa*. Charlottesville: University Press of Virginia.

Christiansen, Catrine, Mats Utas, and Henrik Vigh, eds. 2006. *Navigating Youth, Generating Adulthood: Social Becoming in an African Context*. Uppsala: Nordiska Afrikainstitutet.

Chudacoff, Howard. 1992. *How Old Are You? Age Consciousness in American Culture.* Princeton: Princeton University Press.

Cole, Jennifer. 2010. *Sex and Salvation: Imagining the Future in Madagascar.* Chicago: University of Chicago Press.

Cole, Jennifer, and Deborah Durham, eds. 2007. *Generations and Globalization: Youth, Age, and Family in the New World Economy.* Bloomington: Indiana University Press.

———. 2008. "Introduction: Globalization and the Temporality of Children and Youth." In *Figuring the Future: Globalization and the Temporalities of Children and Youth,* edited by Jennifer Cole and Deborah Durham, 3–23. Santa Fe, NM: SAR Press.

Cole, Jennifer, and Lynn M. Thomas, eds. *Love in Africa.* 2009. Chicago: University of Chicago Press.

Comaroff, Jean, and John L. Comaroff. 1999. "Occult Economies and the Violence of Abstraction: Notes from the South African Postcolony." *American Ethnologist* 26(2): 279–303.

Condorcet, Marie Jean Antoine Nicolas de Caritat, Marquis de. [1795] 1955. *Outlines of an Historical View of the Progress of the Human Mind.* Trans. June Barraclough. London: Weidenfield and Nicolson.

Coontz, Stephanie. 1992. *The Way We Never Were: American Families and the Nostalgia Trap.* New York: Basic Books.

Côté, James. 2000. *Arrested Adulthood: The Changing Nature of Maturity and Identity.* New York: New York University Press.

Dalsgård, Anne Line, Martin Demant Frederiksen, Susanne Højlund, and Lotte Meinert, eds. 2014. *Ethnographies of Youth and Temporality.* Philadelphia: Temple University Press.

Durham, Deborah. 2000. "Youth and the Social Imagination in Africa: Introduction." *Anthropological Quarterly* 73(3):113–20.

———. 2004. "Disappearing Youth: Youth as a Social Shifter in Botswana." *American Ethnologist* 31(4): 589–605.

———. 2005. "Just Playing: Choirs, Bureaucracy, and the Work of Youth in Botswana." In *Makers and Breakers: Children and Youth in Postcolonial Africa,* edited by Alcinda Honwana and Filip de Boeck, 150–71. Oxford: James Currey.

———. 2007. "Empowering Youth: Making Youth Citizens in Botswana." In *Generations and Globalization: Youth, Age, and Family in the New World Economy,* edited by Jennifer Cole and Deborah Durham, 102–31. Bloomington: Indiana University Press.

———. 2008. "Apathy and Agency: The Romance of Agency and Youth in Botswana." In *Figuring the Future: Globalization and the Temporalities of Children and Youth,* edited by Jennifer Cole and Deborah Durham, 151–78. Santa Fe, NM: SAR Press.

Edmonds, Alexander. 2014. "Surgery-for-Life: Aging, Self-Fitness, and Self-Management in Brazil." *Anthropology & Aging Quarterly* 34(4): 246–59.

Erikson, Erik. 1968. *Identity, Youth and Crisis.* New York: W. W. Norton.

Featherstone, Mike, and Mike Hepworth. 1991. "The Mask of Aging and the Postmodern Life Course." In *The Body: Social Processes and Cultural Theory,* edited by Mike Featherstone, Mike Hepworth, and Bryan Turner, 371–89. London: Sage.

Ferguson, James. 1999. *Expectations of Modernity: Myths and Meanings of Urban Life on the Copperbelt, Zambia*. Berkeley: University of California Press.

Ferguson, Jane. 2010. "Another Country Is the Past: Western Cowboys, Lanna Nostalgia, and Bluegrass Aesthetics as Performed by Professional Musicians in Northern Thailand." *American Ethnologist* 37(2): 227–40.

Field, Corinne T. 2014. *The Struggle for Equal Adulthood: Gender, Race, Age, and the Fight for Citizenship in Antebellum America*. Chapel Hill: University of North Carolina Press.

Field, Corinne T., and Nicholas L. Syrett, eds. 2015. *Age in America: The Colonial Era to the Present*. New York: New York University Press.

Fortes, Meyer. 1984. "Age, Generation, and Social Structure." In *Age and Anthropological Theory*, edited by David Kertzer and Jennie Keith, 99–122. Ithaca: Cornell University Press.

Foucault, Michel. 1979. *Discipline and Punish: The Birth of the Prison*. New York: Vintage Books.

Frederiksen, Martin Demant. 2013. *Young Men, Time and Boredom in the Republic of Georgia*. Philadelphia: Temple University Press.

Frederiksen, Martin Demant, and Anne Line Dalsgård. 2014. "Introduction: Time Objectified." In *Ethnographies of Youth and Temporality*, edited by Anne Line Dalsgård, Martin Demant Frederiksen, Susanne Højlund, and Lotte Meinert, 1–21. Philadelphia: Temple University Press.

Freud, Sigmund. [1930] 1955. *Civilization and its Discontents*. London: Hogarth Press.

Ghannam, Farha. 2013. *Live and Die Like a Man in Urban Egypt*. Stanford: Stanford University Press.

Gottlieb, Alma. 2004. *The Afterlife Is Where We Come From: The Culture of Infancy in West Africa*. Chicago: University of Chicago Press.

Grinspan, Jon. 2015. "A Birthday Like None Other: Turning Twenty-One in the Age of Popular Politics." In *Age in America: The Colonial Era to the Present*, edited by Corinne Field and Nicholas Syrett, 86–102. New York: New York University Press.

Gupta, Akhil. 2002. "Reliving Childhood? The Temporality of Childhood and Narratives of Reincarnation." *Ethnos* 67(1): 33–75.

Hall, G. Stanley. 1904. *Adolescence: Its Psychology and its Relations to Physiology, Anthropology, Sociology, Sex, Crime, Religion, and Education*. New York: D. Appleton.

Hanks, William. 1990. *Referential Practice: Language and Lived Space among the Maya*. Chicago: University of Chicago Press.

Hansen, Karen Tranberg. 2005. "Getting Stuck in the Compound: Some Odds Against Social Adulthood in Lusaka, Zambia." *Africa Today* 51(4): 3–16.

Hobsbawm, Eric. 1983. "Introduction: Inventing Traditions." In *The Invention of Tradition*, edited by Eric Hobsbawm and Terence Ranger, 1–14. Cambridge: Cambridge University Press.

Honwana, Alcinda. 2012. *The Time of Youth: Work, Social Change, and Politics in Africa*. Sterling: Kumarian Press.

Illouz, Eva. 2007. *Cold Intimacies: The Making of Emotional Capitalism*. Cambridge: Polity Press.

———. 2008. *Saving the Modern Soul: Therapy, Emotions, and the Culture of Self-Help*. Berkeley: University of California Press.

James, Allison, and Alan Prout. 2015. "Introduction." In *Constructing and Reconstructing Childhood*, edited by Allison James and Alan Prout, 1–5. London: Routledge.

Jeffrey, Craig. 2010. *Timepass: Youth, Class, and the Politics of Waiting in India*. Stanford: Stanford University Press.

Jeffrey, Craig, and Jane Dyson. 2014. "'I Serve Therefore I Am': Youth and Generative Politics in India." *Comparative Studies in Society and History* 56(4): 967–94.

Johnson-Hanks, Jennifer. 2002. "On the Limits of Life Stages in Ethnography: Toward a Theory of Vital Conjunctures." *American Anthropologist* 104(3): 865–80.

Kertzer, David I., and Jennie Keith, eds. 1984. *Age and Anthropological Theory*. Ithaca: Cornell University Press.

Kratz, Corinne. 1993. *Affecting Performance: Meaning, Movement, and Experience in Okiek Women's Initiation*. Washington, DC: Smithsonian Press.

La Fontaine, Jean S. 1977. "The Power of Rights." *Man* 12(3–4): 421–37.

———, ed. 1978. *Sex and Age as Principles of Social Differentiation*. A.S.A Monograph 17. London: Academic Press.

Lamb, Sarah. 2000. *White Saris and Sweet Mangoes: Aging, Gender, and Body in North India*. Berkeley: University of California Press.

Lévi-Strauss, Claude. 1963. "The Structural Study of Myth." In *Structural Anthropology*, vol. 1, 206–31. Trans. Claire Jacobson and Brooke Grundfest Schoepf. New York: Basic Books.

LeVine, Robert. 1980. "Adulthood among the Gusii of Kenya." In *Themes of Love and Work in Adulthood*, edited by Neil J. Smelser and Erik H. Erikson, 77–104. Cambridge: Harvard University Press.

Liechty, Mark. 2002. *Suitably Modern: Making Middle-Class Culture in a New Consumer Society*. Princeton: Princeton University Press.

Livingston, Julie. 2012. *Improvising Medicine: An African Oncology Ward in an Emerging Cancer Epidemic*. Durham: Duke University Press.

Lutz, Catherine, and Lila Abu-Lughod, eds. 1990. *Language and the Politics of Emotion*. Cambridge: Cambridge University Press.

Lythcott-Haims, Julie. 2015. *How to Raise an Adult: Break Free of the Overparenting Trap and Prepare your Children for Success*. New York: St. Martin's Griffin.

Mains, Daniel. 2007. "Neoliberal Times: Progress, Boredom, and Shame among Young Men in Urban Ethiopia." *American Ethnologist* 34(4): 659–73.

Mannheim, Karl. [1952] 1972. "The Problem of Generations." In *Essays on the Sociology of Knowledge*, 276–320. London: Routledge and Kegan Paul.

Masquelier, Adeline. 2013. "Teatime: Boredom and the Temporalities of Young Men in Niger." *Africa* 83(3): 470–91.

McCallum, Cecilia, and Vania Bustamante. 2012. "Kinship, Gender and Individuation in the Day-to-Day Life of the House in a Working-Class District of Salvador da Bahia." *Etnográfica* 16(1): 221–46.

Meillassoux, Claude. 1981. *Maidens, Meal, and Money: Capitalism and Domestic Community*. Cambridge: Cambridge University Press.

Meiu, George. 2015. "'Beach-Boy Elders' and 'Young Big-Men': Subverting the Temporalities of Ageing in Kenya's Ethno-Erotic Economies." *Ethnos* 80(4): 472–96.

Merser, Cheryl. 1987. *Grown-Ups: A Generation in Search of Adulthood*. New York: G.P. Putnam's.

Mitchell, J. Clyde. 1956. "The Kalela Dance: Aspects of Social Relationships amongst Urban Africans in Northern Rhodesia." Rhodes-Livingstone Institute Paper 27.

Moore, Hollis. 2015. "Carcerel Courtship and Marriage: Understanding Young Women's Decisions to Forge Intimate Relationships with Imprisoned Men in Northeast Brazil." Paper presented at the American Anthropological Association annual meeting, Denver CO, November 21.

Munn, Nancy. 1992. "The Cultural Anthropology of Time." *Annual Review of Anthropology* 21: 93–123.

Newman, Katherine. 1988. *Falling from Grace: The Experience of Downward Mobility in the American Middle Class*. New York: Free Press.

———. 2012. *The Accordion Family: Boomerang Kids, Anxious Parents, and the Private Toll of Global Competition*. Boston: Beacon Press.

Nypan, Astrid 1991. "Revival of Female Circumcision: A Case of Neo-Traditionalism." In *Gender and Change in Developing Countries*, edited by Kristi Anne Stølen and Mariken Vaa, 39–65. Oslo: Norwegian University Press.

Önder Erol, Pelin. Forthcoming. "Youth Transitions to Adulthood in Late Modernity: Opportunities and Uncertainties." In *Issues and Themes in Contemporary Society. Volume 2 of a Festschrift for I.P. Modi*, edited by B. K. Nagla. Jaipur: Rawat.

Prout, Alan, and Allison James. 2015. "A New Paradigm for the Sociology of Childhood?" In *Constructing and Reconstructing Childhood*, edited by Allison James and Alan Prout, 6–28. London: Routledge.

Reynolds, Pamela. 1991. *Dance Divet Cat: Child Labour in the Zambezi Valley*. Athens: Ohio University Press.

Robbins, Alexandra, and Abby Wilner. 2001. *Quarterlife Crisis: The Unique Challenges of Life in Your Twenties*. New York: Penguin/Putnam.

Roberts, Ken. 2007. "Youth Transitions and Generations: A Response to Wyn and Woodman." *Journal of Youth Studies* 10(2): 263–69.

Schloss, Marc. 1988. *The Hatchet's Blood: Separation, Power, and Gender in Ehing Social Life*. Tucson: University of Arizona Press.

Schott, Ben. 2011. "Schott's Vocab. 'Moonlight Clan.'" *New York Times*, January 12. http://schott.blogs.nytimes.com/2011/01/12/moonlight-clan/.

Schrum, Kelly 2004. *Some Wore Bobby Sox: The Emergence of Teenage Girls' Culture, 1920–1945*. New York: Palgrave Macmillan.

Settersten, Richard, Frank F. Furstenberg, and Ruben Rumbaut, eds. 2008. *On the Frontier of Adulthood: Theory, Research and Public Policy*. Chicago: University of Chicago Press.

Silva, Jennifer. 2013. *Coming Up Short: Working-Class Adulthood in an Age of Uncertainty*. New York: Oxford University Press.

Silverstein, Michael. 1976. "Shifters, Linguistic Categories, and Cultural Description." In *Meaning in Anthropology*, edited by Keith Basso and Henry Selby, 1–55. Albuquerque: University of New Mexico Press.

Singerman, Diane. 2013. "Youth, Gender, and Dignity in the Egyptian Uprising." *Journal of Middle East Women's Studies* 9(3): 1–27.

Sommers, Marc. 2012. *Stuck: Rwandan Youth and the Struggle for Adulthood*. Athens: University of Georgia Press.

Steedman, Carolyn. 1994. *Strange Dislocations: Childhood and the Idea of Human Interiority, 1780–1930*. Cambridge: Harvard University Press.

Thomson, Rachel, Janet Holland, Sheena McGrellis, Robert Bell, Sheila Henderson, and Sue Sharpe. 2004. "Inventing Adulthoods: A Biographical Approach to Understanding Youth Citizenship." *Sociological Review* 52–(2): 218–39.

Trask, R. L. 1999. *Key Concepts in Language and Linguistics*. London: Routledge.

Turner, Victor. 1969. *The Ritual Process: Structure and Anti-Structure*. Chicago: Aldine.

Twenge, Jean. 2006. *Generation Me: Why Today's Young Americans are More Confident, Assertive, Entitled—and More Miserable Than Ever Before*. New York: Free Press.

Twenge, Jean, and W. Keith Campbell. 2010. *The Narcissism Epidemic: Living in the Age of Entitlement*. New York: Atria Books.

Urciuoli, Bonnie. 2008. "Skills and Selves in the New Workplace." *American Ethnologist* 35(2): 211–28.

Vandegrift, Darcie. 2015. "'We Don't Have Any Limits': Russian Young Adult Life Narratives Through a Social Generations Lens." *Journal of Youth Studies* 19(2): 221–36.

Vigh, Henrik. 2006. "Social Death and Violent Life Chances." In *Navigating Youth, Generating Adulthood: Social Becoming in an African Context*, edited by Catrine Christiansen, Mats Utas, and Henrik Vigh, 31–60. Uppsala: Norkiska Afrikainstitutet.

Weiss, Brad. 2002. "Thug Realism: Inhabiting Fantasy in Urban Tanzania." *Cultural Anthropology* 17(1): 93–124.

Wyn, Johanna, and Dan Woodman. 2006. "Generation, Youth, and Social Change in Australia." *Journal of Youth Studies* 9(5): 495–514.

Zhang, Xia. 2013. "Gnawing the Elderly or Gnawing the Youth: An Analysis of the Crisis of Adulthood in Aging China." Paper presented at the annual meeting for the American Anthropological Association, Chicago, IL, November 22.

CHAPTER ONE

⤳

THE PREDICAMENT OF
ADULTHOOD IN BOTSWANA

Jacqueline Solway

IN BOTSWANA, AS many scholars have noted, social adulthood entails a balance between "making oneself" as an autonomous individual and embedding oneself in a complex network of social relations and obligations (see Alverson 1978; Comaroff and Comaroff 2000; Comaroff and Roberts 1977; Durham 1999; Livingston 2009).[1] As a consequence of rapid urbanization and the increasing dominance of possessive individualism (Macpherson 1962), the balance has become harder to establish, and hence adulthood harder to achieve. I argue further that one generation's difficulty in entering the social phase of adulthood has implications for the preceding generation's ability to exit it, to move beyond the responsibilities of social adulthood to the satisfactions of elderhood. Change in historical experience disrupts expected life cycle transitions, producing tensions and conflicts not only for the members of a given historical cohort but between generations whose historical experience and expectations have differed from one another.

In 2002 I attended a large "white wedding" (*go nyala ka lesire*) in the village in which I had conducted my original fieldwork in the late 1970s and have visited repeatedly since.[2] The wedding was on a long holiday weekend, as most are scheduled now, so that urban-based village sons and daughters as well as friends and relatives could attend. Guests slept in various compounds, in tents set up for the occasion, and in the backs of vehicles. In the 1970s wedding rituals were less ostentatious and scheduled for any time since few villagers had formal sector employment apart from work in the South African mines.

I was particularly struck at the 2002 celebration to see the very same people who had done most of the physical work—food collection, securing of firewood, large pots, dishes, cutlery, slaughtering and butchering of animals, preparation of compound, cooking, serving—for the numerous celebrations that I attended in the late 1970s spend this event sitting comfortably with each other around the fire, enjoying pleasant discussion, and being served tea and bread for hours while younger people carried out the frenzied work. In 2002, many of the latter did not sleep for a night or two preparing the food and the venue for the wedding. A transition of generation had taken place in a twenty-four year period; a new generation took on the status of *bagolo* (sing. *mogolo*)—seniors or elders—in which their role at village celebrations was to be served, cared for, and given due respect for all that they had done over the years. They may be asked for advice but their main role is just to sit back and "eat" (see also Livingston 2007). Some seniors continue to work in the formal sector and many are active in agro-pastoralism (barring bad health), domestic labor, childcare, and kin work on a day-to-day basis but at a more relaxed pace than earlier in their lives.[3]

Seniors are conceived as moving out of adulthood, a status made possible only as a new generation moves into adulthood to take their place. Hence, I argue, the new "crisis in adulthood" experienced in Botswana needs to be conceived inter-generationally and as a process of regeneration (Cole and Durham 2007). In particular, I argue that insofar as young people experience difficulty in moving into adulthood status, so those people who are currently social adults will have difficulty leaving adulthood and "retiring" into the welcome status of bagolo (see Boddy this volume).

I examine the changing terrain upon which adulthood is attained and imagined in Botswana and explore the anxieties, dilemmas, and difficulties encountered by various generations that seek to "move on," in and out of adulthood in contemporary Botswana. The analysis is rooted in the long-standing tension between the efforts of "making oneself" and remaining entwined in ongoing social networks of rights, obligations, and hierarchies that coexist for Tswana. This chapter draws primarily, but not exclusively, on data about middle-class Tswana.[4]

THE "INDEPENDENCE GENERATION"

The couple whose wedding I attended in 2002 were already well into their thirties, had middle-class employment, an urban as well as a village home and two children (born more than a decade apart), who were soon followed by another. Although all historical cohorts are transitional in one way or another, this generation—namely those born primarily in the late 1950s through to 1970—just before and after Botswana's independence (1966), experienced particular change.[5] They had opportunities that their parents did not have and ones that their children, on the whole, do not have or have as easily as their parents did. The independence generation, born when almost all Tswana were rural based, did not imagine what lay ahead for Botswana in terms of vast mineral wealth, skyrocketing rates of urbanization, and tremendous expansion of the formal sector.[6] However, Botswana was growing even then with an expanding infrastructure as well as educational and health-care sectors. This generation's parents' aspirations were often limited to their children obtaining teaching or nursing positions (and/or continuing to farm) but many more opportunities became available for boys and girls by the time the luckier and more successful of the independence generation completed secondary school, an opportunity in and of itself that few of their parents had had.[7]

Not all or even the majority of the independence generation succeeded in gaining middle-class status but a great many did. However proportionately small in number, their patterns of opportunity, consumption, standard of living, and upward mobility have set a model that came to be seen as a norm against which many of their generation and subsequent generations continue to measure themselves and others.[8]

The couple whose wedding I attended in 2002 act, feel, and are recognized as adult (see Durham this volume) and have enabled their parents to move into elderhood. They are still relatively young but many of the independence generation experience difficulties reproducing adulthood in their children despite having invested seemingly much more into their children's upbringing. Many middle-class parents in Botswana spend a great deal of money to reproduce their class status in their children. They invest in private English medium schools and extra instruction in academic and nonacademic subjects, as well as in clothes, and general life style. However, while it appears as though they are investing much more in their own children than their parents did in them, this is true primarily in nominal and not real terms, given inflation and periodic currency devaluations. The independence generation's parents paid for school fees, uniforms, and school supplies and in remote areas had to send their children to stay with relatives or patrons in larger villages to complete even primary school. Many parents did not appreciate the possible future value of education. They often kept one or more children out of school to help in agropastoralism and frequently sent their children to school only when they were already pubescent. To send a child to school was to sacrifice labor and pay fees, money usually derived from cattle sales or migrant labor to South Africa. Thus the upwardly mobile of the independence generation had an advantage as their parents invested what was in those days a relatively substantial sum in both cash and lost labor.[9]

While the majority of the independence generation did not achieve full middle-class status, and many felt left behind by the material successes of their middle-class relatives, I know few who did not make the transition into social adulthood. Just a few years age difference, a change in aspiration, imagination, and luck had an enormous impact on the life course of these people compared to the previous generation. Some of the most poignant moments I observed were in the early 1990s as I watched many older brothers sitting with "nothing to do" see their younger siblings, who had gained valued employment after education, drive up in their shiny new 4×4 pickup trucks. The older brothers had assumed that like their fathers and uncles before them they would pursue oscillating migration to the South African mines. That employment opportunity largely ceased by 1980 as the South African mines required less labor and confined their recruiting to South Africa. A new and more materially prosperous vision of adulthood exhibited by younger kin was often a source of disquiet to their immediate elders.

Many of the independence generation are fretful that their children remain youths, leaving themselves unable to move into a comfortable elder status. This is true across the socioeconomic hierarchy. Current bagolo have a relatively clear sense of what adulthood entails and means and so do most of the independence generation, but shifting societal notions and circumstances have worked to erode what were never precise avenues to adulthood and to throw into question existing meanings of adulthood. There is a "crisis" of succession: insofar as their children remain stuck in a new kind of extended youth, many of the independence generation are left stuck in adulthood and with all of the work that entails.

The independence generation's "fresh contact" with their social universe (Mannheim 1952: 293) was strongly influenced by the new historical possibilities opened and imagined first by Botswana's independence and then by the vast wealth that followed. They came of age at a time, like all times, when existing expectations and structural locations set them on a life course that directed their acquisition of adult status, but they achieved it at a new historical conjuncture, one at which their expectations for themselves and their children took new turns.[10]

ADULTHOOD

Social adulthood in Botswana is no one thing or solitary status nor does it correlate easily with a particular biological marker or any specific accomplishment. Various criteria, such as achieving marriage, parenthood (not simply bearing but raising children), a stable livelihood and an established household may be invoked but not only do many adults lack one or more of these, rarely do they occur in linear order (see Johnson-Hanks 2006, and

Dungey and Meinert this volume). Persons are complex and their positions as adults or non-adults, along with the various "visible" criteria associated with adulthood, are contested.[11] According to my informants and observation adulthood is something recognized or conferred by others and performed by an individual gradually. It emerges through the work of kinship, showing responsibility and respect toward oneself and others; it entails authority and sacrifice. Maturity is both acknowledged and exercised in the process of becoming and being a full moral person (see Sykes this volume). One is recognized as a social adult by expectations and tacit acknowledgment of a person's authority. The status of adulthood was not automatic and not always achieved, or achieved well, yet today people in Botswana speak of a crisis of adulthood.

Adult status in Botswana is an unmarked and unnamed but significant stage of the life cycle with no Setswana equivalent term. Decades ago marriage and having children may have been markers but bearing children has long been disarticulated from marriage (Comaroff 1980; Kuper 1982; Schapera [1940] 1971).[12] Marriage rates for Botswana are low even by regional standards, and they continue to decline. Age at first marriage continues to increase (Kubanji 2014: 224–37).[13] Formal marriage and spectacle white weddings are largely confined to the wealthier that can afford or qualify for loans to fund them.[14] As in the 2002 wedding described above in which the couple already had children, were in their thirties, had cohabitated for many years, and had middle-class status, marriage coincides with and strengthens adult status: it is an indicator but not a prerequisite.

Initiation rituals (*bogwera* for men and *bojale* for women) launched young people on a course to adulthood; these largely were abandoned during the colonial era (Schapera [1953] 1973: 39). There is now a revival of initiation ceremonies and other "traditional" practices, which, among other things, articulate with Botswana's "tribal" (ethno-political) groupings. Renewed initiation rites vary in nature; many include aspects of the didactic functions of training youth for adulthood (Werbner 2009). As Durham notes in the introduction to this volume, these may provide some external recognition of changed status and a subjective self-identification of maturation but they alone do not confer adult status. For urban-based middle-class women a new ritual, the bridal shower, exhibits some qualities of initiation but its practice is limited to the small minority and for women much older than previous initiates (Solway 2016). Bridal showers entail giving gifts to the bride and are in this way commensurate with the spirit of globalized consumerism. Gifting to the bride and groom is new; not long ago all gifts exchanged during the marriage process went to the parental generation. In addition to gifts, brides are presented with questions by other women on how to behave as a wife, toward in-laws, and in wider society. These are pondered, debated, and sometimes reinvented or answered in new ways. In this way the bride as well as the attendees further their initiation into and redefinition of a new stage of adult life.

Botswana's staggering economic expansion in the final quarter of the twentieth century set a high standard of material consumption and lifestyle that youth strive to achieve. However, the opportunities to acquire valuable employment were much more readily available to school leavers two and three decades ago than now, while the level of necessary credentials continue to escalate, making it harder to fulfill the material demands of adulthood thus contributing to its elusiveness.[15]

In the late 1970s youth were expected to work in the yards, fields, and cattleposts of their senior kin; they were expected to attend school and attend to a multitude of tasks. Their lives were neither easy nor filled with leisure. However, much of the responsibility and work of building and maintaining the social good, of social reproduction fell onto the shoulders of their elders. This work of social reproduction remains ongoing and entails caring for young and elderly, involvement in local governance, kinship work such as participating in dispute settlement, arranging marriages, donating money and goods for rituals and other events, providing assistance of all sorts to youth as well as to visitors and others. To perform adulthood properly requires not only material resources to exchange with and/or help others with but also time, wisdom, thought, and the capacity to keep in view that the whole is greater than the sum of its parts. People look to adults for support and to carry out the work of maintaining harmony. It is hard and time-consuming work that for most adults becomes part of their habitus. But for youth, especially but not exclusively those raised in the urban areas as the majority now are, the possibility of taking on these responsibilities is increasingly met with anxiety and ambivalence. It is here that we see the tension entailed in Macpherson's possessive individual, a subjectivity that competes with the embedded social subject in the imagination of Botswana's youth.

Possessive Individualism and Adulthood

In 1962 C. B. Macpherson identified possessive individualism as a means to conceptualize the person within capitalist modernity. He wrote, "Possessive Individualism [is a] conception of the individual as essentially the proprietor of his own person or capacities, owing nothing to society for them . . . Society consists of relations of exchange between proprietors" (1962: 3). As an ideal type it represents an analytical abstraction of a raw and exaggerated vision of liberalism, market society, and globalized modernity. Yet it is also an image of self that circulates throughout the world today.[16] As a vision of life and subjectivity, it is regarded among many Tswana, especially the youth, whether consciously or not, as simultaneously appealing and dangerous. It is the tension between being the possessor of one's own self and property and being a socially embedded individual that lies at the heart of the predicament of adulthood in Botswana.

As already noted, the tension between the desire to make oneself and the need to remain socially entangled has long been identified as a central theme of Tswana society. However, the growth of possessive individualism heightens the tension and produces contradictory tendencies, especially in the relations between the independence generation and their children.

Contemporary marriages illustrate the contradictions facing young people today. Most classic works on Tswana marriage emphasize marriage as a process that entails years if not decades of rituals, and material and labor exchanges. In particular, bridewealth (*bogadi*), usually eight head of cattle or their cash equivalent, was generally completed long after the wedding rituals and occasionally even given by adult children or grandchildren on behalf of their deceased parents or grandparents. The exchange of bridewealth resolves the status of the children and their affiliation to their father's affinal group (Comaroff 1980; Kuper 1982; Schapera [1940] 1971; Solway 1990, 2016). In recent decades a shift has occurred in which wedding rituals and the exchange of bridewealth occur within a few days of one another, thereby collapsing what had been decades of open-ended obligation into a very short space of time. The "gift" contracts. Repeatedly I am told that couples, especially grooms, wish to conclude the marriage process all at once; that they "don't want to owe anything to anyone." Such assertions and actions are manifestations of possessive individualism.

In fact, wedding exchanges are rarely so quickly completed; extended kin provide much support prior to, during and after the weddings and husbands and wives remain engaged with kin, including affines, following the wedding. Although less has changed than it might appear, change is happening. Couples who now often share and pay much of the wedding expenses themselves and grooms who can amass bridewealth with less help from kin are making statements about their relative material and social autonomy. This is especially the case for couples who live primarily in urban settings and derive the greater part of their livelihood from employment, not rural pursuits or on family land and who thereby experience diminished material and social interdependence. Ties still bind but in attenuated form relative to several decades ago. Modern weddings raise the stakes and limit the options for achieving adulthood.[17]

Owning oneself and especially one's property, the amount and scale of which is constantly escalating in diamond rich Botswana, may confer economic status but it does not in itself confer the status entailed in being a social adult and in fact may run counter to it. Most people wish to attain adulthood but are worried about not being able to perform and achieve it effectively and are ambivalent about taking on the responsibility inherent in adulthood status. Part of this ambivalence derives from intensifying pressure and desire to consume, to control oneself, one's time, and one's property. Yet it is not simply selfishness that drives ambivalence (Livingston 2009). In fact, it is increasingly hard to move both into adulthood and out of it, into elderhood.

Next, I present two case studies that illustrate different trajectories among children of the independence generation in their attempts to come to terms with the transition to adulthood.

Mother and Daughter: Refashioning Adulthood

Tshepo is a woman now in her late fifties whom I have known since I first conducted fieldwork. She was in first year at university then but returned to her home village every school holiday where she worked tirelessly in her father and stepmother's household, cooking, cleaning, and looking after her younger siblings, of whom there were many. Tshepo rose eventually to become a senior civil servant, having worked long and hard to reach that level. She attained a master's degree in the UK and thus is familiar with Western lifestyles but she is committed to her life as a Tswana adult. She has a modest house in the capital and a pickup truck as well as a much older car that her daughter uses. The former proves more useful than a car for transporting goods and building materials, something she does for herself and many others. Tshepo has long been a responsible adult actively engaged in kinship work with both her father and mother's extended families. Tshepo retired from civil service recently and she now devotes herself almost entirely to kinship work. She had other post-retirement aspirations but explained that she is deferring these to focus on certain urgent kinship quandaries.[18] She is virtually the sole supporter of her village-based elderly mother since her younger siblings (she is the firstborn) are currently unemployed and is helping to raise her orphaned nieces. She is also involved in her father's extended family, having taken on the task of restoring peace after a fraught and painful inheritance (*boswa*) dispute that has festered since her father's death in 2009. This case set sibling against sibling, household against household, and has divided the extended family within the village and across the country. The case went to court with expensive lawyers on both sides and is now on hold since the premature death of Tshepo's stepmother, a death many attribute to the ugliness of the case and the ancestors' anger. Tshepo attends multiple meetings and events in her home village and elsewhere in an attempt to bring the sides together, dissipate conflict, and restore peace. These are all-consuming tasks but still leave her time to support and care for a cancer-afflicted cousin and others.

Tshepo has two daughters several years apart in age. As a single (never married) mother relying on one income, she struggled to raise them well and to provide the resources to enable them to become middle-class adults. They attended private schools and she paid for her elder daughter, Lerato, to attend a South African university because the subject Lerato wished to study was not available to her in Botswana. Tshepo's younger daughter is now in medical school in Botswana, having completed secondary school with the highest possible results. Lerato, now in her early thirties, is a professional working in the private sector. She earns more money than her mother did. Lerato is a kind and decent young woman, respectful to her mother, but to a point. The last time I spoke to Tshepo she said she asked Lerato to move out (she has previously shared accommodation with friends). While not presenting troublesome behavior such as drunkenness, theft, or extramarital pregnancy that concern many Tswana parents, Lerato does worry Tshepo. She helps little around the house and provides little financial assistance. She uses her mother's twenty-year-old unsafe car while her mother implores her to buy a new one. She is not married.

Tshepo told her, "you are an adult now and should be contributing more" but instead Lerato spends her money on clothes and other personal items as well as on entertainment and restaurants. Over lunch one day, Lerato told me that when she marries she does not want a conventional Tswana wedding with hundreds of people; she wants to know everyone she sees at the wedding. Tshepo and I looked at each other and smiled since we know the anthropological truth that weddings are more about bringing families together than they are about the spouses. But I am not sure Lerato understands marriage in that way. I doubt Lerato means this statement as repudiation of her culture or heritage. Indeed, Lerato was born and raised in town. Her mother took her to the village when she was young, but as she grew older she went as little as possible. She does not know how to behave in the village, how to comport herself, how to wash dishes without a sink and tap, and so on. She is uncomfortable and worries about the hygiene of food prepared in villages.

Lerato does not deny her kin but recognizes them in a different way than Tshepo. For instance, a few years ago, I was pleased to be invited to Lerato's birthday party that was held at an upscale lodge just outside the capital. I was not sure what to expect. Birthdays were not celebrated when I first went to

Botswana. The restaurant reserved a space for us and prepared a nice buffet at
Lerato's expense. Lerato received gifts; mine, suggested to me by her mother,
was a gift certificate at an expensive department store. All the attendees were
women and, with the exception of just a very few friends, they were kin of different generations. These were the women with whom Lerato wanted to spend
her birthday. Lerato's party reflects a rise of consumer culture but also the
importance and the limits of kin. The attendees at this party were invited in-
dividually, gifts were exchanged, and it is likely that Lerato maintains wider
reciprocity relations with these women. But Lerato's commitment to kin and
especially the work of kinship is unlikely ever to approach that of her mother.
Indeed, she looks at her mother and sees an overworked, exhausted woman
with an aversion, in her mind, to having "fun"—to taking more time for herself, seeking entertainment venues, leisure travel, restaurants, and the like.

Lerato is a perfect example of a new middle-class Tswana woman who
embodies the subjectivity of possessive individualism but is, at the same time,
entangled in a web of kin, but in a way that she chooses. Lerato is reluctant to
become an adult in the conventional Tswana manner but might well represent
a new vision of adulthood at least for the urban-born and bred middle class.
Lerato is uncertain whether she has the capacity or the desire to perform
adulthood effectively, at least the role of adulthood into which her mother attempts to place her. It is not material poverty that keeps Lerato out of social
adulthood; rather, she maintains her choice to refuse it for as long as possible
or to construct and to fashion a new way of becoming an adult in urban
middle-class Botswana.

Tshepo is unlikely to see herself replaced by her daughters as the social
adult she was raised to be and she will likely carry on in caregiving to relatives
and kinship work longer than she wishes. As for Lerato, the model of social
adulthood presented to her does not resonate with her own experience or desires. For example, it seems unlikely that she will be able or desire to solidify
adulthood through cattle, as I discuss below.

A "Successful" Transition

David was born in the mid-1970s to his then unmarried teenage mother,
Montle. Montle, an age-mate and friend of Tshepo's, was born in the early
period of the independence generation. Montle began but did not complete
secondary school[19] but attended a special course and subsequent ongoing
training for a low-level health-care sector position. Montle's eventual husband
also benefitted from the emerging opportunities of post-independence bu-
reaucratic expansion. With a few years of secondary education, he was able to

obtain various low-level civil service appointments. Importantly, both Montle's and her husband's employment, although relatively low paid, enabled them to remain in the village where they continued to farm and rear cattle and where they did not have to pay rent. Although they are not rich, all their children attended government schools and they live reasonably comfortably by village standards.

When David was two, Montle married and moved with David to her husband's village, a few hours away. Montle's husband raised David as his own and David considers his father's village home. Many more children followed over a twenty-year period. David was an exceptional student, excelling at all grades and eventually attending the University of Botswana and graduating with a law degree. After university he worked for the government for some years during which time he was sent on a training course to the United States. Eventually, with a partner, he opened a private legal practice in one of Botswana's secondary cities, not too far from David's home village. In his late twenties he married a young woman from his mother's home village (where he was born) who is also a professional. They have young children and visit their parents, especially his, often.

David, now in his late thirties, began his transition into adulthood in his twenties. He is remarkably self-reflective about the transformation and what it means. While he accepted the role, he might have liked to evolve a little more slowly. For instance, during a conversation we had not long after he turned thirty, he explained to me that his father was already devolving responsibility onto him. David was and is expected to lead events such as rituals and more secular activities on behalf of his parent's family. He is called upon to participate in resolving family disputes and problems, expected to be present at his in-laws' and mostly his parents' home frequently, to attend events as a representative of his family (parents' and own household), and to reprimand his younger siblings. In addition, he provides material support to his parents and in-laws. David's father wishes to move into bagolo status and David is facilitating this gradual transition.

David observes that his younger siblings are finding the transition into adulthood difficult. Some try to eke it out in town, others remain in the village with his parents, but most refuse to work in their parents' fields or cattlepost, believing the work beneath them. His siblings are not alone. David speaks of the difficulties facing youth, how many remain with their parents well into their thirties, and how demoralized they feel. He is sensitive to the livelihood precarity faced by his generation in contrast to his parents' generation. For instance, he explained that when the Botswana Defense Force originated in 1977 one needed a junior certificate, acquired after completing junior secondary school, to apply; now applicants need a high secondary school pass just to be considered. Applicants are also encouraged to have a post-secondary degree, diploma, or certificate.

David is fortunate and is aware of his privilege and the responsibilities it entails. He has worked hard and takes little for granted. He completed law school after Botswana's boom and built his career slowly, first working for the government, whose pay is less than the private sector and then opening his practice in a secondary city due to his observation that the capital was already saturated with lawyers. He lives unpretentiously by the standards usually associated with lawyers in Botswana. For instance, he drives an older small car and dresses appropriately for his field but without flash and designer labels.

David may have been pressed into adulthood somewhat earlier than he would have preferred but he has moved into it gracefully. He is deeply immersed in the day-to-day practices of adulthood. He is trusted and recognized for his effective leadership, capacity to make decisions, and to consider the long-term implications of his actions. Perhaps his legal training is an asset here but his own actions and his role model lifestyle contribute to his recognition.

David is deeply involved in kinship work, marriage negotiations, dispute settlement, and material support of kin, all of which are central components of adult status in Botswana. He is married and has established his own household. These are also manifestations of adulthood. His level of material consumption exceeds that of many in his generation but he has chosen a relatively modest path, keeping in check what might be impulses of possessive individualism and demonstrating his maturity and ability to enable his parents to begin to transition into bagolo.

It is also important to note that in contrast to Lerato, David was raised in a village while Lerato was raised in the urban areas. Thus David finds it easier to stay in the village and knows how to behave in the village context. While Lerato was raised to know her extended kin, David lived among them, although he completed most of his schooling beyond the primary level at boarding schools. The majority of young people of David's age and home area have relocated, or tried to relocate to town and the urban based generally have more attenuated links with their home areas than does David. Obviously David and Lerato are also differentiated by gender. In this case, however, I believe that divide is not crucial in explaining their stories; both young men and women find adulthood elusive. David and Lerato are examples of contemporary "young" people who have followed different trajectories in the move to adulthood and have made choices in circumstances both within and beyond their control. David has found a path in which he is able to better balance the competing desires and demands of social embeddedness and possessive individualism;

he has been able to "make himself" while remaining socially entwined. Lerato is finding that path more difficult in her urban milieu. Coming to a stage of life that Johnson-Hanks (2006) refers to as a "vital conjuncture," Lerato remains in the liminal space between youth and adulthood while David has moved into the early stages of adulthood.

Cattle and Adulthood

My current research is on the cattle industry as a lens into the evolving political economy of Botswana.[20] In doing this research, I asked everyone, "Do you own cattle and why?" When I posed this question to urban-based middle-class people, all of whom had alternative sources of livelihood that obviate their need to own cattle for sheer economic reasons, they all answered in virtually the same way. They said it was their "culture" and more specifically they all said that one needs to have cattle in order to be a "social adult." They always used the English term "social adult," explaining that there was no equivalent in Setswana. Most of these people were forty or over and most had been born in villages as part of what I call the independence generation. You were not a "man" I was told, unless you could present an animal from your own kraal for exchange as part of bridewealth or other prestations or to offer for slaughter for a relative's funeral or other rituals. An urban professional in his late forties told me that he began to acquire cattle little more than a decade ago. He explained, "You get to a point in life when your nieces and nephews start to marry and your seniors die and it is simply embarrassing not to be able to offer cattle from your kraal for the occasion." Owning cattle is a deep component of demonstrating masculinity, but it is also important for women. As one elite woman explained to me "when you get to a certain age [forty-plus] you realize the importance of social adulthood in which full participation and recognition requires cattle." She had joined a borehole syndicate and planned to expand her now small herd. She and others (male and female) explained that there is no real substitute for presenting your own animal for social purposes. You can get one from a friend or relative or buy one but it would not confer the same status as one from your own kraal.

Money is increasingly replacing cattle in exchanges but it is not the same. Many people tell me money is "cheap" and has no moral value.[21] If you use money for bridewealth, as many do now—but always calculated and articulated in numbers of livestock—it appears as though you are paying for or buying a bride and not engaging in an ongoing reciprocal network of rights and responsibilities. In Setswana one "gives" but does not "pay" bridewealth. Many parents refuse cash bridewealth and want to "see" the animals that are given for their child. This is so even if an animal is to be sold immediately (see Ferguson 1990). Recently I attended a bridewealth ceremony in a large Kalahari village. I had known the bride's mother's brother (*malome*) for decades. A mother's brother has the honor to be the first to step into the kraal, look at the bridewealth cattle and select, pointing to the one he wants. He was extremely proud of this privilege but told me that since he lived in another village, he was going to sell the animal to avoid transport costs. Indeed, I saw him at the local butcher's a few hours later where he was doing just that. However, his pride in receiving the live animal was not diminished. For women, too, having cattle bridewealth given for them entails a significant rise in prestige. One woman told me that when she returns to her home village she is treated with dignity and respect. It is not the big diamond ring on her finger but the fact that cattle have been exchanged on her behalf (Solway 2016).

The social and moral value of cattle, their capacity to summarize, create, and expand social identities and relationships and their role in mediating the world of humans and the gods or ancestors has been described eloquently and at length by anthropologists working with African pastoralists and will not be repeated here (see, e.g., Evans-Pritchard 1940). What I wish to highlight is the work of cattle exchange in signaling social adulthood. The exchange of cattle is a complex indexical sign; cattle exchange is public, it is recognized by all involved and it evokes past exchanges and thus relationships as well as heralding future ones (Solway 1998). In the past and still today to some extent, cattle exchange and slaughter accompany and mark many life cycle stages and rituals. Even as a weekend, mostly absentee activity for urban-based adults, raising cattle demonstrates that one has the wisdom, organizational and financial capacity, and resources to sustain a herd. More important, however, cattle exchange, like no other form of exchange, binds one within an ongoing web of social relations, rights, and obligations that form the basis of social adulthood. I was told, for example, that if a young person has given an animal to his or her mother's brother, the mother's brother has no choice but to help them if need arises. If the person was in an accident and calls his or her mother's brother, he would have to help and if the latter were unable to do so himself, he would have to find someone to do so in his stead. Adult status can and is achieved in the absence of cattle exchange but it is harder and the status is less complete, especially for a man.

Marriage and the exchange of bridewealth cattle are now restricted largely to the wealthier but other forms of cattle exchange remain important, especially those that mark life cycle transitions. For instance, as in the example above, young people, especially males, are meant to give their mother's brother a male animal; in return the youth are given a female animal to promote herd production. This exchange also leads young people to deepen their relationship with the mother's brother on whose support they rely in many ways. At early stages of the marriage process, cattle, which are not part of bridewealth, are presented to the woman's parents. This still happens even if the marriage is not completed. Among other important cattle presentations is the offering of an animal for slaughter and consumption at ritual occasions, the most important being funerals. Such an offering can also be interpreted as a sacrifice and one that affirms adult status. The vast majority of the independence generation was born in villages where the funerals of their seniors take place. Their own funerals usually take place there as well.[22] Independence generation urban-rural relations remain strong for the most part (Werbner 2004). However, as successive generations become more firmly established in town, rural-urban relations as well as the importance of presenting cattle for funeral slaughter and for demonstrating adulthood are likely to diminish.

Succession and Regeneration

Social adulthood confers status but it also entails significant responsibility. As a social adult one has "a seat at the kinship table" whether one wants it or not. Adults are called upon to engage in dispute settlement and to take part in marriage negotiations. They help raise junior kin and offer material assistance and advice for myriad family concerns. They have both authority and respect and the high status that comes with these. However, these engagements are time consuming and costly in a number of ways. Thus in the final section I return to the problems of succession and regeneration.

Cole and Durham (2007: 13) speak of regeneration as a fraught process and their depiction is apt for Botswana where the regeneration of adulthood and elder status is increasingly problematic. It is not just youth who are "stuck" but adults as well. Many older adults desire that their junior kin "come-up" and relieve them of some responsibilities (see Boddy this volume, for a discussion of thwarted generational succession in Sudan). Adult mothers complain to me that their sons (and daughters) refuse to marry, to become adults even into their forties. Marriage rates in Botswana are among the lowest in the world; there are many factors that contribute to this phenomenon that vary by gender and class, but ambivalence about taking on adult status is a factor.[23]

Current adults look to a period of time prior to old age—a period of bagolo to relax and enjoy the fruits of their productive and reproductive labor. They have helped raise junior kin and if urbanites they have opened their homes to their rural juniors and helped them to become established in town. These same adults have tirelessly participated in marriage arrangements, dispute settlements, and the like, all of which they find rewarding but draining at the same time. They want some relief and care directed toward them but the next generation is not stepping up. Interestingly, many youth on the cusp of adult status tell me that the youth coming up today behind them are different again and that it is difficult to provide for the "new and ill-behaved youth" as their elders did for them. These young people who have established themselves in the urban areas say they earn too little and/or live in too small homes to easily accommodate their younger kin wishing to relocate to town, despite the fact that many of them have themselves benefitted from older urban-based kin's hospitality. Again, regeneration is apt in capturing the new sets of difficulties entailed in moving through the life course.

For members of the independence generation, achieving adult status was rarely easy, but acquiring employment for those with the skills, education, and discipline was easier for them than it is for those of subsequent generations. As the economy began to slow and jobs were swallowed up by those coming of age in the 1980s and 1990s, a form of closure began and employment opportunities contracted. The state has cut back, instituted neoliberal reforms such as the imposition of user fees for some services and in doing so also attempts to create more "responsible" and self-sufficient citizens. Today's youth look at the current adults, especially those with valued employment, with awe but also bear some resentment toward them and to society. They feel robbed of the opportunities their seniors have had and it is difficult for them to be satisfied with the prospects open to them. Many who cannot obtain employment return to the rural areas where it is cheaper to live but the work is hard and considered by many to be degrading. Many others stay in town and take government sponsored very low paying internships that are in principle meant to be a gateway into a formal sector job but such jobs often fail to materialize and youth are stuck in limbo. Life to them is not fair and maybe they are right. They have been raised with ideals both of possessive individualism and embedded social personhood but it can be difficult to realize either, or even to know how to behave in order to perform them. These options seem to many to be in contradiction and competition, as they are everywhere. But in Botswana the contradictions result in several generations being stuck—stuck in youth and stuck in adulthood, in what is a crisis of succession and regeneration.

CONCLUSION

Honwana (2012) and Singerman (2013) depict African youth as locked in a period of "waithood," a liminal period in which youth, often well into the age cohort that ought to be marked by adulthood, are caught with limited options to transition into the forms of adulthood of their parents. Honwana emphasizes changes wrought by the onset of neoliberalism and its attendant unemployment. That youth find it increasingly difficult to obtain adequate jobs is certainly true, but there is more. Even young people such as Lerato who have attained valued employment find adulthood elusive. Lerato wonders what adulthood entails for young professionals such as her. She knows she does not wish to follow her mother's path that she sees as entailing too much sacrifice but neither does she wish to "escape" from her kin. For people like Lerato the path is uncertain and she remains hesitant, perhaps hoping for new opportunities and new imaginaries of what adulthood might entail. In the meantime her mother awaits transition to bagolo.

I have illustrated in this chapter that it is not just youth who are finding the transition to a new life stage difficult but also their parents who wish to move into elder or bagolo status. They also find this stage elusive. The independence generation has transitioned into social adulthood. Most feel the responsibility and authority that comes with adult status; some perform it better than others. For some urban-based middle-class young people, social adulthood, as they conceive it, is a choice, but one made in highly determined circumstances. For others, such as David, it is less of a choice than simply part of their habitus, but they are aware of alternatives and see some of their peers making different choices. They all live in a world in which visions of socially embedded adulthood and possessive individualism circulate and compete. Their decisions are not either/or but matters of degree, of ethical judgment between incommensurable commitments (Lambek 2015). In the case of Lerato and David, being middle class they can aspire to and perform both, but within the constraints and parameters that society sets out for them. The stakes are high for the children of the independence generation and for their parents.

Jacqueline Solway is Professor Emeritus of the International Development Studies and Anthropology Departments of Trent University of Canada. She is editor of *The Politics of Egalitarianism: Anthropological Theory and Practice*.

NOTES

I am grateful to the Social Science and Humanities Research Council (SSHRC) of Canada and to Trent University internal SSHRC awards for supporting this research and to the Government of Botswana for granting me research permits. Michael Lambek has deepened my thinking about generations and provided much editorial guidance. I am indebted to the many people in Botswana who, for decades, have kindly endured my intrusion into their lives and homes, shared their knowledge and offered sustenance to me in more ways than I can begin to list. Deborah Durham has been an outstanding interlocutor offering inspiration, critical dialogue, and editorial wisdom.

1. All personal names in this chapter are pseudonyms.

2. *Lesire* refers specifically to a white dress and *nyala* to wedding. In local vernacular understanding *go nyala ka lesire* connotes a white (*sekgoa*) style/culture and wedding (Solway 2016; van Dijk 2012). Such weddings tend to be expensive grand spectacles. The first in the village where I worked was in 1997.

3. Between the early 1990s and early 2000s when ARVs for HIV treatment became widely available the burden of caring for AIDS patients fell disproportionately upon seniors as they cared for sick young "adult" children as well as grandchildren.

4. Defining a middle class is a fraught and complicated matter in which economic, cultural, subjective and objective characteristics all matter (Heiman, Freeman, and Liechty 2012). "Middle-classness" in Botswana is something people feel, perform, and experience in multiple and often unstable ways—one can move in and out of the status. Emic criteria for Botswana usually include owning a car, increasing levels of material consumption and/or sending a child to private school. In narrow economic terms many Batswana would consider having sufficient income to obtain a bank loan as a bottom-line indicator of middle-class status. Increasingly in Botswana desires for adulthood and desires to be middle class become mutual proxies (see Hughes this volume).

5. Botswana's economic growth has been staggering; from being amongst the poorest countries in the world at independence in 1966, it had the fastest growing GDP per capita for the thirty-five year period prior to 2002 (various World Bank Reports). Through careful planning, Botswana has avoided the fiscal consequences of the Dutch disease that afflict many resource rich countries (see Acemoglu et al. 2003; Leith 2005; Poteete 2009). Its political achievements in liberal multiparty democracy have been equally heralded (see, e.g., Gulbrandsen 2012; Samatar 1999; Solway 2002; Werbner 2004) although detractors are vocal as well (Good 1992, 2008).

6. According to the 2011 census over 60 percent of the population now lives in urban areas; in 1971, already five years after independence, it was less than 10 percent (Gwebu 2014: 179).

7. There were fewer secondary schools prior to independence, they were expensive and usually entailed boarding. Many parents were unable or unwilling to send their children away. Also more opportunities for primary school leavers were available at that time compared to a decade or two later.

8. There are parallels to the age of high mass consumption that characterized the post-war generation of economic growth in developed countries as depicted by W. W. Rostow (1952) in his classic modernization account of stages of growth. It coincided with new forms of media such as television that projected the image of prosperous nuclear family suburban households that became accepted as a stable norm, but that have proven to be ephemeral, especially as Fordist models of growth, production and consumption were dismantled in the 1970s. However, the model of stable nuclear families each owning a car and other basic modern conveniences, even if illusory at the time, has proven to be a model that frustrates those unable to achieve it then and now.

9. See James (2015: 40) for a comparable account of South Africa's "independence generation."

10. Mannheim (1952, 303) observes that while generations share much, their experiences are not homogeneous. See Cole and Durham (2007), Honwana (2012), and Alber, van der Geest, and Whyte (2008) for anthropological approaches to Mannheim on generations.

11. During my 1970s fieldwork, I discussed with people who had the right to sit, speak, and be heard at the *Kgotla* (chief's court, village center and meeting place, seat of authority), which at that time pertained mostly to males as women were historically jural minors, represented

at Kgotla by male relatives although that was changing. No single attribute granted jural major status. Attaining a certain age, being married, and raising a family were important but none in and of themselves were sufficient. One young man, for instance, was married, employed in the civil service and had his own household, fields, and herd. But people told me that he was unreliable, drank too much, and while he might take a seat at the Kgotla, people were not certain that he would be allowed to speak or taken seriously (heard) if he did. He had not yet shown a sufficient degree of responsibility.

12. In the late 1970s the birth of a woman's first child was hardly considered a criterion for adulthood. If the mother was very young the grandmother would often claim her daughter's first child as her own and raise it is as such. Grandmothers explained that their daughters were too immature to raise a child, especially when the child was born outside of or in the early stages of what was then a lengthy marriage process (see Comaroff 1980; Solway 1990, 2016). The practice still occurs, although less frequently; now grandparents who raise their young daughters' first child are more likely to say that their daughters need to complete their education before parenting.

13. According to the most recent Botswana census (2011) only 17.9 percent of women are currently married while 53.4 of women have never been married (Kubanji 2014: 227). Kubanji (228) also reports that average age for women's first marriage is 32 and for men it is 36.1, almost a decade later in life than in 1971.

14. Contemporary white weddings have potlatch quality to them with each new event trying to outdo the previous. Couples often share expenses with their families or pay most of the costs that can exceed five times the couple's annual income (van Dijk 2012: 145). Weddings are a primary instance of the intersection of global consumerist desires and local cultural practices of social reproduction.

15. For instance, in the 1970s many primary school teachers had attained only standard seven, the final year of primary school, while "qualified" primary school teachers had two additional years of teacher's training college. "Unqualified" teachers were eliminated. Now primary school teachers must have completed a university or college of education degree, both post-secondary professional education degrees. Yet primary school teacher is considered a fairly low status position and poorly remunerated. Young people point out small, beat-up cars and tell me such a car is "a teacher's forum," indicating low status.

16. See Handler (1988) for anthropological usage of possessive individualism with respect to nationalism and McKinnon and Cannell (2013: 3–38) for a discussion with respect to kinship and modernity.

17. Not only are contemporary weddings expensive events for the hosts, but invited guests are expected to bring individual gifts, usually household items or cash. This was not the case in the past and serves as another instance in which the material requirements of adulthood have escalated.

18. In order to preserve Tshepo's anonymity I have omitted some details about the difficulties she faced in working her way up the civil service hierarchy. Similarly I have not detailed some of her post-retirement aspirations but wish to emphasize that apart from home improvements, these do not entail consumption but use of time for more personal and creative endeavors.

19. Montle left secondary school for health reasons a few years before her pregnancy. However, many girls of her generation did not complete school because of pregnancy, others withdrew for marriage, and if squeezed for cash, parents often allowed their sons but not daughters to continue school.

20. At independence cattle were the only real form of private wealth and export earner in the country (Morrison 1987). They were and remain to some extent widely, if unequally, owned. Many urbanites keep cattle in the rural areas with kin and/or hired hands. Minerals overtook meat as Botswana's most important export earner less than a decade after independence.

21. See Parry and Bloch's (1989) compelling argument that the exchanges most central to society's long-term reproduction of the social and cosmic order remain the most resilient to monetization.

22. This generation experienced high mortality during the worst of the AIDS pandemic before antiretroviral drugs were available in 2002.

23. While marriage rates are low, aspirations for marriage remain high (see Posel and Rudwick 2014). Many marriage negotiations stall in the process, are delayed, or not completed. In addition, marriage negotiations take longer and are more complicated than in the past when marriage was a process. The stakes are much higher now as weddings are a one-off and expensive event.

REFERENCES

Acemoglu, Daron, Simon Johnson, and James A. Robinson. 2003. "An African Success Story: Botswana." In *In Search of Prosperity: Analytic Narratives on Economic Growth,* edited by Dani Rodrik, 80–119. Princeton: Princeton University Press.

Alber, Erdmute, Sjaak van der Geest, and Susan R. Whyte. eds. 2008. *Generations in Africa: Connections and Conflicts.* Berlin: Transaction.

Alverson, Hoyt. 1978. *Mind in the Heart of Darkness.* New Haven: Yale University Press.

Cole, Jennifer, and Deborah Durham, eds. 2007. "Introduction: Age, Regeneration and the Intimate Politics of Globalization." In *Generations and Globalization,* edited by J. Cole and D. Durham, 1–28. Bloomington: Indiana University Press.

Comaroff, Jean, and John L. Comaroff. 2000. "Millennial Capitalism: First Thoughts on a Second Coming." *Public Culture* 12(2): 291–343.

Comaroff, John. 1980. "Bridewealth and the Control of Ambiguity in a Tswana Chiefdom." In *The Meaning of Marriage Payments,* edited by John L. Comaroff, 161–95. London: Academic Press.

Comaroff, John L., and Simon Roberts. 1977. "Marriage and Extra-Marital Sexuality: The Dialectics of Legal Change amongst the Kgatla." *Journal of African Law* 21(1): 97–123.

Durham, Deborah. 1999. "Civil Lives: Leadership and Accomplishment in Botswana." In *Civil Society and the Political Imagination in Africa,* edited by John Comaroff and Jean Comaroff, 192–218. Chicago: University of Chicago Press.

Evans-Pritchard, E. E. 1940. *The Nuer: A Description of the Modes of Livelihood and Political Institutions of a Nilotic People.* Oxford: Clarendon Press.

Ferguson, James. 1990. *The Anti-Politics Machine.* Cambridge: Cambridge University Press.

Good, Kenneth. 1992. "Interpreting the Exceptionality of Botswana." *Journal of Modern African Studies* 30(1): 69–95.

———. 2008. *Diamonds, Dispossession and Democracy in Botswana.* Oxford: James Currey.

Gulbrandsen, Ornulf. 2012. *The State and the Social: State Formation in Botswana and Its Pre-colonial and Colonial Genealogies.* New York: Berghahn Books.

Gwebu, Thando. 2014. "Urbanization Patterns and Processes and Their Policy Implications in Botswana." In *Population and Housing Census 2011: Analytical Report,* 168–81. Gaborone: Statistics Botswana.

Handler, Richard. 1988. *Nationalism and the Politics of Culture in Quebec*. Madison: University of Wisconsin Press.

Heiman, Rachel, Carla Freeman, and Mark Leichty, eds. 2012. *The Global Middle Class*. Sante Fe: School of Advanced Research Press.

Honwana, Alcinda. 2012. *The Time of Youth: Work, Social Change, and Politics in Africa*. Sterling, VA: Kumarian Press.

James, Deborah. 2015. *Money from Nothing: Indebtedness and Aspiration in South Africa*. Stanford: Stanford University Press.

Johnson-Hanks, Jennifer. 2006. *Uncertain Honor*. Chicago: University of Chicago Press.

Kubanji, Rebecca. 2014. "Nuptiality Patterns and Trends in Botswana." In *Population and Housing Census 2011: Analytical Report*, 224–36. Gaborone: Statistics Botswana.

Kuper, Adam. 1982. *Wives for Cattle: Bridewealth and Marriage in Southern Africa*. London: Routledge & Kegan Paul.

Lambek, Michael. 2015. *The Ethical Condition: Essays on Action, Person and Value*. Chicago: University of Chicago Press.

Leith, Clark. 2005. *Why Botswana Prospered*. Montreal: McGill-Queen's University Press.

Livingston, Julie. 2007. "Maintaining Local Dependencies: Elderly Women and Global Rehabilitation Agendas in Southeastern Botswana." In *Generations and Globalization*, edited by J. Cole and D. Durham, 164–89. Bloomington: Indiana University Press.

———. 2009. "Suicide, Risk, and Investment in the Heart of the African Miracle." *Cultural Anthropology* 24(4): 652–80.

Macpherson, C. B. 1962. *The Political Theory of Possessive Individualism: From Hobbes to Locke*. Oxford: Clarendon Press.

Mannheim, Karl. 1952. "The Problem of Generations." In *Essays on the Sociology of Knowledge*, 276–320. London: Routledge and Kegan Paul.

McKinnon, Susan, and Fenella Cannell. 2013. "The Difference Kinship Makes." In *Vital Relations*, edited by Susan McKinnon and Fenella Cannell, 3–38. Santa Fe, NM: School for Advanced Research.

Morrison, Stephen. 1987. "Development Optimism and State Failure in Africa: How to Understand Botswana's Relative Success." PhD diss., University of Wisconsin.

Parry, Jonathan, and Maurice Bloch. 1989. *Money and the Morality of Exchange*. Cambridge: Cambridge University Press.

Posel, Dorrit, and Stephanie Rudwick. 2014. "Marriage and Bridewealth (Ilobolo) in Contemporary Zulu Society." *African Studies Review* 57(2): 51–72.

Poteete, Amy. 2009. "Is Development Path Dependent or Political? A Reinterpretation of Mineral-Dependent Development in Botswana." *Journal of Development Studies* 45(4): 544–71.

Rostow, W. W. 1952. *The Process of Economic Growth*. New York: Norton.

Samatar, Abdi. 1999. *An African Miracle: State and Class Leadership and Colonial Legacy in Botswana*. Portsmouth, NH: Heinemann.

Schapera, Isaac. [1940] 1971. *Married Life in an African Tribe*. Middlesex: Pelican.

———. [1953] 1973. *The Tswana*. London: International Africa Institute.

Singerman, Diane. 2013. "Youth, Gender, and Dignity in the Egyptian Uprising." *Journal of Middle East Women's Studies* 9(3): 1–27.

Solway, Jacqueline. 1990. "Affines and Spouses, Friends and Lovers: The Passing of Polygyny in Botswana." *Journal of Anthropological Research* 46(1): 41–66.

———. 1998. "Taking Stock in the Kalahari: Accumulation and Resistance on the Southern African Periphery." *Journal of Southern African Studies* 24(2): 425–41.

———. 2002. "Navigating the 'Neutral' State: 'Minority' Rights in Botswana." *Journal of Southern African Studies* 28(4): 711–29.

———. 2016. "'Slow Marriage' and 'Fast *Bogadi*': Transformation in Botswana Marriage." *Anthropology Southern Africa* 39(4): 309–22.

van Dijk, Rijk. 2012. "A Ritual Connection: Urban Youth Marrying in the Village." In *The Social Life of Connectivity in Africa*, edited by Mirjam de Bruijn and Rijk van Dijk, 141–59. New York: Palgrave Macmillan.

Werbner, Pnina. 2009. "The Hidden Lion: Tswapong Girls' Puberty Ritual and the Problem of History." *American Ethnologist* 36(3): 441–58.

Werbner, Richard. 2004. *Reasonable Radicals*. Bloomington: Indiana University Press.

CHAPTER TWO

EDUCATED YOUTH AND THE SEARCH FOR ADULTHOOD IN POST-WAR SRI LANKA

Dhana Hughes

I FIRST MET Saman[1] one humid afternoon at a busy canteen in Colombo in 2013, some four years after the war between the Sri Lankan state and the Liberation Tigers of Tamil Eelam (LTTE) had ended. He was a tall and well-built young man in his mid-twenties, who was impeccably turned out in smart trousers and a neatly ironed shirt. Saman had moved to Colombo from his war-torn, rural village to pursue his education at a state university. Having completed his degree some weeks earlier, he was now feverishly searching for suitable employment. I had recently arrived in Sri Lanka to carry out fieldwork with educated unemployed youth, and was put in telephone contact with Saman by one of his university peers.[2] It had been Saman's idea to meet at this crowded canteen, where I had to strain my ears to hear him above the din of voices and clanging of plates. I found the noisiness of the canteen to be oddly juxtaposed to Saman's quiet and thoughtful manner. I would come to learn that this somewhat chaotic canteen was his favorite "haunt." It was a place that Saman would frequent with the three male friends from university with whom he shared a rented room in the outskirts of the city. They, like Saman, had recently completed their degrees and were searching for what they called "stable employment." Saman and I continued to meet regularly over the following months.

Saman appeared to have spent much time reflecting on his life. As we sat over tea and sweet buns he talked about his childhood marked by poverty and war, his anxieties about finding suitable employment, and his fears and hopes for the future in post-war Sri Lanka. Over the course of our meetings spanning almost eleven months, I found that Saman became increasingly dejected, frustrated, and at points even resentful, at his inability to find what he considered suitable employment, specifically a white-collar government job. He felt that this was preventing him from attaining adulthood, instead keeping him unnecessarily locked in a prolonged state of youth. This was a common theme that emerged across the conversations I had with a range of educated young people from marginalized backgrounds in Sri Lanka.

There is a growing body of rich literature from both the Global North and the Global South, on the difficulties young people experience in attaining life-stage advancement in the face of recent global economic and social changes brought on by the maturation of neoliberalism. World economic restructuring and the decline in public spending have blocked many young people's ability to access social goods associated with adulthood (e.g., employment, housing, marriage), particularly at a time when they are increasingly exposed to media images of adulthood based on education and employment (Aitken 2001; Ruddick 2007). Concurrently, economic recession, violent conflict, and the restructuring of labor markets often push young people into taking on responsibilities for social reproduction (Jeffrey 2010a). Scholars in other South Asian countries, such as India and Nepal, have begun to show how young people respond to the experience of "chronic waiting" between prolonged youth and an indefinitely (or sometimes strategically) delayed adulthood, which characterizes their lives (Jeffrey 2010b; Liechty 2009; Snellinger 2009). Similarly focused ethnographic research in Sri Lanka, based on the perspectives of young people themselves, is lacking. There is an urgent need to pay careful attention to what life-stage advancement means to young people in post-war Sri Lanka, and their aspirations for attaining it as shaped by their lived experiences.

This chapter is based on the life story of Saman, an unemployed young graduate of Sinhala Buddhist background.[3] Saman was the eldest of two boys born to peasant farmers in a rural and marginalized "border village" in the north of the country, which was caught between the ferocious fighting of the LTTE and the state during Sri Lanka's protracted civil war. Saman's story provides a lens through which to understand the wider socio-political forces shaping young marginalized people's imaginings of, and attempts at attaining, life-stage advancement in post-war Sri Lanka. The value of paying detailed attention to the life stories of young individuals such as Saman lies in the rich insight we gain into how a young person's positioning and location produce certain material, social, and structural effects, and into the changing experience of youth and its implications for attaining adulthood.[4] Saman's story is specific to him, and he speaks from a particular location and position. I do not claim that his story represents a universal "Sinhala" or "youth" experience. But it does in many ways resonate with and flesh out the hopes, concerns, and struggles of many young people I spoke to with a similar background to Saman's, particularly concerning their search for secure employment and connected aspirations for adulthood in the post-war period.

Saman's anxieties and hopes around finding suitable employment were inextricably tied to his aspirations to attain a particular version of social adulthood, entailing social class advancement. This took the form of respectable middle-class adulthood, which he understood would be achieved through education and securing a stable white-collar government job. Recent studies of youth overwhelmingly posit fluid and blurred "transitions," with people stepping back and forth between overlapping stages of life. What was striking about Saman was his subscription to a rigid ideal of life-stage advancement, where he saw himself neatly progressing between discrete stages of childhood, youth, and adulthood. Saman viewed life-stage progression as moving in tandem with his social class advancement.

I suggest here that for Saman and his educated, young peers, adulthood appeared to be frustratingly elusive because they understood it in terms of upward social mobility. While this is a familiar trend in many postcolonial, neoliberal societies across the world, in Sri Lanka it was further complicated by the prolonged war and its aftermath, along with the structural inequalities perpetuated by the education system and a powerful state.

Saman's "lived reality" was marked by disruption brought on by violence, poverty, social discrimination, and political corruption. I suggest that educated young Sri Lankans from marginalized backgrounds like Saman find themselves in a perpetual state of "anxious liminality" as they struggle to secure appropriate employment commensurate with their education and associated with the status of respectable adulthood. As the adulthood to which he aspires becomes more and more elusive, Saman responds by further investing in "skilling up" in an attempt to stay on the path to adulthood that he envisions for himself. Significantly, I show how throughout the conflict and beyond, the state has impinged on the lives of young Sri Lankans in ways that have largely frustrated their attainment of what they consider successful adulthood. While Saman and his peers expressed their cynicism and mistrust of the state, blaming it for blocking their social progression, they also continued to invest their hopes for achieving their ideal of adulthood in the state (by means of delivering white-collar employment). Furthermore, Saman's story highlights that it is often educated young people who bear the burden of social reproduction, which is built on ideas of social class advancement, in socially and economically marginalized Sinhala communities.

In recent decades, scholars have critiqued earlier conceptualizations of social maturation, from childhood to youth through to adulthood, within the confines of a rigid life-course model (Jeffrey 2010a). Rather than discrete life stages with definite and straightforward transitions being made from one to another, ethnographic studies have demonstrated that the distinctions and boundaries between childhood, youth, and adulthood are fluid and blurred (Beck 1992; Valentine 2003; Vigh 2006). They have shown that the named life-stage category of "youth" is relational and socially contingent, with "youth" often being an ambiguous, social experience. Durham calls for us to think of youth as a "social shifter," which situates it "in a social landscape of power, rights, expectations, and relationships—indexing both themselves and the topology of that landscape" (Durham 2000: 116; see also Durham this volume). Scholars have illustrated the fragmented and variable nature of transitions from youth to adulthood. Johnson-Hanks's (2002) work is of particular interest here. She has called for a new anthropological approach focusing on "vital conjunctures" in people's lives, to replace the traditional life-cycle model with its emphasis on "totalizing transformations" that move people from one named, stable status to another. By vital conjunctures, she refers to "a socially structured zone of possibility that emerges around specific periods of potential transformation in life," those "experiential knots during which potential futures are under debate and up for grabs" (Johnson-Hanks 2002: 871–82).

In Sri Lanka, youth and adulthood are commonly depicted as discrete stages of the life course, with progress from one category to the other being made through the attainment of a measurable set of variables.[5] The Sinhala term *tharuna* (youth) is understood as "young hopeful" or "one with potential," and depicts youth as a distinct and temporary life stage from which young people are expected to transition to adulthood (see Hettige 1992). Social scientists have identified employment, financial independence, and marriage as being important cultural markers of entering adulthood in Sinhala society (Hettige and Mayer 2002). Stable employment carries particular significance here, as the lack of financial independence poses a serious obstacle to marriage, particularly for men who are thereby prevented from being treated as "real adults" (Amarasuriya et al. 2009). My fieldwork in Sri Lanka found that this view of the life course was widely subscribed to by educated young people.

I would describe the period during which I met Saman as being a "vital conjuncture" in his life, where he appeared to be at "the intersection of structured expectations with uncertain futures" (Johnson-Hanks 2002: 870). Johnson-Hanks explains this concept by drawing from a social context where people move back and forth between nondiscrete age statuses. This reflected Saman's lived experience, which was marked by uncertainty and fluidity. At the same time, educated young people like Saman envisioned the life course as a coherent and ordered progression from the clearly identifiable stage of youth to the fixed destination of socially recognized adulthood. Saman held tightly on to the expectation that the stage of adulthood he envisioned (respectable middle-class adulthood) would come to him in a specific way (via white-collar government employment), at a specific time (upon completion of his education). The optimism, anxiety, and frustration that emerge from his story revolved around this central tension.

BACKGROUND: WAR AND DISRUPTION

In 2009 the protracted conflict between the LTTE and the Sri Lankan state, which had ground on for nearly thirty years, was fought to its bitter end on a narrow strip of beach in the north of Sri Lanka. The conflict, which escalated with state-sponsored pogroms against Tamils in 1983, ended with the elimination of the LTTE leadership and the declaration of "victory over terrorism" by the Sri Lankan state. Young people in many ways suffered the worst of the war, as government soldiers or guerrilla combatants on the front line, and through missed educational and employment opportunities. Sri Lanka's youth demographic (both majority Sinhala and minority Tamil youth) has powerfully shaped the country's post-independence political trajectory.[6] Prior to the war between minority Tamil militants and the Sri Lankan government, the post-independence state had been entangled in two other violent conflicts, both with educated, unemployed young Sinhala militants from marginalized backgrounds led by the Janatha Vimukthi Peramuna (JVP) in 1971 and the late 1980s (Hughes 2013). All three conflicts were underpinned by grievances around state power and politics, discrimination and exclusion, resource distribution, and concerns around education and employment. Significantly, the failure of the state to meet the aspirations of educated young people from poorer backgrounds, and its perpetuation of structural discrimination through the education system, were important factors underpinning the violent revolt of Sinhala youth. Many of these grievances persist, and carry important implications for young people's desires for life-stage advancement.

Sri Lanka is characterized by a highly educated population. Despite the unrelenting war spanning nearly three decades, Sri Lanka continues to have fairly high social indicators and a highly educated population, resulting from the policies put in place by the post-independence welfare state. The post-independence state's provision of universal free education and health care produced generations of well-educated, aspirational youth from the 1960s on. The introduction of free education from primary to tertiary levels; the achievement of gender equality in primary, secondary and tertiary enrollment; and a high youth literacy rate currently at 98 percent raised hopes among youth from poorer backgrounds, like Saman, for a potential escape from poverty and an opportunity for social mobility. But inequitable access to education and stark disparities in the quality of education and distribution of educational resources remain significant problems. While poorer rural youth, like Saman, receive their education in the vernacular (Sinhala or Tamil) in under-resourced schools, their wealthier multi-ethnic peers (mostly from urban backgrounds) are able to access English-medium education in better resourced, privileged state schools or private schools. Moreover, while the former youth cohort pursues higher education in free state universities in Sri Lanka, the latter predominantly attends fee-levying foreign universities, which carry more prestige. These factors are a manifestation of structural social discrimination, which has a significant impact on young people's employment outcomes and futures, further perpetuating socio-economic disparity in Sri Lanka.

Rapid economic liberalization from 1977 on, while bringing economic growth, new income opportunities, and the expansion of the private sector, has also resulted in sharp economic and social inequalities, an increase in state patronage in the distribution of economic and political resources, and a contraction of civilian state employment (see Hettige and Mayer 2002; Moore 1990; Venugopal 2011). The private sector, widely touted as the "engine of growth," remains small and has failed to step in where the state left off to create secure employment opportunities to meet the needs of the youth population on an equitable basis. Many young people find themselves trapped in temporary, poorly paid, non-decent work in the growing informal sector.

The centralized state, however, maintains a powerful presence in the lives and imaginings of young people like Saman. The colossal political upheavals wrought by educated, unemployed Sinhala youth in recent decades, apparently fueled by their "thwarted aspirations" (Hettige 1992), remain etched in the minds of political leaders who are reliant on the votes of the large, rural Sinhala constituency. Consecutive governments have tended to adopt reactionary (mainly politically driven) measures to deal with the volatile problem of graduate unemployment, most often through spurts of mass graduate recruitment into a bloated public sector. The most recent (political) gesture was made by the state in 2012 when it recruited some 52,000 unemployed local graduates to the white-collar government sector. The graduates appointed far exceeded the existing vacancies, and were recruited largely in response to loud public protests over graduate unemployment.[7]

Ethnographic fieldwork for this research was conducted in 2013/2014 during the post-war period of rule by the Rajapaksa regime, which was characterized by authoritarianism, nepotism, corruption, state violence, and triumphant Sinhala nationalism. The four years that followed the end of the war in 2009 further witnessed the rapid growth of infrastructure development projects, provincial council elections held in the north, a creeping militarization of society, two US-led resolutions against Sri Lanka at the UN Human Rights Council, and calls for an international inquiry into human rights violations, among other developments.[8] In 2015 President Mahinda Rajapaksa faced a sensational, and unexpected, electoral defeat. The new government led by President Maithripala Sirisena initially raised hopes for democracy, accountability, and sustainable peace. These hopes, however, have dissipated rapidly as allegations of corruption, nepotism, and lack of accountability mark the administration of President Sirisena.[9]

SAMAN'S ASPIRATIONS FOR ADULTHOOD

Saman remained in Colombo doing various temporary service-sector jobs, such as working in fast food restaurants, while he continued to seek government employment. He spent the money he earned from these jobs on his board and lodging, sending the rest to his family. It was barely enough for him to get by, he lamented. He complained that he had little time for leisure activities. On the rare occasions in which he did have time to spare, he would spend it watching TV with his friends and drinking tea in local cafes (including the canteen where I first met him). His social circle was largely comprised of young people who had completed their degrees and were in search of stable employment, like him. Saman strived to stay on the path of progressing to middle-class adulthood as he sought to improve his marketability in the employment field by attending various courses such as English, IT, and human resource management. When I asked him why he chose these particular courses, he told me somewhat vaguely that his friends, who had also signed up to the very same courses, had told him that these skills would make him attractive to employers.

Saman yearned for adulthood, and the social and economic security he imagined it would bring. His understandings of adulthood were shaped by poverty, war, and education. While Saman viewed his childhood and youth as stages of struggle and insecurity, he had anticipated his "transition" to adulthood to be smooth by dint of his education. Adulthood was seen as a fixed destination, which promised the rewards of socioeconomic stability and a life of relative ease, free from the struggles of his childhood and youth.

The adulthood that Saman envisaged was not an individual destination, but one that was tied to the aspirations of his family, and embedded in powerful cultural ideals such as social status and respectability. As an educated young person, then, finding work was not simply about getting a fulfilling job with decent pay. It was about finding a job that was considered suitable by

Saman's family and the village "community."[10] Importantly, it was not just about lifting his family out of poverty, but also about raising their social status and respectability at the same time, through the elevation of his own social status. Saman and his family had believed that education would enable him to move up the rigid Sinhala social class hierarchy by awarding him white-collar state employment. For young people from marginalized backgrounds, like Saman, and for their families, the "transformative potential of education" (Jeffrey et al. 2004) lay in its promise of social class advancement.

Saman believed that a government job would bring him income security, a pension, decent employment conditions, job stability, and, more importantly, social status and respectability, which are culturally tied to ideals of the Sinhala rural middle class. This would enhance his marriage prospects and also hold the potential for intergenerational social mobility, whereby Saman could cultivate the social connections necessary to improve the social and economic prospects of his children. Saman confided that he would like to marry and start a family within the next five years, but had not yet met the right woman. Anyway, he went on, he needed a stable government job first, because the long-term economic security and social status that it symbolized would render him more marriageable. It was important for Saman (and his family) that his future wife was educated to his level, and ideally in white-collar government employment herself.

It should come as no surprise that many young people who had been forced to suffer the insecurity and "assaults on dignity" (Farmer 1996) wrought by poverty valued the long-term stability, security, and enhanced social status apparently offered by white collar government employment (i.e., the pension, stable income in the form of a monthly salary, and long-term job security) over private sector employment. The latter, despite its potential for higher pay, was considered risky and unstable. The government jobs that Saman and his educated peers clamored for were largely described to me in abstract terms, rather than adhering to any particular occupation, department, or specialization within the vast government sector. A government job was considered desirable if it was white-collar and involved working in an office. This, they believed, would confer respectability and social status on the educated young person and by extension her/his family in the eyes of their rural Sinhala communities.

SAMAN'S STORY: GROWING UP THROUGH WAR

Saman carved out his childhood as a distinct stage of his life, which was characterized by war, poverty, and disrupted education. His enduring memories were of fear, insecurity, disruption, loss, and a focus on surviving violence. The unfortunate location of his home village resulted in a heavy state military presence and frequent attacks on the village by the LTTE. Although he came from the Sinhala ethnic majority, he was part of the local minority (along with Muslims) in his village, which was inhabited predominantly by Tamil people. Growing up in a multi-ethnic community, he firmly believed, had enriched his childhood. The majority of his childhood friends were Tamil-speaking (a language he spoke fairly fluently). He told me, "we played together and our families were close." He recalled attending village funerals as a child, where both Hindu and Buddhist rituals were performed. Saman also had Tamil relatives, as previous generations had married across ethnic lines in the village, a practice that dissipated as the war amplified and drove a wedge of mistrust between ethnic communities.[11] He explained that before the war, people in his village were largely united like any small rural community leaving room for mundane problems between neighbors. Their main focus was grappling with poverty. Saman told me somewhat bitterly, "We never asked for this war, but it was we who had to suffer it."

As the violence escalated, resentment and mistrust festered between Sinhala and Tamil people, fracturing community relationships, and entrenching self-identification with increasingly polarized ethnic groups. With the increasing militarization of his village came the loss of his Tamil friends, as many Tamil inhabitants moved out of the village following harassment by state soldiers. Saman emphatically stated, "a great injustice was done to our Tamil neighbors by the soldiers." He attempted to make sense of this by taking account of the prevailing climate of violence and chaos, and the pressure of combat (and its brutalizing effects) on the "young boys" (soldiers) who were handed weapons and deployed for prolonged periods in remote jungle-ridden villages (such as his), to fight a relentless war. Saman's experience of conflict during his own childhood, along with the brutalizing effects of war and sensitization to violence he had witnessed among young men from a similar background to his who had followed the path of soldiering, shaped his own aspirations for the future. Saman longed for a future based on imaginings of a stable, secure adulthood, free from poverty and violence.

The war resulted in student and teacher absenteeism, disrupted lessons, and inadequate resources. For periods of time, the village school functioned as a shelter for displaced people who streamed in from the surrounding areas, which further impacted adversely on his school education. Sleepless nights spent hiding in the jungle, in the top of trees, or in bunkers underground resulted in poor school attendance and performance. On average, Saman was only able attend school two to three days of the week. He told me:

Sometimes you were hiding in the same jungle in which LTTE cadres and the army were roaming. We couldn't tell the difference between them in bitter night in the thick of the jungle. If someone called out to us as children we knew never to respond and to stay silent. Because we couldn't know for sure who they were. When we were underground hiding in the bunkers we could feel the footsteps of people walking overhead, and hear voices. We would feel frightened. But we were also young, so because our parents were there we would also get some sleep, curling up on their laps. But only now I think about how frightening it must have been for our parents.

Despite the obstacles thrown in the way of his school education, Saman was determined to see his education through, goaded by his parents and schoolteachers. He credited them with pushing him to study hard and drilling into him the aspiration to leave the village and make something of his life. Saman failed his *Shishatvaya* exam, on which he had pinned his hopes of obtaining a transfer to a better school outside the conflict zone.[12] Nevertheless, at the age of fourteen, Saman managed to gain acceptance to a school in a neighboring town with the help of some distant relatives, who also agreed to accommodate him until he completed his A levels. Although he failed at his first attempt at A levels, he successfully re-took the exams and was accepted to a university in greater Colombo.

Saman's childhood determination to get a university education was driven by a desire to leave his village, and to get a decent job that would enable him to lift his family out of poverty and suffering, to move them away from the village, and to concomitantly raise their social status. He had come to realize from a young age that if he were to remain in his village and not pursue higher education, the only option available to him as a young Sinhala man of poor background would be that of enlisting in the security forces, a fate he resisted amid a brutal war involving a high probability of death or life-altering disability. Alternatively, engaging in rice farming in the face of a crisis in the rural economy, and the violent targeting of peasant farmers by the LTTE, would not offer him the escape from structural and physical violence that he desired. He explained:

I saw how my parents suffered . . . In our area people suffered greatly because of the war and poverty. So I had to think seriously at a very young age about staying in the village or leaving. If I stayed on, I would have had to join the army to fight in the war. That was the only opportunity available to the Sinhala youth like me in my area. You join either the navy, the airforce, the army, or the homeguards.

As the war escalated in the 1990s, the army grew to be Sri Lanka's largest employer. The military came to occupy a critical position in rural villages as a source of livelihood for young Sinhala men from poorer backgrounds, against the backdrop of stark economic inequality, a widening rural-urban gap, and a crisis in rural agriculture (Venugopal 2011). Despite the nationalist rhetoric espoused by powerful political elites portraying soldiers as "patriotic heroes" fighting to defend the nation from terrorism, many young Sinhala men signed up to fight on the frontline of a brutal war out of sheer economic desperation (Gamburd 2004). In the short term, political leaders used the war to solve the connected problems of rural poverty and unemployment, while at the same time providing a convenient means of averting the reoccurrence of Sinhala youth insurgencies in the rural south. These concerns undoubtedly contributed to the post-war state's decision to maintain a bloated military.

Moreover, while soldiering offered young men from impoverished backgrounds with lower education levels a means to attain social adulthood (by providing salaried work and the ability to support their families, which in turn rendered them marriageable), it pushed them from structural violence into the arms of physical violence. Importantly, soldiering did not enable the social class mobility to which Saman aspired, and believed to be achievable through higher education. The heavy responsibility for intergenerational social mobility sat firmly on Saman's young shoulders. Saman saw the end of war as promising new opportunities for the future. Yet the hope he held out for secure employment and a better future was also tinged with a sense of dejection. As Saman and his peers saw it, the encroachment of politics on access to state employment, and increasingly private sector employment, contributed to a disappointing gulf between their aspirations and their lived realities. Saman was not passive in the face of conflict; he creatively tried to steer his life through the constraints imposed on it. He spent much time reflecting on the dynamics of the war and its end. While he, like everyone else I spoke to, was relieved that the war was now over, Saman continued to be troubled by the violence and the way in which it was brought to a finish. Saman construed the war as being imposed on his village by external forces, by powerful and manipulative politicians on both sides of the ethnic divide. He blamed former political leaders and those belonging to the higher echelons of the military for perpetuating and dragging out the war for personal profit, while poor young men from both sides of the ethnic divide continued to die on the battlefront. Saman commented: "The war could have ended several years ago through negotiations. But the political leaders of the time and some of the big people in the military dragged it out over the years. That is why we have a common saying that the war was cultivated and eaten by big people (*loku minissu yuddhe wawāgena kāwa*)."

Gamburd (2004: 154) glosses the oft-repeated Sinhala phrase "the big people cultivate and eat (from the war)" as "people in power grow and harvest the ethnic conflict, perpetuating it for their own benefit." Despite vociferously criticizing the harassment of his Tamil neighbors by the soldiers in his village, Saman maintained that his support and gratitude lay with the military. He told me that this was simply because it was the military that had protected his village and his family from destruction by the LTTE. As a child he had lived in constant fear of his family being murdered by the LTTE; as farmers working in paddy fields they were particularly vulnerable to LTTE attacks. At the same time, however, he was adamantly opposed to the "war victory" triumphalism espoused by the state. He reflected:

Two things can come out of war. Either one side is destroyed or both sides are destroyed. That is the final outcome of war. In our country what happened was that one side was destroyed. This was not a war against an external enemy . . . but one that grew from within the country. So we haven't won the war. What happened was that a segment of our people was destroyed. So we haven't won this war. It was a disaster. What has happened is that we have moved backwards rather than forward.

POST-WAR ECONOMIC DEVELOPMENT: "ROADS DON'T EASE PEOPLE'S HUNGER"

With the end of the war in 2009, Saman had felt a sense of relief and hope. He had believed that the future looked positive for young people like him, with peace promising new opportunities. It seemed to him that the struggles he had endured during his childhood and youth would now give way to a smooth transition to stable employment and a secure future. This mirrored his expectations for the country. He hoped that with the end of the war Sri Lanka would leave behind its violence and struggles, bringing forth social and political progress, and sustainable peace, within which he could attain the kind of adulthood he sought.

The Rajapaksa government's post-war development programs brought water and electricity to his village, and new infrastructure had improved people's mobility.[13] While he maintained that these large infrastructure projects were necessary for the country's overall development, Saman emphasized that economic development alone was insufficient to build a healthy and prosperous post-war society: economic development had to be combined with social and political development. He told me:

Development is happening, I accept that . . . We are behind the rest of the world by thirty years due to the war . . . [But] development is not just building roads or removing coconut trees from one area and bringing them to plant here. . . .[14] Development is about education, health, nutrition, jobs. Development means bringing together and developing the society, the economy, and politics. It's not just about what you see on the surface.

Saman's concern about the inadequacy of infrastructure projects alone to foster development was captured in his comment: "roads don't ease people's hunger."[15] Saman grew increasingly frustrated as the post-war new dawn he had anticipated for educated young people like himself was failing to materialize. He went on to tell me that the employment opportunities promised by large infrastructure projects were elusive to poorer youth like himself who lacked the necessary political connections. There were some employment opportunities available on construction sites, he said, but these were often poorly paid and temporary; moreover, many of the workers employed on these projects were from overseas (predominantly from China). Saman's critique of the state's post-war development program was further built on concerns around corruption, transparency, and accountability. He commented on "kick-backs" and lucrative development contracts being awarded on the basis of political patronage to a select few. The large majority of young people I spoke to expressed similar concerns over the lack of transparency and accountability for post-war development expenditure, and through this conveyed their lack of trust in the politicians responsible for implementing the post-war development program.

Saman identified unemployment combined with the soaring cost of living and economic hardship as the most urgent problems facing young people in post-war Sri Lanka. Saman and his family had invested their hopes for social class mobility in education, and it was to this end that he had expended his efforts in the face of numerous obstacles that war and poverty had thrown his way. But in reality Saman's life as an educated young man was marked by a series of disappointments. Education had thus far failed to yield the desired white-collar employment and attendant entry to middle-class adulthood it had seemed to promise. Saman described his current existence as one of *degidiyawa* (uncertainty) and anxiety about what the future would bring. He had applied for several advertised state and private sector jobs, but had not as yet been successful in securing one.

Saman told me that if it were up to him he would gladly work in either the private sector or the state sector, as long as the work was interesting and the pay was decent. But he stated emphatically that finding a job in the state sector was imperative in order to meet the expectations of his family and village community. He explained:

The expectations of my village and family are such that I as a degree holder should do a job that is suitable to my degree. So I am not able to take certain jobs. My parents and the village people expect that I do a government job as opposed to a private sector job. The village people invariably look to see what [job] this person [Saman] is doing. So while I will do whatever job I can get, I want a government job. . . . We may be able to earn a better income, if instead we were to do some agricultural work . . . that is if it is done properly. But the problem we face is, how can we go back to the village and do this? The village people think . . . they don't understand what a degree is . . . they think that getting a degree is the most significant thing that one can possibly achieve in life. So their expectations are for a high-end job. . . . So the main reason I want a government job is social acceptance/status. When you look at Sri Lanka's social culture, people place more value on a state job than on salary.

Skilling Up

Saman maintained that his inability to speak English prevented him from finding white-collar work in the private sector. He told me that this increasingly applied to some sections of the state sector as well. At the same time, political patronage and corruption (e.g., money required for bribes) shut him firmly out of state employment. English is widely taken as a prerequisite for white-collar employment in the private sector. This puts youth from poorer backgrounds educated in the vernacular in state institutions, like Saman, at a distinct disadvantage from the outset. State schools in rural and marginalized areas (like the one Saman attended) suffer from neglect and chronic resource shortages, most prominently the lack of qualified English teachers. Importantly, English language capability is loaded with power and meaning, functioning as a marker of social class, rather than simply being a technical skill requirement. English is commonly referred to as "the sword" (*kaduwa*), a weapon of power wielded by the privileged classes to oppress "the masses." How it is embodied and performed carries significant implications for the life chances of young people (see Amarasuriya 2010). White-collar employment in the private sector is dominated by English-speaking, privately educated, multi-ethnic urban youth of privileged backgrounds. Moreover, the families of urban elite youth utilize their class networks as leverage to access employment in the private sector for their children, which in turn puts young graduates like Saman, who lack the relevant social and cultural capital (e.g., social contacts), at a disadvantage.

Scholars have focused on the temporal experience of waiting as unemployed youth attempt to deal with the liminality they are faced with, perpetuated by the mismatch between aspirations and social realities (Jeffrey 2010b; Katz 2004; Mains 2007). What struck me about educated unemployed youth in Sri Lanka, such as Saman, was just how busy they were. Much of their time was occupied with skilling up in the form of attending various courses (e.g., English, IT, human resource management), in between job hunting and engaging in various forms of temporary work. Skilling up here appeared to be "a mode of being" for unemployed youth (see Snellinger n.d.). It was an important means through which they gave meaning to, and negotiated, a world ridden with *degidiyawa* and anxiety. Through skilling up, young people attempted to re-empower themselves by garnering a sense of certainty and investing in hope for the future.

Saman was faced with managing multiple expectations in his search for secure employment. He had to manage the pressure of job hunting in a competitive environment where the odds are stacked against youth like himself from socially and economically marginalized backgrounds; of economically supporting his family; of securing respectable employment befitting an educated young man, which would open the door to middle-class adulthood; and of improving the social status of his family. His failure to meet these expectations gave rise to a sense of shame, which in turn led him to reduce his visits home. He told me that he was fed up with his neighbors and relatives asking him why he had not yet found a (government) job. He could not tell them that he was working in a fast food outlet through fear of losing face, and instead lied that he was teaching part-time at a university. Saman expressed frustration at their lack of understanding of the competition and other difficulties that marred the process of finding state employment. Not only were his own aspirations and respectability at stake here, but also those of his family. Loss of face and shame carry powerful cultural weight in Sinhala society, and this along with the sense of having failed in his duty to ensure the upward social mobility of his family would be a heavy burden for Saman to bear.

"Political Buddies" and the Politicization of Employment

Saman cited the stranglehold of politicization on the employment sector, which entailed appointments based on political patronage, nepotism, and corruption (e.g., jobs in exchange for bribes), as the central challenge faced by young people like him in their search for secure employment. Saman described this as an injustice (*asādhāranakama*) wrought on educated young job seekers like himself.[16] While political patronage primarily applied to securing work in the state sector, the increasing entanglement of politicians and their relatives in private businesses post-war saw the creeping politicization of the private sector, too. There was remarkable uniformity across the responses of educated unemployed young people I interviewed, in their identification of political patronage, corruption, and nepotism as being fundamental barriers to finding suitable state employment. Politics (*deshapālanaya*) was widely construed by young people to be a dirty and dangerous game, and involvement in it was considered immoral and even shameful. Entanglement in politics could potentially compromise the dignity and social status conferred upon an individual by education. Many young people drew my attention to the fights and shoot-outs that often broke out between rival politicians and their "thugs," and to the violent and belligerent antics of politicians' offspring. This situation engendered a sense of disillusionment, disenchantment, and apathy on the part of educated unemployed youth like Saman when it came to politics. The following extract of a conversation between Saman and me gives an insight into his perspectives on the nature and extent of this significant problem.

> SAMAN: "When you take an *amāthayansha* (ministry), the *lēkham* (secretary) is your wife. Then the people who fill every executive-level post there are your family members, your older brother, younger sister, older sister, younger brother. So the state sector functions as a *paul vādaya* (family dynasty). Nepotism is rife in the state sector. It runs through the top-most levels down to the bottom. Even the auxiliary staff in hospitals are appointed politically (through political patronage). The health minister's co-villagers are recruited to hospitals as *kamkaruwo* (laborers). You can't even get a *kamkaru* (laboring) job without political connections."

> DH: "How would you develop such connections to secure a job?"

> SAMAN: (laughs.) "That is what we call '*kadē yanawa*' . . . [17] You go during the elections with a bundle of the politician's posters and stick them up everywhere, then you get a loudspeaker and travel around the village in a vehicle propagating their election message, and you get a crowd together to attend his/her political rally.

On a separate occasion, I was having tea with Saman and two of his friends who were trying to explain to me the barriers they faced in securing state employment due to the prevalence of political patronage. They were eager to tell me about *henchāyo*, which they translated into English as "the politician's buddy."[18] The henchāyo, they told me, did all of the politician's work, from his private "dirty" work to carrying out his political wishes. Saman's friend Tissa explained that the henchāyo was " 'like the politician's servant." "The henchāyo even polishes the politician's shoes. That's the kind of character the henchāyo has!" Saman added. Both Saman and his friend stated that if an educated youth was to become a henchāyo they could "go to a better place" (i.e., get a desirable state job). When I asked whether they would consider taking on the role of a henchāyo in order to obtain a state job, I was met with incredulous laughter. In between gasps for air through their laughter Saman responded: "We can't keep our good character and engage in such work!"

Saman, along with many of his peers, expressed concerns about the future degeneration of the economy, and country as a whole, resulting from large swathes of incompetent state workers, recruited on the basis of political patronage and bribes rather than skills and qualifications, steering its administration. They pointed to widespread inefficiency and corruption in state administration, and to the huge losses incurred by clumsily managed public bodies (e.g., the national airline carrier, the electricity board), as preliminary evidence of this. Saman derided both the nature of the work itself and the quality of workers in the state sector: "When you look at government jobs in Sri Lanka, the government worker goes to work at 9 am, at 10 am they drink tea, then they push the files here and there; they pile up the files one by one, by 11 am they have a little sleep in their chair, then at noon they have lunch, then after a tea break by 4 pm they go home."

When I asked him why he still desired a government job, Saman reiterated that he had to meet the expectations of his family and village community, while acknowledging that it would de-skill him. He also added that a state job provided freedom/flexibility (*nidahas*) due to the short hours and light workload. The main barrier that now stood between Saman and secure state employment was political interference, as he saw it. What he wanted from the state was simply the removal of this debilitating barrier and the creation of a level playing field for educated young job seekers. But he remained disenchanted with the political system and its representatives, and had little faith in their capacity to effect change. Saman stated: "The state must stop the interference of politics in employment. But this will never happen, no matter what government comes in . . . no matter what party comes into power, it is the same. The last government did the same, this one is the same, and the future governments will also do the same. You can't break this system."

Saman was uncertain and anxious about the future, but he was also hopeful. His anxiety was fueled by concerns about his youthful years being wasted away, those years that he considered most valuable in terms of the potential contribution he could make to "serving the country." Moreover, he felt unable to move forward with his life due to his lack of secure employment, in terms of economically supporting his family, building a house, and marrying and starting his own family. Without decent employment, he seemed to find himself caught in a liminal place between youth and adulthood. Saman, nevertheless, maintained hope for the future, and held firmly onto the belief that in five years' time he would be in "a good place" with a secure white-collar state job and married with a family. He drew my attention to the most recent round of graduate recruitment to the state sector. Despite his disaffection with the state and politics, Saman continued to rely on it to deliver the promised fruits of education and the adulthood he so longed for.

Spencer (2007) has drawn attention to the ambivalence that the state engenders among people in Sri Lanka, both as a source of social hope and disappointment. The villagers with whom he conducted his fieldwork in the 1980s viewed the state as "a source of resources . . . , a source of social capital . . . , a source of oppression . . . , an arena for disputes . . . , and a screen onto which villagers could project their visions of their own future" (Spencer 2007: 141). Rather than being experienced as an external abstract entity, the state encroached on Saman's personal and social life through the "dirty politics" of political patronage and corruption, obstructing his goals of securing employment and raising the social situation of his family, and further blocking his transition to adulthood. Saman's relationship with the state, too, was one of ambivalence. Despite his moral critique of dirty politics, Saman invested hope for his future in the state and in its potential to provide him with a fundamental resource (employment) and social capital (status, stability). But, to engage with the state and its "dirty politics" in order to secure a state job was to sully his social standing and dignity (bestowed by education) as an educated young man, and compromise his moral principles.

CONCLUSION

This chapter has followed the life story of Saman, an unemployed young graduate who grew up amid war, paying particular attention to his aspirations for employment and search for adulthood in post-war Sri Lanka. In doing so, it considers what adulthood means to educated young people from marginalized Sinhala backgrounds like Saman's, and how they go about navigating the complicated social and political terrain they are faced with in the post-war period, in order to secure their desired life-stage advancement. The chapter finds that Saman's imaginings of adulthood are inextricably tied to ideas of social class progression in the form of attaining middle-class adulthood, which are linked to powerful cultural ideals of respectability and social status. He considers secure government employment enabled by education to be central to attaining this vision of adulthood. Adulthood appears so elusive to Saman because he understood it in terms of social class advancement. While in reality Saman's life trajectory is marked by disruption and a sense of constantly moving backward and forward, he imagines the life course to be ideally one of linear social progression from childhood, to youth, to adulthood. Saman's story illustrates that education can be a contradictory resource, which can draw people tighter into structures of inequality while also providing some opportunities (Jeffrey et al. 2004). Saman yearns for a state job to counter the current liminality of uncertainty and anxiety, tinged with shame (i.e., the shame of facing his family and neighbors), that he occupies as an educated unemployed youth. He attempts to exert a sense of control and certainty over socio-political dynamics that make the adulthood he desires appear elusive, by busying himself with skilling up. In doing so, he firmly invests hope in the future for securing a state job and thereby middle-class adulthood through his efforts. Skilling up and holding out for the future then function as an important coping strategy to deal with the uncertainty and anxious liminality that he is faced with. It also allows him to hold on to the sense that he is following the ideal model of progress from youth to adulthood, even while the period is unstable.

Saman's story further provides a complicated and contradictory picture of the changes wrought in the lives of young people by conflict, and the ways in which violence is enmeshed in people's social and political lives as they seek to attain their desired version of social adulthood. Many of the struggles and challenges that educated young Sri Lankans like Saman must grapple with in their search for adulthood are not new. But they have taken on new forms, new meanings, and new complexities as a consequence of the interactions between a bitter and long drawn-out civil war, the dynamics of state power, the global economic crisis, and the maturation of neoliberalism. Life stories give us rich insight into the ways in which people make meaning of, and interact with their worlds. Saman's reflection on his life trajectory gives rise to a sophisticated and nuanced social critique of the conflict and sociality; politics and the state; and of youth and life-stage advancement in post-war Sri Lanka. In doing so, Saman's story pushes against simplistic Manichean depictions of war and nationalistic constructions that pit homogeneous and undifferentiated ethnic entities against each other.

Dhana Hughes is Honorary Research Fellow in Anthropology at Durham University, UK. She is author of *Violence, Torture and Memory in Sri Lanka: Life after Terror.*

NOTES

1. Saman is a pseudonym.
2. "Educated" for the purposes of this research was defined as those with A level qualifications and above. The fieldwork was conducted as part of a wider collaborative research project studying the politics of educated unemployed youth in India, Nepal, and Sri Lanka, funded by the Economic and Social Research Council Grant ES/JO11444/1.

3. Sinhala people comprise the majority ethnic group in Sri Lanka and are predominantly Buddhists. Tamil people are the largest minority and are predominantly Hindu. The experiences of Sinhala youth caught up in Sri Lanka's civil war are notable for their absence in existing literature, which has focused on the experiences of Tamil people.

4. This research is based on ethnographic fieldwork I conducted in Colombo with educated unemployed young men and women between the ages of eighteen and thirty, over a period of twelve months. I conducted semi-structured interviews and informal conversations with around thirty unemployed youth, accompanied by participant observation with a small number of key research participants. Here, I focus specifically on Saman's life story.

5. This turn of phrase is borrowed from Durham's introduction to this book.

6. The National Youth Policy of Sri Lanka defines youth as those between the ages of fifteen and twenty-nine.

7. The appointees complained of the lack of work, the lack of permanent contracts, meager pay, and the lack of basic facilities (e.g., desks and chairs for them to sit on).

8. See International Crisis Group, http://www.crisisgroup.org/en/regions/asia/south-asia/sri-lanka.aspx.

9. The government's failure to investigate war crimes, the soaring cost of living and entrenched socioeconomic inequality, and the "gifting" of lucrative political posts to family members (e.g., the influential diplomatic post of British high commissioner being handed to the prime minister's cousin) are among developments causing upset among those who voted in the present government.

10. I use quotes when using the term "community" in recognition of the diversity that this term encompasses, and to emphasize that Sinhala and Tamil "communities" are not monolithic, homogenous entities.

11. Other studies have also pointed to the perpetuation of ethnic divisions resulting from the conflict (see Thaheer et al. 2013).

12. *Shishatvaya* is a competitive exam for year five students based on which children with high scores could transfer to better schools.

13. Note that Saman lives in an area that was under state control. There is some evidence to suggest that areas under LTTE control during the war did not benefit equitably from postwar development (Thaheer et al. 2013).

14. Saman refers here to the post-war "Colombo beautification" project.

15. The Rajapaksa government launched two major infrastructure development projects in the former conflict zones called *Uthuru Wasanthaya* (north) and *Nagenahira Navodaya* (east). Research conducted with war-affected "communities," however, found that these projects had little positive impact on their everyday lives, in terms of their livelihoods, health, education, and well-being. Moreover, the top-down exclusionary imposition of development, the lack of village-level infrastructure development, and the prevalence of political patronage, corruption, and nepotism benefitting a small, politically connected southern Sinhala elite, were causes for concern (Thaheer et al. 2013).

16. Frustration with the prevalence of political patronage in employment is not new. The Presidential Commission on Youth, which inquired into the causes of the JVP-led youth insurgency of the late 1980s, also found that the politicization of society, including the employment sector, led to a deep sense of injustice among youth, which fueled youth unrest and violence (Presidential Commission on Youth 1990).

17. *Kadē yanawa* suggests doing various things, regardless of whether they are moral or not, to win favor. It may be interpreted as "selling one's soul."

18. *Henchāyo* here appears to be derived from the English word "henchman."

REFERENCES

Aitken, Stuart. 2001. *Geographies of Young People: The Morally Contested Spaces of Identity.* London: Routledge.

Amarasuriya, Harini. 2010. "Discrimination and Social Exclusion of Youth in Sri Lanka." In *The Challenge of Youth Employment in Sri Lanka,* edited by Ramani Gunatilaka, Markus Mayer, and Milan Vodopivec, 199–215. Washington, DC: World Bank.

Amarasuriya, Harini, Canan Gunduz, and Markus Mayer. 2009. *Rethinking the Nexus between Youth Unemployment and Conflict.* London: International Alert.

Beck, Ulrich. 1992. *Risk Society,* Newbury Park, CA: Sage.

Durham, Deborah. 2000. "Youth and the Social Imagination in Africa: Introduction to Parts 1 and 2." *Anthropological Quarterly* 73(3): 113–20.

Farmer, Paul. 1996. "On Suffering and Structural Violence: A View from Below." *Daedalus* 125(1): 261–83.

Gamburd, Michele. 2004. "The Economics of Enlisting: A Village View of Armed Service." In *Economy, Culture and Civil War in Sri Lanka,* edited by Deborah Winslow and Michael Woost, 151–67. Bloomington: Indiana University Press.

Hettige, Siri, ed. 1992. *Unrest or Revolt: Some Aspects of Youth Unrest in Sri Lanka.* Colombo: Goethe-Institut Sri Lanka.

Hettige, Siri, and Markus Mayer, eds. 2002. *Sri Lankan Youth: Challenges and Responses.* Colombo: Freidrich Ebert Stiftung Foundation.

Hughes, Dhana. 2013. *Violence, Torture and Memory in Sri Lanka: Life after Terror.* Abington: Routledge.

Jeffrey, Craig. 2010a. "Geographies of Children and Youth 1: Eroding Maps of Life." *Progress in Human Geography* 34(4): 496–505.

———. 2010b. *Timepass: Youth Class, and the Politics of Waiting.* Stanford: Stanford University Press.

Jeffrey, Craig, and Jane Dyson, eds. 2008. *Telling Young Lives: Portraits of Global Youth.* Philadelphia: Temple University Press.

Jeffrey, Craig, Patricia Jeffery, and Roger Jeffery. 2004. "A Useless Thing! Or Nectar of the Gods? The Cultural Production of Education and Young Men's Struggles for Respect in Liberalizing North India." *Annals of the Association of American Geographers* 94(4): 961–81.

Johnson-Hanks, Jennifer. 2002. "On the Limits of Life Stages in Ethnography: Toward a Theory of Vital Conjunctures." *American Anthropologist* 104(3): 865–80.

Katz, Cindy. 2004. *Growing Up Global: Economic Restructuring and Children's Everyday Lives.* Minneapolis: University of Minnesota Press.

Liechty, Mark. 2009. "Youth Problems: An Introduction." *Studies in Nepali History and Society* 14(1): 35–37.

Mains, Daniel. 2007. "Neoliberal Times: Progress, Boredom, and Shame among Young Men in Urban Ethiopia." *American Ethnologist* 34(4): 659–73.

Moore, Mick. 1990. "Economic Liberalisation versus Political Pluralism in Sri Lanka?" *Modern Asian Studies* 24(2): 341–83.

Presidential Commission on Youth. 1990. "Report of the Presidential Commission on Youth." Government of Sri Lanka.

Ruddick, Sue. 2007. "At the Horizons of the Subject: Neo-liberalism, Neo-conservatism and the Rights of the Child." *Gender, Place, and Culture* 14(5): 513–27.

Snellinger, Amanda. 2009. *"Yuba, Hamro Pusta* (Youth, Our Generation): Youth and Generational Politics in Nepali Political Culture." *Studies in Nepali History and Society* 14(1): 39–66.

———. n.d. "Space within Limits: How Nepali Student Activists Orient Themselves in the Political Landscape." Unpublished manuscript.

Spencer, Jonathan. 2007. *Anthropology, Politics, and the State: Democracy and Violence in South Asia*. Cambridge: Cambridge University Press.

Thaheer, Minna, Pradeep Pieris, and Kasun Pathiraja. 2013. *Reconciliation in Sri Lanka: Voices from Former War Zones*. Colombo: ICES.

Valentine, Gill. 2003. "Boundary Crossings: Transitions from Childhood to Adulthood." *Children's Geographies* 1(1): 37–52.

Venugopal, Rajesh. 2011. "The Politics of Market Reform at a Time of Civil War: Military Fiscalism in Sri Lanka." *Economic and Political Weekly* 46(49): 67–75.

Vigh, Henrik. 2006. *Navigating Terrains of War: Youth and Soldiering in Guinea-Bissau*. New York: Berghan Books.

CHAPTER THREE

⤲

LEARNING TO WAIT

Schooling and the Instability of Adulthood for Young Men in Uganda

Claire Elisabeth Dungey and Lotte Meinert

"I AM JUST here doing nothing," said Paulo, a young man in rural Uganda early in 2015, frustrated with his life of farming. Paulo contrasted a life of digging with another life, one with a higher status and the prospect of being able to take better care of his family. Throughout his years in primary and secondary school, he had learned that it was important to wait for "a better future in adulthood," which involved getting a job, building his own hut, getting married, having children, and taking care of his family. Years later, Paulo had a small business repairing mobile phones. He also got a job and felt he was becoming an adult; but he lost the job again, and the business was not going well, so he was back to digging. He seemed to be slipping in and out of the status of adulthood.

In this chapter, we argue that young men in Uganda are trained in school to learn to wait and to tolerate hardship of various kinds, and that this leads them toward a kind of educated, docile, but often frustrated adulthood. However, it is also during moments of waiting for stability that young men creatively find ways to maneuver, moments in time that are not just characterized by sitting around waiting for things to happen, or "doing nothing," as Paulo put it.

What does it mean to become an adult in a context where everything might be unstable? And how do young men learn to habituate the practice of waiting? In his classic ethnography of working-class lads in Britain, Paul Willis ([1977] 2000) discusses how manual labor indexes a status in the "real" adult world for these young men and how therefore they resist mental labor and school authority. Willis points to the paradox that it is partly the working class lads' own culture that directs them to eventually take on lowly paid jobs.

He emphasizes, however, that the implicit curriculum in school promotes dispositions that ensure the less privileged a continued low status (Willis [1977] 2000: 3). While our young Ugandan interlocutors do not articulate manual labor as more significant than "mental labor," they do appropriate the implicit curriculum of waiting in school as a strong disposition—"true," in Willis's words. Our point is that waiting in school is a learned habitual practice, which is also given moral weight, but that it may contribute to the young men not accomplishing what they hope for in adulthood. Similar to Kipnis's study (in this volume) of how young people in China refuse factory work due to the higher status of jobs where they have to think for themselves, young men in Uganda tend to resist doing manual labor and regard it as "doing nothing." In order to embrace the "real adult world," they hope and expect that enduring hardships and waiting at school will pay off.

Based on fieldwork in Kisoro between 2011 and 2013 (Claire Dungey) and in Tororo in 1997, 2007, and 2015 (Lotte Meinert)—both rural areas in Uganda—we describe how students are trained and disciplined in their school career, through waiting and through enduring hardship, to believe that their education will translate into a paid white-collar job and a stable adulthood, and not into the low and unstable status of farming the land. Similarly, Hughes (this volume) also found that young people in Sri Lanka anticipate upward class mobility and desk jobs after education; when these do not materialize they often find themselves back in the agricultural fields and frustrated. If you ask children and young people what they want to do with their futures, they do not mention digging as a first choice. Jobs that are perceived to be "significant" are usually mentioned as nouns—for example, doctors, lawyers, office workers, nurses, or schoolteachers. These jobs come with a respected identity, even if they are poorly paid and frequently paid in arrears. Uneducated villagers are often perceived by the educated to be ignorant and lower down in the social hierarchy than those who have been to school. Uneducated villagers frequently do day labor for richer and educated families, which earns them a small income that is often insufficient to sustain a family. Sometimes they do manual jobs such as digging, often referred to by a continuous verb tense implying a temporary state (e.g., "I am digging") rather than a noun identifying a profession (e.g., "I am a digger"). This kind of work is not a status that is earned or wished for; it is simply something you do while waiting and hoping for better options. The trained practices of waiting in school are seldom called "nothing activities" by the students themselves, even though they spend extensive periods waiting for the teacher. The waiting practices in school are of many different kinds: the students might wait for relatives to get money for school fees. Moreover, there is waiting for exam results in order to be able to go to the next level of education, and they wait for books, tables, basic equipment for schooling. Teachers often try to instill values of waiting and time management as a way of preparing children for a so-called successful adulthood. The waiting in school is perceived to be for something—for a job and a status. Yet there is also an awareness that jobs do not come by themselves or simply from waiting.

THE NEW GENERATION

When understanding why school institutions in Uganda end up promoting the idea that students need to wait for better times and to endure hardships, it is important to keep various contextual factors in mind. Periods of war and political and economic instability have swept through the country, especially during the regimes of Milton Obote (1966–71) and Idi Amin (1971–79), resulting in significant breakdowns of infrastructure. During the periods of insecurity most schools continued to operate, despite the lack of textbooks and other essentials for education. According to Paige (2000), many parents perceived schooling as fundamental in teaching children so-called good morals, as well as creating stability and safety in the country. Schools, however, have not only been used to promote stability, but also to foster a distinction between manual labor and book knowledge, which reaches further back in history. Missionaries introduced formal schooling in Uganda at the end of the nineteenth century, and promoted the abandonment of precolonial education based on "learning in practice," such as through rituals that were passed on from parents to their children (Hansen 1984; Ssekamwa [1971] 2001). School institutions have played a powerful role in shaping young people's perceptions of academic knowledge learned from books as opposed to practical skills learned in the home (Meinert 2009). In 1997, Universal Primary Education (UPE) was established in Uganda under the rule of President Yoweri Museveni (1986–) and was made mandatory for all children above five years of age. This changed the life situations for many families in Uganda since it instilled the idea—by law—that childhood should involve going to school (Meinert 2009). Policy makers, teachers, and also parents hoped that schoolchildren would learn, among other things, to stop the spread of HIV and that school would promote modernity and development. The UPE program meant that government schools became overcrowded and under-resourced, which caused many of those who could afford it to opt for private schools instead (Meinert 2009).

School policies with a neoliberal turn encourage children and young people to become job creators rather than job seekers to fight widespread unemployment (Baguma and Furnham 2012). Ironically, however, students are not given opportunities to develop proactive skills that would promote creative job making, even though teachers emphasize the importance of these skills. The students are taught to listen to the teacher, whose answer is "always right," and to wait patiently for this knowledge. In this context, creativity is often downplayed and regarded as causing too much disruption, nor is critical problem-based thinking promoted or cherished. Although young men's school expectations can be disappointed when they end up in agricultural work or a small-scale business, we do not wish to suggest that they do not learn important skills at school, since waiting practices also make life more bearable with hopes and expectations of future opportunities. Paradoxically, it is often because they have undergone the disciplining and waiting at school that other people begin to acknowledge them as educated and cultivated. Cultivated waiting will not, however, automatically get them a job and thereby the opportunity to take care of a family and be considered an adult.

From Prolonged Adolescence to the Instability of Adulthood

Numerous scholars, particularly in African contexts, have pointed out that young people wait in a prolonged and often frustrated youth, characterized by economic and social uncertainties, in which marriage and other expected responsibilities associated with adulthood are postponed and delayed (Jeffrey 2010; Mains 2013; Ralph 2008; Singerman 2007; Sommers 2012; Utas 2005).

Honwana (2012, 2014) uses the concept "waithood" to describe the suspended period between childhood and adulthood in which youth "wait for adulthood." Honwana emphasizes that waiting is not passive lingering, since young people in waithood are not simply waiting inactively for something to change, but continually experimenting and improvising their life situations. For example, see Solway's chapter (this volume) where adults find themselves unable to proceed to the valued status of elder as a consequence of their children failing to enter adulthood.

We agree that youth or waithood is often a period of experimentation and creativity as well as frustration, and this may be perceived as a suspended period, similar to how liminality is often conceptualized as a period of creativity (see Turner [1969] 1987). Yet there is a risk that conceptualizing youth as waithood implicitly anticipates that adulthood is a stable position, with the move to adulthood being a teleological pathway, and adulthood being a status that can be achieved as long as the money and the resources are available. With our material from Uganda we shed light on the various ways in which adulthood is an uncertain period, one of waiting and of gaining and losing status. Adulthood, we suggest, is a state and position that can relatively easily be lost, along with a job, a wife, a house, children, and other responsibilities. Young people can in some contexts be viewed as adults and in others as children: for example, if they have their own children while still undergoing education, they are regarded as children because they are students. Others lose their adult status when they manage to build a house by gradually saving up, but are forced to leave the unfinished house for a while to wait for resources, or are unlucky enough to have their house destroyed during a war-related event or in a conflict with a neighbor. Young adults might slide back into a youth status if they do not live up to certain criteria. Older adults who do not live up to the same may be considered adult, but somewhat financially unstable. This leads us to explore what might be a Ugandan index of adulthood.

Indexing Adulthood

In the Ugandan Children's Statute of 1996, a child is defined as a person under the age of eighteen. The UN Convention on the Rights of the Child as well as the African Union's Charter of the Rights and Welfare of the Child were incorporated into Ugandan law (GOU 1996: 10; see also Berntsen 2010). However, this legal definition does not accurately describe the distinction between childhood and adulthood in everyday social situations. Understandings of adulthood depend not only on age but also on other indexical factors, such as gender and skill level (Durham 2004; Argenti and Durham 2013). While most of us would agree that the time period of adolescence is characterized by various physiological changes, there is no clear-cut definition either of when a person moves from adolescence to adulthood or of what these classifications mean in cultural terms (Christiansen et al. 2006).

During the 1990s, in particular, youth cultures became a popular study focus in the social sciences, with cross-cultural comparisons of meaning systems and cultural practices (Hutchby and Moran-Ellis 1998; James and Prout 1997; Qvortrup 1994; Wulff 1995). In these, the category of youth was often taken for granted, since youth was studied exclusively as a group, and not in relation to other generations or family members. Perhaps partly for this reason, studies of youth have tended to focus on "stuckness" and on how young people face difficulties in moving to the seemingly stable category of adulthood (Amit and Dyck 2012; Frederiksen 2013; Frederiksen et al. 2014; Hansen 2005; Honwana 2012; Jeffrey 2010; Mains 2007; Ralph 2008; Singerman 2007; Sommers 2012).

The uneasiness of adulthood is not, however, a novel phenomenon: the transition to and position of adulthood were experienced as problematic in the past as well. Van Gennep's ([1909] 1960) and Turner's ([1969] 1987) studies of rites of passage and transitions give us an indication that the status of adult has long been perceived as difficult to achieve, requiring a ritual to manage the transition and mark the new position. Less attention has been paid to the struggles to maintain the position of adult. Studies of masculinity (e.g., Barker 2005) have largely focused on the expectations and difficulties of being men versus being women, and less on the generational aspect of being adult men. Our contribution sheds light on what it means to aspire to be an adult man in a Ugandan context; this is not merely an uneasy "rite of passage" (Van Gennep [1909] 1960) with bumps along the way, but a very slippery and contested status to maintain.

In Uganda, as in other places in Africa, it is generally recognized that people can move and are moved back and forth between different generational positions, so that a fifteen-year-old can sometimes be regarded as an adult compared to a seventy-year-old "child" (Alber, Geest, and Whyte 2008; Durham 2004; Fortes 1984; Rasmussen 2000). Moreover, it is important that a person can be seen as an adult in some contexts but simultaneously as a child in another context, which makes the category of adulthood situational and flexible (Johnson-Hanks 2006). Karen Sykes (this volume) draws attention to moral agency exercised intersubjectively within extended households and between generations in Papua New Guinea: in Uganda, too, household and intergenerational morality can outweigh age as a feature of adulthood. The practice of waiting is also part of relational obligations over the life course.

In our exploration of the hurdles young men face in the transition from youth to adulthood, we take our inspiration from Deborah Durham's (2000, 2004) conception of "youth as a social shifter," and also regard adulthood as a social shifter (see Durham's introduction to this volume). A shifter is an indexical term that can only be understood in the context of a particular use where the meaning constantly shifts depending on the context (Durham 2000, 2004). Male adulthood in rural Uganda involves a range of interrelated dimensions that contribute to indexing a person as more or less of an adult man. The main dimensions include housing, marriage, children, providing for a family, and taking on community responsibilities.

The following list is not meant to be exhaustive, but is instead a heuristic tool with which we ask questions. First, building a hut or house is and has long been an important criterion for being considered an adult man. This may include having the skills and being able to get the materials to build a grass-thatched hut or iron sheet-roofed house, or having the finances to pay for the labor and skills of someone else to build the hut or house (Meinert 2005). Second, marrying involves having enough money to pay bridewealth and/or collect bridewealth contributions from family members. The cost of bridewealth varies greatly between families and regions; people often say it has reduced remarkably over time, but many young men still struggle to accumulate it. Previously boys were given calves to rear for their future bridewealth and these were added to cows from fathers and uncles. Now, bridewealth cows are often converted into money and vice versa. Young men try to save money for bridewealth, but seldom succeed in doing so. Third, having children is an important criterion for achieving adulthood. If the marriage does not result in children, it can be canceled and bridewealth returned. If you end up dying without having had any children, you might be considered an incomplete person. There will be no one to continue the lineage and inherit your property, and no one to bury you. Fourth, providing materially for a family is an extremely important measure for men to be considered as adults. This includes being able to provide food for the family, but also providing housing, clothing, children's educational costs, health-care costs and other expenses. Many young rural men feel that they are unable to provide well for a family through digging and subsistence farming, because what is now considered good housing, food, clothing, and education requires money and even monthly paid salaries, for teaching staff for instance, are often delayed. Finally, a man is expected to help his brothers and sisters and his parents in the form of labor, support or finances. His family-in-law will also expect continued support, sometimes in the form of ongoing bridewealth, or financial help in the case of health problems or similar issues. These expectations are often greater when a man has been to school and has the potential to gain a higher income because of his degree. Degree papers, however, are often issued late in Uganda, and need various signatures that are hard and expensive to get.

SOCIAL AGES AND LIFE-SITUATION

In Kisoro and Tororo, the move from childhood and youth to adulthood is a flexible process, dependent on social achievement and life-situation, something that is also reflected in language use (Dungey 2015; Meinert 2005, 2009: 29–30). You can still be defined as a child (*umwana/ikoku*) as long as you are in school, and as a girl or boy if you are unmarried.[1] Hence, you find children in their twenties, but also men (*abagabo/ejakait*) and women (*abagore/aberu*) who are defined as adults due to early marriages yet are still teenagers. Johnson-Hanks (2006: 52) points out that, in Cameroon, "what establishes someone's status as a child or an adult is not having achieved a set of life-history transitions, but rather the role that she inhabits in a given situation." In Uganda, the specific situation a person is in—for example, visiting her parents or meeting her lover—also establishes the status as child or adult. Yet besides the situational definition, there is simultaneously an achieved status that depends on life-history transitions, and this can sometimes create awkwardness and conflict.

Although teachers point out that it is important to know the age of children when they are enrolled at school, it is rarely considered important outside of school, unless a particular age is supposed to indicate particular competencies and expectations. Even age in chronological years is considered relative to the given situation and purpose. Many young people do not keep track of their age in years. Schoolchildren sometimes changed their ages according to their skill level, occasionally saying they were thirteen years old for several years in a row if they had still not passed the exam that would progress them to another level. The ages people mentioned to others were usually regarded as approximate, and not particularly significant, unless children were sponsored by foreign donors, in which case children below a certain age could receive help. Most young women referred to themselves as *abakobwa/apese* (girl) until they were married, whereas men called themselves both *abahungu/esapat* (boy) and *abasore/etumunant* (young man).

While unemployment and underemployment are well-known parts of everyday life for both men and women in Uganda, there is a powerful discourse that young men, in particular, should be able to change their futures and get jobs through education. Mains (2013), who conducted a study of education and temporality among young men in Ethiopia, emphasizes how formal education is often taken to be synonymous with success and progress, not just because education is seen as progressive in nature, but because of its importance in securing employment, which leads many to expect a linear improvement in their lives. Although young men in Uganda also hope for a linear improvement, the reality is that their situations are very uncertain and seldom progress in a straightforward fashion; they end up sliding back and forth into and out of adulthood. Next, we turn to how the disciplined training at school in the practice of waiting is often regarded as essential for achieving "successful" adulthood as opposed to "doing nothing" activities at home.

Keeping Busy and Having No Time

Hedwig, a secondary school student from Tororo who had started going to a boarding school in the capital, Kampala, commented that in the new school the students had no time, since they studied until late at night and got up very early in the morning. Hedwig saw this as an indication of the high quality of education in this school. However, much of this time was spent waiting for teachers, meals, electricity, and books. We suggest that having no time and keeping busy at school are practices created to set an atmosphere of seriousness and dedication, and perhaps a way to prepare children and young people for the "right" kind of adulthood—one that is busy with an office job, a family, and other responsibilities. Some teachers in the schools we visited argued that it was important to keep young people busy in order to prevent them from getting into trouble, such as smoking or drinking alcohol. Thus, keeping busy seemed to have both a disciplinary and a formative purpose, aiming at creating "proper" adults.

In Uganda schools, one of the main forms of waiting is queuing in a line for food. When the food arrived late because of the kitchen staff in one of the schools Claire studied, a teacher did not acknowledge this and ordered the students to come to class without finishing their meals. Writing on the topic of queuing and waiting, Schwartz ([1975] 2014) argues that the queuing process has a structure in its own right, often with the perception "first come, first served." Visitors were generally the first to get food, whereas schoolchildren had to learn the disciplinary practice of waiting: if they did not stand properly in line, they were beaten.

Schwartz ([1975] 2014), among others (Bourdieu 1977; Flaherty 2011), argues that there is often an interrelationship between rank and waiting, whereby the least powerful has to wait for the person of higher rank, while the more powerful person has the power to keep others waiting. Our point is that students learn to wait for the more powerful, often the teacher, but that they still appropriate and manipulate time in their own ways, for instance, by playing in the corridors and coming late for class. Moreover, students emphasize that waiting and keeping busy is important for being a dedicated student and preparing themselves for adulthood. In this way it inserts the students into the social hierarchy and teaches them to respect teachers.

In the dormitory or at home with their families in Kisoro, many of the students pointed out how they were "doing nothing." The boarding school students usually had a day off on Saturdays where they had no formal classes. Sometimes they would do readings in their beds, wash their clothes, talk in groups, act out wedding scenes, or play football but they would also get minimal time for this during the week. Free time in this sense was not conceptualized as "something" but it was still part of the rhythm of time in school, but without the same status. Students, however, pointed out how time spent in the classroom was important and hence something, and Hedwig, for instance, conceptualized this time as valuable. At home, time was often spent on hard manual labor, which was frequently emphasized as nothing. This is related to a social hierarchy where household work is often conceptualized as not worth mentioning, just like manual labor. Book knowledge, by contrast, and the fact that you were "a serious student" were clear indicators that you were doing something. Even if you spent your time in school writing notes without understanding or waiting for food, you were still doing "something," since you were participating in the rhythm of school time.

Some students grew bored while they were waiting for a teacher and practiced drum rhythms impatiently, or ran up and down on the tables to temporarily speed up time. Moments of waiting in school could be characterized as forms of "time-work" (Flaherty 2011), in which students manipulate time in various ways and experience time as something they do not have, or do not have enough of. Very often students were late for their classes and would come to the classroom at different times in the morning, sometimes receiving punishments. In day schools, this was often due to parents being late, perhaps waiting for transport for their children. They might have been delayed by not having any water at home. Students would then have to help their parents fetch water before they could bathe, which was required by the school.

Many teachers told students, especially the day students, that they were sleeping too much and that they were wasting their time, so they would not be able to support themselves when they grew up. The residential students usually got up between 4:30 am and 7:00 am and went to bed at 10 pm at night depending on their age, the teachers' management of time, and whether or not the students could avoid punishment for being late for class. The idea that children should get up early was closely connected to the conception that a rural Ugandan needs more than one job to subsist and still needs time to take care of their children. Even though a child might be tired, getting up early was seen as necessary.

One social studies teacher emphasized how the Primary Seven[2] students could not lift themselves out of poverty if they did not work hard and continued to resist getting up at 4 am (as he himself did). He told the students they should not simply let their parents "wait for the president" (meaning they should not expect things for free). Here he emphasized waiting—and receiving without doing anything—as a negative value that would bring about dependency. To a certain extent this dependency concept included household work, since this type of work in his view could not give a sufficient income: they would still have to rely on gifts or help from family members. Waiting in school, however, was a different matter: this was necessary in order to show respect for your elders and to recognize the fact that some people had more power than others.

This teacher, who spent little time sleeping himself, emphasized how time spent without supervision by adults was not good. He used a proverb from the Bible (Proverbs 16: 27) to emphasize his point—"an idle mind is the devil's workshop." However, he was often late himself and could turn up at the school as late as 7 am. Many teachers managed their own affairs during so-called classes.

The case below follows two brothers and their reflections on their lives since 1997 and what it took to be an adult after leaving school. Our point is that the waiting time they experienced at school was hopeful waiting for something, whereas the waiting they experience in their lives later was more of a frustrated waiting for "nothing." Both brothers had reached a certain level of adulthood—with jobs, wives, children—and then lost it all again.

"I Didn't Go to School for Nothing"

Paulo, whom we met at the beginning of this chapter, and Orieba are brothers. Both of them live in Tororo district in eastern Uganda, bordering Kenya. Kwapa sub-county, where they both grew up, is a rural area where people live mainly from subsistence farming, and where small trading centers show signs of a slowly growing trading economy. Paulo, the younger, was probably around thirty years old in 2010, and Orieba, the older, was around thirty-eight and the firstborn of his mother's six children. Yet in January 2015, when Lotte last visited their village, Paulo had become the "more adult" of the two because, as Paulo said, "Orieba is still unstable. . . . At least me, I have been able to sustain a home for my family." Paulo was settled on a piece of land entrusted to him by their father, and he had built a small house and kitchen hut for his wife and their two children. Still, Paulo did not feel he himself had succeeded as an adult. "I am just here doing nothing," Paulo said, gesturing nothing with his empty hands. He explained, "I struggle to feed my family, but there is no job. It is just digging." Paulo had tried to start a small business repairing mobile phones, and at some point a businessman had even taken him to Juba in Sudan to work, but the man was cheating, so Paulo ended up going home without any profit. "So you see, I am just like that—digging—but at least it feeds the family . . . and soon my firstborn will go to school."

Orieba, the older brother, had gone to Malaba, a nearby border town to Kenya, and Paulo kept repeating that "Orieba is still unstable." Orieba was unstable in the sense that he had lost the house he had built for his wife and children. A young man with whom Orieba had a conflict had set the house on fire, and Orieba had not been able to resolve the conflict or build a new house, so his wife had moved away with the children. Now Orieba had another wife and a child, but he had not been able to satisfactorily care for them, because he had started drinking heavily and was not serious about growing his vegetable garden. "You know drinking also made him unstable, and he would beat his wife too much," Paulo explained. Eventually the second wife also moved back to her own family. Orieba started taking care of a shop for someone in Tororo, but after a short time he was accused of stealing money in the shop and had a police case on his neck. For some years he had been hiding, although Paulo knew that Orieba was in Malaba: "We want him to come home. But because he did not send money for his children and wives, maybe he is shy. Maybe he does not feel like a man. But we want to help him . . . and we are worried that he is sick with AIDS."

Over the years the younger brother had grown structurally older than the older brother. Paulo had achieved and maintained some level of adulthood, according to local standards, while Orieba got stuck in youth trouble, and after achieving some aspects of adulthood seemed to slide back into youth status and was still not considered an adult even as he approached his forties. Both brothers had gone through primary and secondary school in the rural area and had endured the hours of hard studying and of waiting, hopeful, for the teacher. Especially Orieba had had high hopes of where education would lead him.

When Lotte first met the brothers in 1997, Orieba was very articulate about his wish to go to an urban school. He wanted to be a businessman, not a farmer in the rural areas like his father. Paulo was more timid about his expectations of where schooling would lead him, but like so many others he hoped for a salaried job. In 2007, when Paulo had almost completed secondary school, he decided to drop out because his results were not good enough and school fees "did not come by themselves," so he tried to set up a small business repairing mobile phones.

Eventually, both brothers had to rely on agriculture—Paulo with some regret, but not bitterly like Orieba, who proclaimed that he did not go to school "for nothing." When Orieba was around seventeen years old, he said: "[My father] is just a poor farmer. I have seen that with farming you will just stay poor even if you work very hard. I will study hard to become a businessman who can move in town to buy and sell things."

Reflecting back on how they were taught in school decades earlier, when they were part of the fortunate crowd who had the chance to go to school and were therefore expected to end up getting a job, it is not surprising that the two brothers were frustrated. Schooling had promoted the idea that small-scale agriculture was "no real future" for the educated, but would make you "stay poor" without achieving something in your life. Orieba and Paulo's case from eastern Uganda, as well as the following case with Adam from southwestern Uganda, point to some of the difficulties young men face when trying to grow up and "become adult" after many years of building up expectations toward a "different future" through schooling.

Waiting for Something

Adam was a twenty-three-year-old former student who was looking for a job when Claire met him in Kisoro in 2013. Adam came from a rural area outside the district town Kisoro, which is close to the border with Rwanda. Because the area Adam lived in was mainly rural, he could rely on crops from the garden. However, he did not know how he would manage unless he could get a job soon. He often explained that he was waiting for a transition into another position from which he would be able to take care of his family members. Adam continued living in Kisoro with his mother while searching for a job. He could eat at home, but was concerned that his mother could not continue to cook for him and they both had difficulties in gaining access to enough money to buy food.

One of Adam's main concerns was that he would be left alone with the responsibility to care for his younger brother, since his mother was terminally ill, and he did not have any family members who could assist him with money. As a result, he often visited his friends at mealtimes, when he could be sure of getting something to eat. Sometimes he asked them for money when he needed to pay for expenses such as his brother's school fees. Adam had been searching for a job unsuccessfully for several years, but planned for his future in which he could sustain himself and become a "big person" (*umuntu mukuru*), somebody with money who could help others as well. According to him, this was what constituted a "successful adult," although many did not advance to that level even if they were regarded as adults. Since his father's death several years before, Adam had faced many difficulties.

Adam's family had been well-to-do and had depended on hiring workers to do the farm work. But with the death of his father, who had been a doctor in the area with a high income, the family no longer had money coming in. Adam's family lost the respect they had once gained for having an income. They had to rely on others for help, but most of their family members were no longer alive. It was clear that the transition from being rich to poor had had an impact on how Adam viewed himself. He did not wish to continue living in Kisoro; he felt trapped without an income and without being able to fulfill his future aspirations. He had an idea that he would like to move somewhere else, somewhere his life might be less complicated and not characterized by a lot of waiting. Moving would require, he noted, that he had money and/or received a scholarship to study.

If you were a "somebody," Adam explained, you would have close relatives who could get you a job if they were well respected in the local community, as his father had been. A "nobody," by contrast, could work hard both at school and at manual labor, but not be recognized as a somebody. Becoming a somebody was also related to schooling. Adam had passed both primary and secondary schooling with good results and had studied business at university for three years. Despite this, Adam was still waiting for better days. After Claire completed her fieldwork, Adam's mother was admitted to the hospital on several occasions and died not long afterward. Adam then became responsible for taking care of his younger sibling. He got occasional jobs, but these jobs were always temporary. He still had the permanence of the house, but had trouble gaining access to his inheritance. According to Adam, it was a problem that rather than an adult who could manage by himself, others saw him as a child who was dependent on others. Since the initial version of this chapter was written, Adam has had a child and gotten a job in a sports company that will undoubtedly bring new evaluations, expectations, and obligations.

The Instability of Adulthood

Orieba was a person who seemed to slip in and out of adulthood several times, which made his brother and other family members consider him "unstable." We may twist this to suggest a perspective that considers adulthood—and manhood in particular—an unstable position. Orieba was not particularly unstable as a person, and many others experienced the same problems he did. After Orieba had turned eighteen and was in secondary school, his girlfriend, who was about sixteen, got pregnant. Unfortunately, both she and Orieba were forced to drop out of school. Earlier in Ugandan history, girls had had to drop out of school, but boys who had impregnated a girl were allowed to stay at school. Yet with the introduction of the defilement law, young men became particularly vulnerable.[3] Paradoxically, the defilement law, which was meant to protect young women, turned out to act against both young girls and boys (Meinert 2005: 193). For Orieba, the pregnancy and the defilement law meant that he had to leave school and go into hiding, because he was uncertain as to whether the girl's family would file a case against him. Fortunately, they did not, and when the child was born, Orieba carefully came out of hiding, but he was unprepared to take care of his new family. He still had only his bachelor hut in his father's compound, he had not been able to do any farming while in hiding, and he had no money. After some time the girl and baby moved into Orieba's family's home and Orieba was expected to take care of them as husband and father. He managed to build a new house and tried to grow tomatoes and onions, which are cash crops, rather than the usual subsistence crops of maize and millet. The first year the harvest was reasonable and Orieba proudly recounted how he had bought clothes and other necessities for the baby and mother, because "now he was a father." About two years later, things had changed quite dramatically. The couple had another child, but the wife's family started demanding bridewealth. Orieba's father and uncles were reluctant to contribute to the bridewealth because they did not approve of the so-called unplanned marriage. Orieba was frustrated, and on top of that his crops did not do well that year. He wanted to leave farming, go back to school, and see if he could get what he considered a proper job. Judging from his red eyes and his wife's comments, he had also taken to drink. One day when the family came back from a trip to Tororo, they found their house burned down and all their property inside destroyed or lost. After the fire Orieba became desperate and started to drink heavily, and eventually the wife and children moved back to her family. He joined a rural school for about one and a half years, but kept dreaming and talking about going to a city school, which he thought would increase his chances of getting a job after graduation. Before he had a chance to realize his city plans, he had to leave school again. He had an affair with an older woman in the village, who got pregnant and moved into Orieba's house with her other two children. Orieba was back to trying to be an adult, taking care of another new family. According to Orieba, the relationship seemed stable, and they farmed the land around Orieba's home to sustain the family. Yet after a couple of years her family started demanding bridewealth, and his first wife's family also demanded that Orieba help support that family. Orieba spent the money he made from growing tomatoes and onions on drinking. His wife complained openly about him.

Orieba, like so many other young men in the area, obviously had difficulties living up to local expectations of adulthood and being a man. When Orieba took on adult responsibilities, he often could not sustain them. At certain critical moments in his potential transition from youth to adulthood, he faced social turbulence and structural resistance. Orieba was definitely not the first young man to get a girl pregnant out of wedlock, but he did so at a particular time when the defilement legislation was new and particularly tough on young men who were already in vulnerable positions. When one thing went wrong, other problems often followed. Young men who coped with their girlfriends' pregnancy by going into hiding rather than taking up the role of a husband and father frequently came to determine the direction of their life events in the future. These were moments that Johnson-Hanks calls "vital conjunctures." For many of the young men in Uganda the conjunctures tipped the wrong way, which meant that they could not realize themselves as responsible adult men. Life conditions and opportunities for young women in Uganda were not much different at this time. The fact that young women who became mothers often gained some kind of recognition by having a child outside of marriage if they stayed with the father in a stable relationship was an important social difference between young men and women. Adulthood has had particular impact on young men hoping for adulthood because of structural issues such as the defilement law. In the following example we describe one young man's more optimistic approach toward schooling: his conviction that he would eventually be considered an adult—as well as a "big person"—if he only waited.

The Return of Education

Many Ugandans experience schooling as formative and transformative with significant consequences for the lives of both individuals and families (Katahoire 1998; Meinert 2009). Yonah, a man in his mid-twenties, was a university student studying for a diploma in business and finance when Claire met him in 2012. He began school around the time of the Universal Primary Education Program in 1997 when there was a widespread expectation that schooling would change young people's lives in the future. After finishing his primary and secondary education, he studied for a diploma degree at a university in the neighboring town, and waited for the chance to study at a bachelor degree level. Yonah was considered a grandchild of an elderly couple with whom Claire stayed; since he was living with them, he was called a child, because he was dependent on their assistance and accommodation. Yonah believed that a permanent job with a reasonable income would improve his status and therefore others would begin to consider him an adult who could take on the responsibility of caring for a wife.

In 2013, Yonah had finished his diploma studies and had gained an internship in one of the main banks in the area, which he mentioned proudly. Employment in a bank meant a lot to Yonah, and he hoped that his friends there would assist him in getting a permanent job that would allow him to rent his own accommodation and hence be considered more an adult. Yonah repeatedly said that going to school was significant even if it delayed marriage and the prospect of being seen as an adult thereby. He believed that schooling would translate into a job one day despite the high unemployment rates, as long as he was patient and waited. The knowledge of a return or even the chance of one should motivate students to go to school, in his opinion, despite the high unemployment rates. According to Yonah, some uneducated people in Uganda believed that schooling was a waste of time. He did not want to take this belief seriously as he did not believe an educated person could think like that. Yonah had a very positive perception of schooling despite all the waiting time, which speaks to the overall theme of the chapter where waiting is seen as resourceful in achieving adulthood. He explained that it was all about waiting for the moment when you would become educated, and when people would treat you with respect. "For the sake of getting what you want just you bear with the situation. For the conditions which you are in, they are not favoring you. . . . Even if they give you [a] hard time, you accept because you know what you are becoming after. And you will not be the one who will be facing that challenge only. It will be common."

Yonah's words point to how "waiting time" can be less difficult when the students wait together in the hope of a different future. While Yonah perceived waiting time at school to be significant for moving into adulthood, this was not a perception that was shared by all. Adam, whom we described above, disliked his time at school, since the students had to spend all their time waiting or being hurried, without having sufficient time to study and think, and he did not believe that waiting would necessarily translate into a job and stable adulthood. This perception, however, was often less outspoken.

School Practices of Waiting and Keeping Busy

Adam believed that schooling had been a transformative experience where he had gained knowledge, connections, and prestige, but he found it problematic that he was not allowed to be creative at primary and secondary school, unlike university where he could be more independent. Once he had made a football out of sterile gloves from his father's medical practice as a child, but the teachers told him never to bring it back. In this case creativity was inhibited, which seemed paradoxical when students were constantly taught the importance of being job creators. Since then, Adam had learned that going to school was all about waiting for the teacher, writing answers the teacher's way, and never challenging ideas. He wanted to start a business, but explained that at school he had only learned the required skills from an academic perspective that was very distant from how you had to deal with these things in practice. Real life was much more complex than what was described in the books, he explained, because of corruption. You never knew whether your boss might misappropriate funds and keep them to himself or his relatives. As an eight-year-old, Adam had been sent to a private boarding school in the hope that he would gain a better education than at the government day schools. According to Adam, schooling was all about following a particular rhythm. This would be the same every day, and this was even more pronounced at boarding school, since they spent more time at school:

I have been to boarding and I didn't like it [for] so many reasons [like] waking up early. Almost every other time you are being given so much to write, you don't have time to revise whatever you wrote. You don't have time with your parents, you don't have time to play, from class at 5 [pm], you go freshing up, go for supper at 6 [pm], supper, go to class at 7 [pm], leave class at 10 [pm] after prep. You are too tired after prep, then sleep, 4:30 [am] you are up. So you are in class by 5 [am]. Go for porridge at 7 [am]. Most of the time, you are hungry . . . So I wouldn't send my child to boarding school.

Unlike many students who were still at school, Adam argued that primary and secondary school had been a waste of time in terms of gaining knowledge, even though he had got his school-leaving degree. However, one of his friends admonished him not to be too critical of the education he had, since he had been given the chance to go to boarding school, whereas she had only attended a day school in the village, clearly echoing the perception that it was worthwhile to go through hardships and wait for a "better" future. Adam's friend perceived private schooling as a privilege that should be endured despite the strict timetable and the long waiting hours. There was a widespread discourse at that time in Uganda that more hours at school would make students better even if those hours were spent waiting for the teacher. Many felt there was a lack of time at home, where children had to help with household work such as collecting water or firewood or digging in the fields, but also because home did not have expensive electric lighting or paraffin lamps that would allow students to study in the evening. Many schoolteachers explained that it was better for children to be at boarding school instead of day school where they would go home every day, as their peers could influence them to study harder and they could focus on their studies instead of household work. However, what Adam complained about was not so much the so-called privilege of having more time to study, but rather the lack of time caused by a rhythm of waiting in which students had no time to study. Our point of comparing these two stories is to show how students learn to wait and often emphasize how waiting is significant for achieving adulthood.

Conclusion

Invoking Paul Willis's classic study *Learning to Labour* about working class lads in Britain ([1977] 2000), we have argued that the implicit curriculum of "learning to wait" in Ugandan schools has an impact on young men not accomplishing what they hope for in adulthood. Paradoxically, school practices of preparing children to expect an office job when they grow up, as well as practices of waiting and "keeping busy," actually seem to contribute to young men getting stuck and losing adult status in later life. They are taught to endure hardship and wait patiently and are kept busy in a way that does not prepare them to become proactive job creators or creative farmers. The economic situation in Uganda means that there are very few paid jobs for young people, and educated young people who have been to school are seldom satisfied with being farmers. Young men who are not able to provide for a family are not considered socially adult, no matter what age they gain in years.

Adam for instance was still waiting for better times to come and become independent in terms of money and achieve a sense of adulthood. Orieba and Paulo tended to slip in and out of adulthood and were frustrated with "doing nothing." Other young men who were still at school were still waiting hopefully for a different future, sometimes repeating classes despite being well into their twenties. At times waiting was regarded as morally significant and a practice to be mastered to be educated, but at other times students experienced waiting as highly frustrating as they could not achieve a stable adult status in the eyes of others. In our view these practices of waiting end up contributing to the unstableness of adulthood for young men.

This creates a great deal of frustration and disappointment among young educated men who went through schooling and withstood the waiting and disciplining, believing and hoping it would get them job opportunities and something they consider worth going to school for. Despite the frustration experienced in relation to school, however, there is also widespread optimism among young people that they will eventually get a job after finishing schooling, after waiting, and hence become "proper adults" who can manage to take care of their families. Whereas a plethora of recent youth studies have been particularly insightful in pointing to the waithood and stuckness that often characterize the youth years, we have pointed to the practice of waiting in school as accommodating and paradoxically preparing young men for the instability and uncertainty of the status of adulthood in Uganda.

Claire Elisabeth Dungey is a Post-Doctoral Fellow at Brunel University, London, doing research in rural Lesotho concerning schooling and aspirations.

Lotte Meinert is Professor MSO in the Department of Anthropology, Aarhus University, Denmark. She is author of *Hopes in Friction: Schooling, Health and Everyday Life in Uganda* and coeditor of *Time Objectified: Ethnographies of Global Youth*.

NOTES

1. The terms in parentheses are for Kisoro and Tororo, respectively.
2. The final year in primary school in Uganda.
3. The defilement law was introduced in Uganda in 1990 as a measure to safeguard especially young girls against older men at the peak of the AIDS epidemic, but in reality most older men were often in a position to get themselves out of trouble by bribing police and other

officials. As a consequence, the defilement law hit young men and women and their families hardest (Parikh 2012). Under the defilement law, a person over eighteen years who had sex with a person under eighteen had committed a capital offense. For many years this meant that the majority of inmates in Ugandan prisons and remand homes were young men accused of defilement (Meinert 2005). Often the girl's family took the case to the police in the hope that they would be able to settle some kind of compensation with the boy's family, but as soon as the case was filed and official, the families were not allowed to negotiate compensation directly.

REFERENCES

Alber, Erdmute, Susan Reynolds Whyte, and Sjaak Van der Geest. 2008. "Generational Connections and Conflicts in Africa: An Introduction." In *Generations in Africa: Connections and Conflicts,* edited by Erdmute Alber, Susan Reynolds Whyte, and Sjaak Van der Geest, 1–26. Portsmouth, NH: Transaction.

Amit, Vered, and Noel Dyck. 2012. "Pursuing Respectable Adulthood: Social Reproduction in Times of Uncertainty." In *Young Men in Uncertain Times,* edited by Vered Amit and Noel Dyck, 1–34. New York: Berghahn Books.

Argenti, Nicolas, and Deborah Durham. 2013. "Youth." In *The Handbook of Modern African History,* edited by John Parker and Richard Reid, 396–413. Oxford: Oxford University Press.

Baguma, Peter, and Adrian Furnham. 2012. "Attributions for and the Perceived Effects of Poverty in East Africa: A Study from Uganda." In *Humanitarian Work Psychology,* edited by Stuart Carr, Malcolm MacLachlan, and Adrian Furnham, 332–50. New York: Palgrave Macmillan.

Barker, Gary. 2005. *Dying to Be Men: Youth, Masculinity and Social Exclusion.* London: Routledge.

Berntsen, Tor Arne. 2010. "Negotiated Identities: The Discourse on the Role of Child Soldiers in the Peace Process in Northern Uganda." In *Culture, Religion and the Reintegration of Female Child Soldiers in Northern Uganda,* edited by Bård Mæland, 39–56. New York: Peter Lang.

Bourdieu, Pierre. 1977. *Outline of a Theory of Practice.* Cambridge: Cambridge University Press.

Christiansen, Catrine, Mats Utas, and Henrik Vigh. 2006. "Introduction: Navigating Youth, Generating Adulthood." In *Navigating Youth, Generating Adulthood: Social Becoming in an African Context,* edited by Catrine Christiansen, Mats Utas, and Henrik Vigh, 9–30. Uppsala: Nordiska Afrikainstitutet.

Dungey, Claire Elisabeth. 2015. "Shades of Friendship: Schooling and Morality among Ugandan Youth." PhD diss., Aarhus University.

Durham, Deborah. 2000. "Youth and the Social Imagination in Africa: Introduction." *Anthropological Quarterly* 73(3): 113–20.

———. 2004. "Disappearing Youth: Youth as a Social Shifter in Botswana." *American Ethnologist* 31(4): 589–605.

Flaherty, Michael. G. 2011. *The Textures of Time: Agency and Temporal Experience.* Philadelphia: Temple University Press.

Fortes, Meyer. 1984. "Age, Generation, and Social Structure" in *Age and Anthropological Theory,* edited by David Kertzer and Jenny Keith, 99–122. Ithaca: Cornell University Press.

Frederiksen, Martin Demant. 2013. *Young Men, Time, and Boredom in the Republic of Georgia*. Philadelphia: Temple University Press.

Frederiksen, Martin Demant, and Anne Line Dalsgård. 2014. "Introduction: Time Objectified." In *Ethnographies of Youth and Temporality: Time Objectified*, edited by Anne Line Dalsgård, Martin Demant Frederiksen, Susanne Højlund, and Lotte Meinert, 1–21. Philadelphia: Temple University Press.

GOU (Government of Uganda). 1996. *Children Statutes: Statute Supplement*. UPPC, Entebbe.

Hansen, Bernt Holger. 1984. *Mission, Church, and State in a Colonial Setting: Uganda, 1890–1925*. London: Heinemann.

Hansen, Karen Tranberg. 2005. "Getting Stuck in the Compound: Some Odds against Social Adulthood in Lusaka, Zambia." *Africa Today* 51(4): 2–16.

Honwana, Alcinda. 2012. *The Time of Youth: Work, Social Change, and Politics in Africa*. Washington, DC: Kumarian Press.

———. 2014. "'Waithood': Youth Transitions and Social Change. Response to Syed Mansoob Murshed." In *Development and Equity: An Interdisciplinary Exploration by Ten Scholars from Africa*, edited by Dick Foeken, Ton Dietz, Leo Haan, and Linda Johnson, 28–40. Leiden: Brill .

Hutchby, Ian, and Jo Moran-Ellis. 1998. "Situating Children's Competence." In *Children and Social Competence: Arenas of Action*, edited by Ian Hutchby and Jo Moran-Ellis, 7–26. London: Falmer Press.

James, Allison, and Alan Prout. 1997. "A New Paradigm for the Sociology of Childhood? Provenance, Promise and Problems." In *Constructing and Reconstructing Childhood: Contemporary Issues in the Sociological Study of Childhood*, edited by Allison James and Alan Prout, 6–28. London: Falmer Press.

Jeffrey, Craig. 2010. *Timepass: Youth, Class, and the Politics of Waiting in India*. Stanford: Stanford University Press.

Johnson-Hanks, Jennifer. 2006. *Uncertain Honor: Modern Motherhood in an African Crisis*. Chicago: University of Chicago Press.

Katahoire, Anne Ruhweza. 1998. "Education for Life: Mother's Schooling and Children's Survival in Eastern Uganda." PhD diss., University of Copenhagen.

Mains, Daniel. 2007. "Neoliberal Times: Progress, Boredom, and Shame among Young Men in Urban Ethiopia." *American Ethnologist* 34(4): 659–73.

———. 2013. *Hope Is Cut: Youth, Unemployment, and the Future in Urban Ethiopia*. Philadelphia: Temple University Press.

Meinert, Lotte. 2005. "På vej mod voksenlivet: Modernitet og mobilitet blandt unge ugandere." In *Lokale liv, fjerne forbindelser: Børn og unge i migrationsprocesser*, edited by Laura Gilliam, Karen Olwig, and Karen Valentin, 283–300. Copenhagen: Hans Reitzels Forlag.

———. 2009. *Hopes in Friction: Schooling, Health, and Everyday Life in Uganda*. Charlotte, NC: Information Age.

Paige, Rhodes John. 2000. *Preserving Order amid Chaos: The Survival of Schools in Uganda, 1971–1986*. New York: Berghahn Books.

Parikh, Shanti. 2012. "'They arrested me for loving a schoolgirl': Ethnography, HIV, and a Feminist Assessment of the Age of Consent Law as a Gender-Based Structural Intervention in Uganda." *Social Science and Medicine* 74(11): 1774–82.

Qvortrup, Jens. 1994. "Childhood Matters: An Introduction." In *Childhood Matters: Social Theory, Practice and Politics*, edited by Jens Qvortrup, Marita Brady, Giovanni Sgritta, and Helmut Wintersberger, 1–24. Aldershot: Avebury.

Ralph, Michael. 2008. "Killing Time." *Social Text* 26(4): 1–29.

Rasmussen, Susan. 2000. "Between Several Worlds: Images of Youth and Age in Tuareg Popular Performances." *Anthropological Quarterly* 73(3): 133–44.

Schwartz, Barry. [1975] 2014. *Queuing and Waiting: Studies in the Social Organization of Access and Delay*. Chicago: University of Chicago Press.

Singerman, Diane. 2007. "The Economic Imperatives of Marriage: Emerging Practices and Identities among Youth in the Middle East." Middle East Youth Initiative Working Paper no. 6.

Sommers, Marc. 2012. *Stuck: Rwandan Youth and the Struggle for Adulthood*. Athens: University of Georgia Press.

Ssekamwa, John Chrisotom. [1971] 2001. *Development and Administration of Education in Uganda*. Kampala: Fountain.

Turner, Victor. [1969] 1987. "Betwixt and Between: The Liminal Period in Rites of Passage." In *Betwixt and Between: Patterns of Masculine and Feminine Initiation*, edited by Louise Mahdi, Steven Foster, and Meredith Little, 3–19. Peru: Open Court.

Utas, Mats. 2005. "Agency of Victims: Young Women's Survival Strategies in the Liberian Civil War." In *Makers and Breakers: Children and Youth in Postcolonial Africa*, edited by Filip de Boeck and Alcinda Honwana, 53–80. Oxford: James Currey.

Van Gennep, Arnold. [1909] 1960. *The Rites of Passage*. Chicago: University of Chicago Press.

Willis, Paul. [1977] 2000. *Learning to Labour: How Working Class Kids Get Working Class Jobs*. Farnham: Ashgate.

Wulff, Helena. 1995. "Introducing Youth Culture in Its Own Right: The State of the Art and New Possibilities." In *Youth Cultures: A Cross-Cultural Perspective*, edited by Vered Amit and Helena Wulff, 1–18. New York: Routledge.

CHAPTER FOUR

⤫

ADULTHOOD AND YOUTH IN A RAPIDLY URBANIZING CHINESE COUNTY

Andrew B. Kipnis

As DEBORAH DURHAM explains in the introduction, adulthood is often a hege-monic, unmarked category of assumed normalcy against which categories like youth are measured. This chapter looks at adulthood in relation to the category and social reality of youth, understood here as a threshold between childhood and adulthood. Youth is marked by sexual maturity but unmarried social sta-tus, as well as being finished with school but lacking a stable occupation. Such a definition reflects several particularities of the place where I did my research, but is also commonplace in many parts of China and today's world. In teasing out what is particular about the place I did my research, I hope also to show how certain particularities serve to accentuate the commonplace.

As would be true anywhere in the world, the precise meanings of abstract concepts like "adulthood," as well as the manner in which they are marked or unmarked, depend upon the context in which they are used. In China, as in much of the world, "adult education" (*chengren jiaoyu*), for example, is a marked category contrasted with the unmarked category of "education," which needs no modifier when it is children who are being educated.[1] But outside of educa-tion, I struggle to think of contexts in which the term "adult" (*chengren*) is commonly used in China. In contrast, the terms "youth" (*qingnian*) or "young people('s)" (*nianqing ren[de]*), are often used when referring to the activities, spaces, and objects of consumption used or undertaken by youth or to the people involved. Thus Durham's depiction of adulthood as an unmarked cat-egory of assumed normalcy seems particularly apt. In my fieldsite, adulthood seemed most apparent (but still unstated) in the social pressures adults ap-plied to youth to settle down, enter steady careers, and get married. The Chinese words for adult and youth themselves imply such a transition. Chengren could be literally translated as a "fully formed" or "completed" person. Qingnian means literally the "green years" and relies on an agrarian metaphor, as the color green is associated with still growing, unripened plant life, and by implication, also springtime. So the terms imply that the transition from youth to adulthood is a ripening to a point of completion, at which point a steady life follows.

The social pressure to settle into fully formed adult lives was highlighted by the ways in which youth resisted. Indeed, youth resistance to settling down, accepting a steady job, and marrying socially defined young people as youth. When an individual did settle down and marry, others would stop describing that person as a youth. In a rapidly changing place like my fieldsite, the social assumptions this pressure revealed could be considered a second-order fantasy. That is to say, the assumption that marriage, a settled career and a steady life are what constitute adulthood could be seen as doubly removed from reality because it reflects a nostalgia about how adults wished their social world was when they were young rather than how that social world actually was, and because the worlds of today's youth (as well as their fantasies and desires about that world) differ again from the those of the last generation. But in another sense, these assumptions have come to constitute reality. By encouraging youth to pursue settled lives, they help to construct a conservative familial order.

I see the lived categories of adulthood and youth in my fieldsite today, and China more broadly, as forms of "recombinant modernity." That is to say, these categories gain importance in relation to the historically recent transformations typically associated with modernity (industrialization, compulsory education, urbanization, marketization, the end of arranged marriage, etc.); but these categories are also constructed with bits and pieces of ideas, social assumptions and patriarchal ideologies with much longer social histories.[2] They are neither simply aspects of a longstanding but gradually evolving cultural tradition (Gadamer 1975, 1976; MacIntyre 1984; Pandian 2008), nor seemingly spurious "invented traditions" (Hobsbawm and Ranger 1983). They are new constructs fashioned from recycled materials.[3]

ZOUPING'S MODERNITY

The place of my research is Zouping, the name of both a county in Shandong province of the People's Republic of China, and the city which is the capital of the county, or the county seat. Over the twenty-five years from 1985 to 2010, the county seat experienced nearly a tenfold growth in both population and built-up area; it was home to less than 30,000 people in 1985 but more than 350,000 by 2010. The population growth of the county seat has resulted from the spatial incorporation of surrounding villages, the migration of villagers from other parts of the county to the county seat, and the in-migration of people who originally lived outside of the county. Over this period, the county of Zouping can be said to have modernized in many classic senses of that term. It has gone from a place where the majority of people are farmers who live in villages to one in which the majority are factory workers who live in urban apartments. At the same time there has been an expansion of the number of years children spend in education from an average of less than eight to one of more than fifteen.[4] Equally important, there has been a demographic transition, an increase in the size of bureaucracy and government, an increase in wealth enabling growth in consumer spending and advertising, and a vast improvement in transport and communications infrastructure which has made the county, the country, and the world a much smaller place.[5]

Consider a stereotypical but generally accurate view of life for young people in Zouping's villages one hundred years ago. Though these children might have been taught various skills, there would have been little formal schooling for the majority. Given populations of a few hundred people in most villages, there would at most have been a handful of other children of the same age that a given child recognized in her or his village. These peers along with everyone else in the village would have been considered a familial relative in one way or another rather than a "friend" or a "schoolmate" (Kipnis 2013). Marriages were completely arranged, predominately virilocal, and often occurred at a very young age, twelve for boys and fourteen for girls. After marriage, the young couple would reside with and be subservient to the boy's parents. Occupations for all would revolve around village agriculture and be determined by the resources which the boy's parents could command. As they grew older, the young couple might gain power and responsibility, but these gains would be marked by changes in kin terms rather than age categories. Rather than reaching "adulthood," one became an elder brother's wife, a father, a paternal grandmother, and so on. In such a village, the category of "youth" as it exists in Zouping today, meaning a group of unmarried young people of roughly the same age, not related to one another, somewhat independent of their parents, who had completed several years of schooling but not yet entered stable occupations, would lack significance.[6] Consequently, the category of adult—those who had achieved marriage and some sort of career stability—would also have lacked significance.

Several interlinked circumstances commonly associated with modernity allow for the growth of the category of youth. First, the rise of industrial economies creates opportunities for people (or forces them) to work out of the agricultural sector and work for someone other than their own parents.[7] These opportunities both insert uncertainty into the question of a job choice and reduce the authority of parents over children. Second, the rise of education systems removes children from their parents' house and puts them together in classrooms where they socialize with children of the same age. In Zouping, as schools have progressively become larger and more centralized (located in towns and the county seat rather than villages, and often requiring boarding for secondary students), the extent to which they immerse children in large, nonfamilial groups of peers is striking.[8] Third, the end of arranged marriages gives youth a significant domain in which to exercise agency. Fourth, the concentration of people in urban areas (along with the time-space compression that more efficient technologies allow) enables large numbers of people of the same age to socialize easily. Fifth, rise in income for youth enables marketers to target and create their consumption needs. These five factors can reinforce each other. Schools, for example, prepare children for careers other than agriculture; schools and urban socialization allow youth to meet potential marital partners without parental supervision. But they do not always co-occur. Industrial economies can arise without school systems and school systems can grow in places without industry. Non-arranged marriage can exist or emerge with or without industrialization or urbanization or a large education system. In Zouping, however, these five factors have roughly (though not exactly) co-evolved, with sharp changes in all five areas between 1985 and 2010.

The category of youth reaches a high degree of visibility in China with the publication of the magazine *New Youth*, from 1915 to 1926, first in Shanghai and then in Beijing. Targeting the young and educated in these metropolises, the magazine advocated left-wing politics and a social revolution against established society and "Confucian" familial values. It had a particular penchant for critiquing the familial institutions of village life, such as arranged marriage, which negated the social significance of being "a youth." In 1923 it became the official journal of the young Chinese Communist Party.[9]

In places like Zouping, the sorts of "modernity" that give rise to journals like *New Youth* arrive later than in Beijing and Shanghai, and are not exactly the same as the modernities of early twentieth-century urban China, though the political campaigns against arranged marriages and the related changes to family law which form part of the context of Zouping's modernity were directly inspired by the ideas present in the early communist writings in *New Youth*. In today's Zouping, children attend school in large classrooms full of unrelated children of the same age (Kipnis 2011). After graduation, those who do not go to university often find themselves living in Zouping's Development Zone, where spaces of entertainment, like roller skating rinks, enable them to congregate together. Peers in factories or service sector workplaces also organize social gatherings, like birthday parties, to which only other "youth" are invited. As elsewhere, the social (self-)segregation of youth is common. Completely arranged marriages are outlawed, and young people often attempt to find their own spouses, though matchmakers or nosy friends, relatives and acquaintances are usually involved in some way. Youth also struggle with uncertainty about their future occupations as they experiment with various jobs.

The social category of youth, as it exists in Zouping and many other places, is existentially marked by a double uncertainty and openness: uncertainty about marital partner and uncertainty about occupation. This uncertainty implicitly frames adulthood as a place of steadiness or certainty, no matter how uncertain actual adult lives might be. For young people, uncertainty can be experienced as both freedom and a burden or problem. As one's chronological age progresses, pressures from familial elders to resolve these problems increase. The precise age at which youth ends is difficult to pin down; it varies from place to place and in some places seems to increase as "modernity" progresses. That is to say, as the average number of years spent in educational institutions increases, so does the average age of marriage and the average age of becoming a parent. In places like Australia, one hears young people declare "one's thirties are the new twenties" and as Durham explains in the introduction, in some countries, even people in their forties and fifties feel themselves to be young (though this may have more to do with local understandings than the arrival or intensification of "modernity").

In places like Zouping, where heterosexual marriage is practically mandatory and a four-year university degree is considered a high level of education, pressures to end one's youth are already quite high by the age of twenty-four. As soon as one enters a stable occupation, Zouping's collective matchmaking apparatus exerts its influence through both the enthusiasm of its agents and its extreme efficacy in identifying potential partners. Matchmakers demand that one find a spouse of appropriate occupation and status; before one's occupation and status are determined, it follows, finding a spouse can be difficult. The problems of occupational niche and marriage thus interrelate.

Many people considered themselves to be matchmakers, and continually kept their eyes open for eligible young people. Matchmakers were given gifts at weddings and often became a lifelong friend of the married couple. Several matchmakers told me that they worked according to the principle of "matching doors and households" (*mendang hudui*). Both this principle and the role of matchmaking itself remix tradition and modernity. In the past, matchmakers would act primarily as go-betweens for the parents of the bride and groom; now they more typically worked directly with the young people themselves. In the past, the economic and social circumstances to be matched were those of the extended families and households of the couple. Now they were primarily about the careers and personal characteristics of the young people themselves. But the role and logic of matchmaking still evince considerable continuity with the past. Most crucially, the very idea of matching economic and social statuses implies an assumption of continuity in people's lives. If people's economic prospects are seen as rapidly changing, then such matchmaking would make no sense. Thus, no matter how unpredictable the world is (and, indeed, for most of the twentieth century, China and Zouping endured a wild array of revolutions and upheavals), matchmaking both past and present presumes a predictable world.

Finally, for almost everyone I knew in Zouping, parenthood rapidly followed marriage. The birth control policy allowed all legally married couples at least one child right away, so newlyweds were the only group of people who did not have to deal with the legal complications of pregnancy. (While many couples are allowed more than one child, they must first obtain a legal certificate before conceiving their second.) Those who did not have a child quickly were usually struggling with infertility. Providing a child with a stable home and place of residence for the duration of her education becomes another reason for adults to seek stability.

LIVED SUBJECTIVITIES OF THE YOUTH/ADULTHOOD DICHOTOMY

Although there have been explicit studies of what certain groups of Chinese people think "adulthood" consists of, I find them overly abstract.[10] The Zouping people I knew never spoke explicitly about abstract definitions of youth and adulthood. But there were noticeable differences in the ways in which youth and adults spoke of their lives. Youth often spoke of dreams for the future that were quite different from their present circumstances. By contrast, adults had a few basic narratives for the future (I formally interviewed over 150 Zouping households with one or more adults present). Either they said they would keep doing what they were doing for as long as circumstances allowed it; or, especially if they were renting, they said they would work until they had saved enough money to purchase their own home; or, for some migrants from other places, they said they would work in Zouping until they retired or their children graduated from school, and then would move back home. Finally, if they were dissatisfied with their current lot, they would complain bitterly, but express no particular alternative future. In one way or another, Zouping adults depicted their future in steady terms.

The social openness which defines youth increases the importance of social imaginaries, desires, and fantasies. As Brad Weiss (2002: 97) puts it in his discussion of youth in urban Tanzania, "fantasy" is a crucial component of attempting to fabricate life from "possible lives." Youth in Zouping often expressed dreams of doing something very different from what they were doing in the present, even if those dreams were sometimes vague.

A second difference between ways in which youth and adults depicted their lives was their use of the term "habituation" (*xiguan*). I first noticed the importance of this term when interviewing long-term, married, "adult" factory workers. These workers responded to my reports of complaints often made by youth (depicted below) about working conditions in the factories, such as that factory work is too hot, too noisy, too tiring and so on, by saying that they had already habituated to those conditions (*xiguanle*) and that their concerns were elsewhere. As Anna Lora-Wainwright observes, "Xiguan implies a habit that has been fostered by long-term experience, but it also suggests the ability and willingness to engage in a particular activity" (2013: 154). As an act of will, this sort of habituation requires accepting some aspects about how the world is, of taking the repetitive nature of factory work as well as what Bourdieu (1984: 370) calls "the gravity of the social field" as an acceptable truth, and getting on with the process of bodily accustoming. What a strict mind/body dualism might see as either a simple, unconscious bodily process of acclimatization or a conscious mental decision to accept or reject a particular social circumstance is a deeply interwoven fabric of both.

In Zouping, having not yet habituated to factory work was almost a defining element of the category of youth. In part this was because two common types of young Chinese people—members of the "ant tribe" and "second-generation migrant youth"—are rare in Zouping. In large Chinese cities like Beijing, hordes of impoverished, underemployed recent university graduates are known as the "ant tribe" (*yizu*), because of their large population and their small and humble living arrangements (Si 2009). They generally look for white collar or service sector jobs and do not even consider factory work. But Zouping does not have any academic universities, and most of the university graduates who either come to or return to Zouping do so because of the offer of a middle-class, white-collar job. As these jobs are usually permanent, the taking of such a position effectively ends their youth.

One example can illustrate the ways in which middle-class young people rapidly cease to be youth, as well as Zouping matchmaking and the pressure to marry. Because of previous research projects in schools, I knew many primary school teachers, the majority of whom were women. Several of these women were married to locally powerful officials, and I began viewing the handsome, powerful official and beautiful primary school teacher as an idealized couple. Both partners in this pairing are college educated and white-collar, but the men have power, relatively high incomes, and demanding but sometimes risky careers, while the women have stable, slightly less demanding careers with moderate incomes and expertise in dealing with children. At one primary school I visited, the principal had just hired a new art teacher, who was a fresh college graduate. She was twenty-two, attractive, and single. Within weeks of her arrival, some of the other teachers in her group office began teasing her by speaking loudly about finding a "big official" (*daguan*) to pair off with the office "beauty" (*meinü*). Two of these teachers told me that they already had matches for her in mind.

In addition to not often being middle class, youth in Zouping were generally not second-generation migrant workers. Second-generation migrant workers are those who have grown up in cities that refuse them urban household registration status (a form of local citizenship that grants full access to local schools, government regulated employment, and welfare rights; for more on household registration in China see Wang 2005). Their life dilemmas are not only those of being unaccustomed to factory work, but those of both being alienated from their so-called rural "homes" (which they barely knew) and being denied full citizenship rights in the cities where they feel they rightfully belong (Liang 2013: 196–98; Pun and Lu 2010). Zouping had few second-generation migrant workers for two reasons. First, it has not been a place that attracts migrant workers for long enough to have had a second generation of such workers grow up there. Second, its household registration regime (like that of many smaller cities) is relatively relaxed. If migrant workers wish to settle permanently in Zouping, they usually can. In sum, Zouping's youth contains neither college educated members of the "ant tribe" nor second-generation migrant workers. Zouping's youth usually work either in factories or in the service sector, and those who work in the service sector have usually at least considered factory work.

I got to know Zouping's youth in three ways. I met young people working in the factories of the development zone (the largest of which was called Wei Mian) by going to the roller skating rinks and other places where at least some of them congregate in the evenings. Those in this group who chose to speak with me cannot be considered a representative sample, but I did manage to conduct unstructured interviews with twenty of them. In addition, I interviewed over thirty young people working in hotels, restaurants, and retail stores. This group likewise cannot be considered a representative sample, though I did make sure to include youth working in venues located in all parts of the city and a variety of service occupations. Finally, I interviewed and attended classes with two cohorts of fifteen- to nineteen-year-old students at a Zouping technical high school (*zhiye xuexiao*) whose mission was to directly prepare students for the local workforce. The school had close links with various business groups and work units in Zouping, and most graduates did receive offers of blue- or pink-collar jobs in the county seat upon graduation. Roughly two thirds of the students in this school came from Zouping county; the rest were recruited from other parts of the province or country and tended to come from particular places (Xingtai in Hebei province or Guyuan in Ningxia province, for example) where the school had managed to set up relationships with local education officials.

Technical school students illustrate the dilemmas of the youth more than academic students because academic students are supposed to put everything else in their lives aside to study for the Higher Education Entrance Exam. In Zouping, academic students were reprimanded if caught indulging romantic inclinations and had no time to work part-time jobs. Every waking second of every day was supposed to be devoted to study. Consequently, the forms of openness and uncertainty which characterize the transition to adulthood were stifled for this group. By contrast, the technical school encouraged students to work part time (during school breaks and on weekends) and even helped arrange temporary positions for them. Gaining work experience, even at jobs not directly related to their majors, was considered an important part of their preparation for working lives. While it did not encourage its students to become romantically involved with each other, neither did the technical school take any measures to prevent student romance. A minority of students openly conducted relationships with each other, holding hands or even kissing between classes. At the time of my research, roughly 80 percent of Zouping's sixteen- to eighteen-year-olds attended academic senior middle schools, roughly 10 percent attended the technical school, and roughly 10 percent did not attend any school (Kipnis 2011). Numerically the technical school students were thus a somewhat exceptional category; they were considered by most in Zouping as only quasi-students rather than the real thing. Thus I consider them here as youth rather than as simply students. The majors at the school were quite gender segregated and I requested to sit in on the classes of one male-dominated major and one female-dominated major. I was granted access to a class of thirty-five machine electronics (*jidian*) majors, thirty of whom were men, and a class of twenty kindergarten teaching majors, all of whom were women. I conducted fifteen-minute interviews with everyone in these classes, so, in total I interviewed more than one hundred Zouping youth.

Factory Working Youth

The roller skating rinks of the Development Zone were frequented almost exclusively by factory working youth and could be sites of some risk taking.

Skaters crowded the available space and beginners struggling to keep their balance created a natural obstacle course for the daring and more experienced, who weaved in and out of the slower skaters at high speeds, sometimes executing spins and skating backwards. Accidents resulting in cuts and bruises happened often enough, though I never witnessed or heard of a serious injury. Many youth whom I interviewed there spoke of the physical exhilaration they felt when skating fast. I came to see this sort of exhilaration not as a form of what Bourdieu calls "social flying, a desperate effort to defy the gravity of the social field" (1984: 370), but as a form of flying nonetheless. What was negated here was the physical constriction and discipline of factory work. In other words, the gravity defied was that of habituation rather than habitus.

One woman I interviewed was twenty-three in 2009, and came from a village in Dezhou, a poorer prefecture in northwestern Shandong. She had an older brother and younger sister, but her father left them when they were young and she was raised by her mother alone. "Do you know what it means to be a 'single parent family' (*danqin jiating*) in the countryside," she asked rhetorically. She came to Zouping eight years before when she was fifteen with an older girlfriend from her home village and found a job spinning cotton in Wei Mian. She remained a temporary worker, rejecting many offers of becoming a "contract" worker (that is, a relatively permanent worker with slightly higher benefit levels, but implied commitment to the company). "I make about 2,000 yuan a month working rotating shifts, which is the same as I would make as a contract worker; besides I always dream of leaving here, so I don't want to be a contract worker," she said.[11] Even after eight years of work, she told me that she had still not become accustomed to working at Wei Mian. She found it too hot and noisy and tiring. In Wei Mian, because of the method of cotton spinning used, they keep the temperature in factories over ninety-five degrees Fahrenheit year round. The machines are noisy enough to make conversation difficult, and rotating shifts require six eight-hour shifts a week. Since rotating shift work involves day, evening, and night shifts, it can be very disruptive of sleep patterns. But she did it anyway because of the poverty of her family. "My younger sister is still in school, my mother's health is not great and my older brother needs to get married. I have to help out. I just hope one day all of these crises will end."

She lived in a Wei Mian dorm room and said that it took a long time to make any friends. "I was here for three years before I really trusted anyone. You have to work so hard you have no time for friends and then some people leave on a moment's notice. Plus sometimes the company lays people off. I am a good worker so they never lay me off. I started skating three years ago, and I only first dared to go because I had a few friends who went at the time. But I really like it now, I go fast and it makes me feel excited (*xingfen*)." Though the group of friends I saw her with at the rink included several boys, she said that she did not have a boyfriend. Her dream was to be able to go back to Dezhou and marry someone there. That way she could be near friends and family. Once the lives of her brother and sister are settled, she will not have to worry about making so much money anymore and then will be the time to move back home.

This woman was one of the oldest youth I interviewed. Her familial circumstances were difficult and perhaps she would marry once she returned home. But at the present moment, her refusal to become a permanent contract worker, her inability to habituate to factory work, and her lack of a boyfriend and immediate marital prospects reinforced each other to perpetuate her youth.

A young man whom I interviewed also said he could not habituate to factory work, but he put up with it in order to save enough money to get married. He was nineteen when I interviewed him and had an older sister who was already married. He made 2,000 yuan a month working six or seven days a week in one of the smaller textile factories (not Wei Mian). He said that the money was alright, but that he was always tired and that he had to work seven shifts a week whenever things got busy or his manager wanted something done quickly. "Overall, my situation isn't good, to make money I have to take a job I hate; if I move back home, I won't make money and I'd never have a family." He elaborated that his parents did not have the money to help him get married. They had told him that he needed to save enough money for a down payment on an apartment before anyone would consider marrying him. But he added that he had not really thought much about marriage and was not even sure whether he would like to marry someone in Zouping or back in his hometown. So again, even though this man lived in difficult circumstances and seemed to be saving for marriage, he lacked immediate prospects and was not habituated to factory work.

He was a daring but not too skillful skater and I saw him fall several times. His knee was skinned and bleeding when I interviewed him. When I asked him about it he said, "That's nothing, one time I fell so hard I was limping afterwards for a month. This is my only way of venting my feelings (*chuqi*). Working in the factory is too repressive (*bieqi*)."

Youth in Service Positions

Between 2009 and 2011, one could see help wanted advertisements for waiters and waitresses, salespeople, and hotel workers posted in the windows of service businesses all around Zouping. These ads typically mentioned salaries in the range of 1000 to 1500 yuan a month. Almost any of the thousands of young people working in these jobs in Zouping knew that she or he could have earned more money than that working in Wei Mian or one of the other factories. They consciously chose lower paying service work because they saw some aspect of factory work intolerable. Service work was usually treated as a type of holding position for young people. Most young people in service positions had dreams of eventually doing something else and matchmakers generally did not pressure them to marry (though their parents might). I met no married male service workers and only a few married female ones.

One single woman I interviewed in 2010 was twenty and worked serving soft-serve ice cream in her aunt's shop, making 900 yuan a month. She was born and raised in Zouping, attended an academic high school there and then left town for two years to obtain a relatively unprestigious short-course university (*dazhuan*) degree in machine electronics. After receiving her degree, she worked for three months in Wei Mian. She had earned over 2,000 yuan a month working day shifts on the factory floor but she did not like it. Because of her degree, Wei Mian then offered her 1,300 yuan a month to take a relatively easy pink-collar job in one of the factory's back offices, but she turned that down as well. She explained that working at Wei Mian "turned one into a robot (*jiqiren*). The people there never speak to one another and never have any of their own ideas. They just listen to orders. The management at Wei Mian doesn't want to develop anybody's ability and doesn't like people who are independent thinkers." She added that the Xiwang Group (another major employer in Zouping) was much better in this regard and encouraged worker input, but that it was hard to get a job there. "Serving ice cream is also better than working at Wei Mian," she concluded, because it gave her the chance to interact with customers and use her brain to think about how to respond to different types of people. "I want to talk to people, to use my brain, to think about the most appropriate thing to say in a given situation."

Refusing factory work because of the desire "to think for oneself" and "not be a robot" suggests another common aspect of modernity—the difficulty of school/work transitions. Education in Zouping (outside of the vocational schools) was unrelentingly academic. It was oriented above all to succeeding on the Higher Education Entrance Exam. For most of the first eighteen years of their lives, young people in Zouping are encouraged to structure every waking moment around preparing for that exam. Teachers spur students to study hard with sayings like "If you do not study hard you will end up spending your life as a factory worker." While some might argue that the tedium of Chinese schooling is the perfect preparation for factory life, in fact the experience of schooling seems to discourage habituating to factory life. Throughout China, the more years of schooling one attends, the less likely one is to accept factory work. If Chinese academic schooling involves considerable memorization, it requires the memorization of consistently new material, and thus models a life in which one constantly moves onto new tasks rather than repeatedly doing a single series of tasks. Ideologically, it constructs a hierarchical world in which white-collar jobs are at the top of the hierarchy, and academic success leads to those jobs. It also encourages youth to be aspirational by suggesting that all dreams are possible just as long as one applies oneself to the tasks of studying. But rarely are all dreams possible in the world of work. Though service work also requires repetition, the social interaction breaks up the repetition in ways that factory work does not.

In terms of school/work transitions, Zouping's modernity is particularly unbalanced. The recent expansion of the school system educates about 80 percent of children through senior middle school in an environment in which all are encouraged to pursue university degrees and white collar careers (see Kipnis 2011: 32), but more than two-thirds of the jobs available in Zouping are in manufacturing (see Kipnis 2016). The gap between the desires fostered in the education system and local employment realities is bridged in three ways. First, some educationally successful Zouping students leave Zouping and find employment in larger cities. Second, some relatively uneducated migrant workers from poorer parts of China come to Zouping. Third, some relatively educationally unsuccessful Zouping students (like this one) only obtain a short-course university degree and return to Zouping, but struggle to habituate to factory employment.

This woman also seemed to be resisting pressure to get married. On another day she told me of the marriage pressures on single factory workers. She said,

Once you settle in Wei Mian, people start introducing you to potential partners (*gei ni jieshao duixiang*). Before you know it you are married, have a baby and live in the Wei Mian housing compound and then that's it; your whole life is over. That is what happened to my older sister. She lives in the number four Wei Mian apartment compound. She is so boring; it is hardly worth talking to her anymore. I want to develop myself and do something with my life. The only people my age who work in Wei Mian all come from desperate situations.

This depiction of her older sister suggests that another aspect of settled adulthood is residential stability, most preferably in a place one owns. In Zouping, both white- and blue-collar careers can lead to apartment ownership and settlement in a single place.[12] But some youth want to explore moving around the country and living in different cities, which generally precludes apartment ownership.

A young man I interviewed came from a village in Manchuria at the age of nineteen in 2009 to work in Wei Mian, but quit after two months because he could not stand the heat and noise. When I met him in 2010 he earned 1,100 yuan a month working as a doorman in a hotel where I stayed for a while. He lived in one of the dorms the hotel provided for single workers. He said, "Earning money isn't everything; I have to live my life. If work is torture then how can you continue? Now I feel free. I think I will go to Shanghai soon and try my luck there. I've been to Beijing but I really want to see what Shanghai is like."

The settled-ness of marriage also implies sexual monogamy. Though many men visit prostitutes, sexual conservatism and patriarchal attitudes often resulted in the surveillance of young women's sexuality. Some young women, however, did experiment with their sexuality, whether for their own pleasure or for the income to be made as a sex worker.

The doorman also once approached me about the hotel's "massage" business. Though I politely turned down his offer, when we were chatting a few days later he told me of the dilemmas Zouping's sex industry posed for both young women working at hotels and sexually conservative young men like himself. He said that the hotels always hire young women who are good looking in service positions and that the hotels also all have some form of sex business. While the hotel service positions only pay about 1,100–1,200 yuan a month, sex workers can earn three, five, or even ten times that much. "So all the young women working here have to decide how much their purity (zhencao) is worth to them." Those that do work as prostitutes, he said, usually avoid working in their home counties to try to preserve a bit of their reputation. "I, myself, am quite conservative (hen baoshou)," he added. "When I am ready to get married I will go back home and ask my parents to help me find someone. Given what I've seen working here, I don't think I could trust any woman I met while working as a migrant laborer."

The place of female sexual purity in this man's imagination illustrates well the recombinant modernity of the category of youth. In the days when marriages were completely arranged and occurred in the early teenage years, few people worried about the virginity of unmarried women. Marriage closely followed sexual maturity, so there was little opportunity for consensual sex before marriage. But patriarchal attitudes toward female sexuality were still important, with the chastity of widows being an especially prevalent concern (Evans 1997). So Zouping's modernization has shifted the category of women to which moralities of chastity apply, but not the content of the moral discourse itself. In so doing, Zouping's modernity has also given rise to one of the common dilemmas of youth (particularly young women), that is, how to handle one's premarital sexuality.

Technical School Youth

The machine electronics class was the only place where I found young people saying positive things about factory work. In part, their positive attitudes could be attributed to the fact that they had not yet experienced full-time factory work. But perhaps some of these youth were people who would habituate to factory life quickly, accept contract worker status, marry and settle down. Most of the nonlocal students told me that they hoped to find factory work in their hometowns, but worried that the opportunities for factory work were not so numerous there. Most of the Zouping students were aiming to get work in Zouping's factories. Thirty-one of the thirty-five students grew up in villages and most of them disliked academic schooling. During the more academic of their classes, which focused on topics like the physics of electricity or the principles of wiring machines, some of the students slept at their desks while others kept their heads up but played with their mobile phones or read items not related to the lessons (for an even more extreme example of dysfunctional vocational school education in China, see Woronov 2011). But the students all enjoyed the practical classes, during which they would move to the school's workshops and wire up various machines. Like the young woman who worked serving soft-serve ice cream, but from an opposite point of view, these students demonstrated the antipathy between academic schooling and willingness to habituate to factory work in China.

The kindergarten teaching class differed from the machine electronics class in several respects. Not only was the latter class entirely female, but the attitudes of the students toward studying was also different. The students all said they liked school and remained alert during classes. Many of the students also had fond memories of their academic junior middle schools, but (at least those from Zouping) simply could not compete with their classmates in terms of test scores and were encouraged by teachers to go to technical school. Their attitudes may simply indicate that those who selected the kindergarten teaching major desired academically oriented white-collar occupations.

One seventeen-year-old electronics student I interviewed not only expressed the antipathy between academic success and factory work, but also the assumptions of social hierarchy which underlie the matchmakers' desire to pair off partners of equivalent social status. This boy hated regular school, but liked fiddling with electric machines, so this major was good for him. He was from a village north of the county seat and his father worked at a factory while his mother farmed. He hoped to get a job at one of the electricity producing factories in the development zone. He said the pay was good—over 2,000 yuan a month, but it was not only the money that motivated him. He told me that many of his former junior middle school classmates were now attending academic senior middle school and that most of them would go on to university. "Attending university, however," he said with a smile, "does not guarantee a job, and most of them won't find one." As a result they'll have to come back to Zouping's factories for employment. Since he will already have had five or six years of experience by the time his former classmates entered the factories, he could end up training them. "I'll make them call me 'Master' (*shifu*) for the rest of their lives," he concluded.

Imaginations of social hierarchy often presume fixity—a hierarchy that is imagined as reversible in a few months is not conducive to hierarchical social interactions. As Louis Dumont (1977, 1980) argues, liberal societies, no matter how unequal they are, enable social interaction to take place as if everyone is either equal, or that any hierarchical differences are easily reversible. In hierarchical societies, social interaction proceeds as if hierarchies are permanent, no matter how fragile structures of inequality may in fact be. The electronics student's fantasy, that all his former classmates (previously superior to him in academic competitions) will call him Master for the rest of their lives, reflects a hierarchical imagination of the social universe. This hierarchical social imagination is the same as that of the matchmakers who compare "doors and households" and feeds assumptions of adulthood involving fixity.

An interview with one of the students in the kindergarten teaching class demonstrates that girls as well as boys can embrace patriarchal views of female sexuality. As with my other interviews with these students, I conducted it in the classroom during break periods with several classmates listening in. This sixteen-year-old girl took the opportunity to launch a monologue that was directed more at the other students than me. She said that she was dismayed by the behavior of some of the other students in her school and that she disliked girls who engaged in underaged romance (*zaolian*) (one of the girls present had been holding hands with her boyfriend an hour earlier) and boys who smoked and drank in the toilets. Such behavior was not tolerated at her old junior middle school and she was not sure why it was allowed to go on here.

She also articulated a desire to move up China's place-based social hierarchy by becoming a kindergarten teacher in as large a city as possible. Beijing or Shanghai would be perfect. It would be acceptable if she ended up working at a kindergarten in the county seat, but she definitely did not want to work at one of the kindergartens in the township where she was from. "Big cities are fashionable and exciting, and I would like to live in as big a city as possible." Given that the employment restrictions of the household registration policy in places like Shanghai and Beijing would make this dream difficult, this particular fantasy seems to fit closely with Bourdieu's description of "dreams of social flying."[13]

CONCLUSIONS

Zouping's rapid and rather classic modernization has increased the importance of the transition from youth to adulthood. The single most important marker of adulthood in Zouping seems to be marriage, but that is only because marriage in Zouping implies (in the majority of cases and in the imaginations of matchmakers) so many other things. To get married one should have a settled career and, ideally, be settled in terms of one's place of residence. After marriage, one should rapidly have a child. And marriage implies sexual monogamy, a norm which is especially expected of women, and which can lead to patriarchal pressures to police young women's sexuality. The youth depicted in this chapter often resisted the many forms of regularity this transition implies. They resisted habituating to factory careers, they resisted getting married, they expressed a desire to experiment with living in different places, and sometimes they experimented with romantic and sexual relationships before marriage. While resisting the transition to adulthood, they often spend their time outside of work socializing with other youth, sometimes engaging in physically risky forms of entertainment, like roller skating.

But for the majority of people in Zouping, youth's duration is relatively short. Pressures to accept a job (which were not too hard to find in Zouping at the time of my research), settle down, and get married were high. I did not meet any unmarried young people in Zouping over the age of twenty-five. Remaining unmarried in Zouping during the 1980s suggested the poverty of a man's family and was considered a source of shame (there was a relative shortage of women in Zouping [Kipnis 1997], so women rarely remained single). During the current era of economic prosperity, fewer and fewer impoverished households exist. Although there are certainly unmarried Zouping people, I suspect that the high level of pressure to marry drives most older youth who wish to remain single to leave Zouping for life in one of China's larger cities.

I theorize the implicit category of adulthood in Zouping—that of a steady, married life—as a form of recombinant modernity. It is a modernity because in the age of arranged, virilocal marriages in an agricultural society, the categories of youth and adulthood were not that important. The simultaneous rise of nonagricultural careers, non-arranged marriage, and compulsory education establish the youth/adulthood transition as a problem space. It is a recombinant modernity because the assumptions and practices recycled in practices of

marriage—presumptions of a hierarchical society in which the status of marital partners should be matched and female chastity should be maintained—
have their roots in the village, agricultural society of a previous era.

While certainly not universal, I believe that aspects of the ideal category of
adulthood in Zouping—marked by marriage, a steady career, and regularity—
are far from rare in today's world. Zouping's compressed and classic modernization has enabled rather common aspects of adulthood to come to the fore.
Boddy's chapter (this volume) shows how young people in Sudan work around
such ideals in circumstances where attaining them is unrealistic for the majority. Zouping's abundance of manufacturing jobs has meant that steady employment is available for the majority, if one is willing to habituate to it. The rapid
expansion of the educational system has marked the school/work transition as
problematic and has developed the contradiction between the ethos promoted
in academic institutions and the realities of factory work. The rapid urbanization has created spaces, both physical and imaginary, for youth to socialize. The
rapidity of these transformations has allowed aspects of the ethos of an earlier
era to persist in the form of conservative familial values, and relatively strong
social pressures to adhere to a highly normalized life course.

In many ways the situation in Zouping resembles that depicted by Mary
Brinton (2011) for Japan during the 1970s and 1980s. She describes this period
as one when the school-to-work transition proceeded relatively smoothly,
where the vast majority of young people (to a much greater extent than in
other industrialized countries) got married and had their first child in their
twenties, and when people thought of their identities in terms of *ba* or social
location. Ba referred to social environments, such as families or the workplace,
which involved more or less lifelong commitments. If Japan as a whole (during
this period) can be described as a place where marriage, regularity and steadiness mark a nearly universal form of adulthood, then it is not so surprising
that a small city like Zouping can exhibit an even greater degree of regularity.
In both cases, this way of living adulthood arises during a period of rapid industrialization and urbanization, under economic circumstances which make
seemingly permanent, full-time employment possible for the majority, and in
a place with a history of "Confucian" attitudes toward education. Brinton further describes how the erosion of permanent employment in Japan during the
1990s and 2000s reduced the regularity of marriage patterns, diminished the
importance of ba, and made school/work transitions more problematic. Perhaps Zouping, too, will one day face such a transformation.

Despite the similarities between Zouping of the 2000s and Japan of the
1970s and 1980s, I want to push against part of Brinton's analysis. Even though
"youth" in Zouping is relatively short, and marriage and employment are quite

regular, I would prefer to focus on the difficulty of the school/work transition rather than its ease. Though this transition may be easier in Zouping than in some places, it is still marked by resistance and the difficulties of habituation. Youth do not just jump into adulthood at the first opportunity, even when there are opportunities to do so. Brinton too depicts a few cases of *furītā*, or Japanese young people who shunned permanent work even when it was available in the 1980s, though she chooses not to pursue this topic (Brinton 2011: 5–6). Many of the Zouping youth described in this chapter might be depicted in the same terms, if only for a relatively short period. In short, the settled lives of adulthood are not often seen as desirable by youth.

Modernity, almost everywhere, has yielded a separation of the worlds of work and those of school, as well as between those of marriage and youthful singledom. In many of the chapters in this volume (e.g., those by Boddy and Solway) the certainties of a stable adulthood seem completely illusory. But even in places like Zouping, the types of dreams fostered in the school environment are not matched by workplace realities. In Zouping, where both places in educational institutions and places in manufacturing jobs are available to the vast majority, where the ethos of education devalues factory labor, and where conservative, patriarchal attitudes toward marriage and sexuality drive some to accept the steadiness of married life earlier than they might otherwise, these contradictions are especially prominent.

Andrew B. Kipnis is Professor of Anthropology in the Department of Anthropology at the Chinese University of Hong Kong. He is author of *From Village to City: Social Transformation in a Chinese County Seat.*

NOTES

1. Technically speaking, adult education in China refers mainly to those courses for which admittance does not rely on the standard exams for admittance to secondary and tertiary institutions. The people attending such courses can range in age from seventeen to sixty and can include people that in other contexts would be referred to as "youth."

2. I am not making an etymological argument about the origin of the terms themselves. Anne Kinney (2004) shows that childhood and children have been written about during the Han dynasty (206 BCE–220 CE), though she makes no reference to the modern term for "youth." But Kinney also shows that writing about children as a distinct social category occurred primarily in texts referring to education in the Confucian classics. So, as with industrial modernity, practices of academic education give rise to ideas about the difference between children and adults. Though educational institutions of one form or another have a long history in China, it is only with the industrial modernity of the twentieth century that education becomes a mass instead of an elite institution.

3. I theorize the notion of recombinant modernity at length in Kipnis (2016).

4. These fifteen years include three years of preschool. Many of the "youth" I interviewed received less than fifteen years of education because 1) they were born fifteen to twenty years ago and the average number of years spent in school has increased rapidly in the past decade; 2) they were born and raised in impoverished places outside of Zouping, which average fewer years of schooling; and 3) they were among those children who received less schooling than average. For more on education in Zouping, see Kipnis (2011).

5. While the government attributes declining birthrates to the birth control policy, most demographers argue that "modernization" factors have been more important and that the strictly enforced "one-child" policy has been a cruel, unnecessary, and counterproductive policy of an authoritarian government. See, for example, Greenhalgh and Winckler (2005), as well as Whyte et al. (2015).

6. Philippe Ariès (1962) famously argued that "childhood" did not exist at all during the Middle Ages in Europe, and thus must be analyzed historically as a category. His work has been criticized for missing some of the ways in which childhood was marked in the Middle Ages, though he certainly demonstrates that the advent of modernity has led to a proliferation of discourse about the category. I would argue that a similar and perhaps even stronger argument about the category of "youth" could be made.

7. In some places, children had opportunities to live outside of their family homes even in predominately agricultural village societies, but not so much in China.

8. For detail on the centralization of Zouping's schools, see Kipnis (2006, 2011).

9. Of course the Communist Party also recruited older people. But just as it saw poor people as its natural allies (though its leaders often came from wealthier backgrounds), so did it see youth. For more on *New Youth*, see Schwarcz (1986).

10. See Nelson et al. (2004), for example. Conducted by a group of social psychologists, this study was based on a questionnaire that gave university students a list of characteristics which they could designate as either important or unimportant for defining "adulthood." The article derived from the research does not even give translations of the words used for "adult" and "adulthood."

11. Her salary, roughly US$325, was relatively high in local terms in 2009. A few years earlier, factory workers averaged only half that amount. A frugal single worker, living in the dorm rooms which the factory provided for free, could easily save more than half of this salary. Married Wei Mian couples are able to purchase their own apartments from the company at a subsidized price, and many couples with both partners on such a salary do so and often own their own car as well.

12. Unlike China's largest cities, the price of apartments in Zouping was, at least at the time of my research, relatively affordable to couples with two salaries.

13. Xin Liu (1997) calls the social hierarchy of places in China generated by the household registration policy a "power geography."

REFERENCES

Ariès, Philippe. 1962. *Centuries of Childhood*. London: Jonathan Cape.

Bourdieu, Pierre. 1984. *Distinction: A Social Critique of the Judgement of Taste*. Translated by Richard Nice. London: Routledge & Kegan Paul.

Brinton, Mary C. 2011. *Lost in Transition: Youth, Work and Instability in Postindustrial Japan*. New York: Cambridge University Press.

Dumont, Louis. 1977. *From Mandeville to Marx: The Genesis and Triumph of Economic Ideology*. Chicago: University of Chicago Press.

———. 1980. *Homo Hierarchicus: The Caste System and Its Implications*. Chicago: University of Chicago Press.

Evans, Harriet. 1997. *Women and Sexuality in China: Dominant Discourses of Female Sexuality and Gender since 1949*. Cambridge: Polity Press.

Gadamer, Hans Georg. 1975. *Truth and Method*. New York: Seabury Press.

———. 1976. *Philosophical Hermeneutics*. Translated by David E. Linge. Berkeley: University of California Press.

Greenhalgh, Susan, and Edwin A. Winckler. 2005. *Governing China's Population*. Stanford: Stanford University Press.

Hobsbawm, Eric, and Terence Ranger, eds. 1983. *The Invention of Tradition*. Cambridge: Cambridge University Press.

Kinney, Anne Behnke. 2004. *Representations of Childhood and Youth in Early China*. Stanford: Stanford University Press.

Kipnis, Andrew B. 1997. *Producing Guanxi: Sentiment, Self, and Subculture in a North China Village*. Durham: Duke University Press.

———. 2006. "School Consolidation in Rural China." *Development Bulletin* 70:123–25.

———. 2011. *Governing Educational Desire: Culture, Politics and Schooling in China*. Chicago: University of Chicago Press.

———. 2013. "Education and Inequality; Education and Equality." In *Unequal China: The Political Economy and Cultural Politics of Inequality*, edited by Wanning Sun and Yingjie Guo, 111–24. London: Routledge.

———. 2016. *From Village to City: Social Transformation in a Chinese County Seat*. Berkeley: University of California Press.

Liang, Hong. 2013. *Chu Liangzhuang Ji* [Records of those who left Liangzhuang village]. Guangzhou: Huacheng Chubanshe.

Liu, Xin. 1997. "Space, Mobility, and Flexibility: Chinese Villagers and Scholars Negotiate Power at Home and Abroad." In *Ungrounded Empires: The Cultural Politics of Modern Chinese Transnationalism*, edited by Aihwa Ong and Donald Nonini, 91–114. New York: Routledge.

Lora-Wainwright, Anna. 2013. *Fighting for Breath: Living Morally and Dying of Cancer in a Chinese Village*. Honolulu: University of Hawai'i Press.

MacIntyre, Alasdair. 1984. *After Virtue: A Study in Moral Theory*. Notre Dame: University of Notre Dame Press.

Nelson, Larry J., Sarah Badger, and Bo Wu. 2004. "The Influence of Culture in Emerging Adulthood: Perspectives of Chinese College Students." *International Journal of Behavioral Development* 28(1): 26–36.

Pandian, Anand. 2008. "Tradition in Fragments: Inherited Forms and Fractures in the Ethics of South India." *American Ethnologist* 35(3): 466–80.

Pun, Ngai, and Huilin Lu. 2010. "Unfinished Proletarianization: Self, Anger and Class Action among the Second Generation of Peasant-Workers in Present-Day China." *Modern China* 36(5): 493–519.

Schwarcz, Vera. 1986. *The Chinese Enlightenment: Intellectuals and the Legacy of the May Fourth Movement of 1919*. Berkeley: University of California Press.

Si, Lian, ed. 2009. *Yizu: Daxue Biyesheng Juju Cun Shilu* [Ant tribes: True reports on the residential districts of college graduates]. Nanning: Guangxi Shifan Daxue Chubanshe.

Wang, Fei-ling. 2005. *Organizing through Division and Exclusion: China's Hukou System.* Palo Alto: Stanford University Press.

Weiss, Brad. 2002. "Thug Realism: Inhabiting Fantasy in Urban Tanzania." *Cultural Anthropology* 17(1): 93–124.

Whyte, Martin King, Wang Feng, and Yong Cai. 2015. "Challenging Myths about China's One-Child Policy." *China Journal* 74: 144–59.

Woronov, Terry E. 2011. "Learning to Serve: Urban Youth, Vocational Schools and New Class Formations in China." *China Journal* 66: 77–99.

CHAPTER FIVE

༄

INVENTING THE RULES

Redefining Moral Agency among the First Post-Independence Generation in Papua New Guinea

Karen Sykes

ŽIŽEK (2010) WROTE that political maturity in the last days of Western capitalism comes with the moral awareness that it is possible to break the rules in order to create a democratic society, rather than to follow its rules. This valuable insight links culturally specific ideas about political agency and moral maturity for citizens in Western democracies, and it allows us also to unhinge ideological assumptions used to evaluate adulthood as political maturity. I do not want to further Žižek's argument in this chapter so much as to examine its underlying assumption that the people of some nations fail to achieve political maturity, while others find it through breaking its rules. In the case of post-independence Papua New Guinea (PNG) national and kinship politics coexist as citizens and *wantoks* (speakers of the same language) create critical commentaries on assumptions about their political maturity (Sykes 2014, 2001). The experiences of the first generation born after PNG independence in 1975 are not recognized in the nationally homogenizing quantitative records produced by international and national agencies. Closer ethnographic study shows that adulthood, or its nearest equivalent in PNG, is not associated with contributions to a national political maturity, nor with individual and psychological states of development. Adults are recognized when they are moral agents, whose maturity is realized interactively in newly emergent households.

Although many anthropologists would contest Žižek's vision that capitalism is in its last days in postcolonial nations, they might recognize that capitalism is in a later stage than it was in the late nineteenth century, especially given the rise of a neoliberal ideology that places personal responsibility for political action center-stage (Gershon 2010; Macpherson 1962; Sykes 2007). Since the 1970s in Europe and North America, late capitalism as neoliberalism has married post-Fordist ideologies of managerialism with democratic political processes for the delivery of social services to citizens. During the same decades in the postcolonial nations, late capitalism in the form of decolonization has married young democratic institutions with the robust institutions of offshore, multinational corporations. As a postcolonial state, democratic PNG relies on investments by offshore extractive industries operating within its borders. Yet its citizens are subject to international and national judgments of a failed political maturity that confound national politics with the morality of generational relations of the household.

It is not so much that the post-independence generation "cannot grow up," a frequent global complaint Deborah Durham queries in her introduction to this volume, but that they are not especially concerned with childhood or adulthood as stages of personal or political development. Nor are they all pursuing traditional markers of the life cycle, even when their elder generation, born before independence, wishes they would. In several chapters of this book, especially those by Jacqueline Solway and Anna Kruglova, we see the challenges of recognition faced by those growing up in the first decades after major political transformation. In PNG they are crafting new ways of acting as moral agents for a collective future, which is what all adults do. The problem is that as adult moral agents who take care of others' needs their activity does not register in official records of educational and economic growth in the nation. In PNG the official records of international development agencies and national departments are concerned with the progress of the PNG nation, whereas the members of that generation frame their understanding of moral agency in terms of their household, which escapes the eye of the demographer. In this regard they are not caught "between adolescence and later life" as their post-Soviet counterparts might be. Neither are they a generation caught in a protracted adolescence-cum-"unstable adulthood," as are the Ugandan graduates described by Claire Dungey and Lotte Meinert in their chapter in this volume, who learned in school to wait to accomplish the goals they set for personal development.

One way to recover the ethnography of this generation from the prejudices and presumptions of international experts and even the PNG nationalists, who can only see failure, is to identify and critique the nationalist categories of analysis, in much the same way as historians of the last part of the twentieth century critiqued the analytic tools of sociologists as too nationalist, and impoverished by the theory they deployed (Thompson 1978). Instead, the aim is to know this generation as "present at their own making," to paraphrase Thompson's famous study of *The Making of the English Working Class* (1963), which provides a scintillating reappraisal of the social class of artisan weavers known as "Luddites," who opposed the new technology in an industry that turned their craft into unskilled jobs in mechanized labor. As a unit of analysis the post-independence generation is fundamentally a group circumscribed by the extended kinship relations of the household, and its shared experiences of the historical circumstances of independence; its morality is neither that of a social class whose logic is a deep structure reaching across centuries, nor is its agency formed only in a short-lived social event, or political revolt. Instead, the post-independence generation is a social cohort that perceives itself most clearly in relation to the previous generation of nationalists that fought for independence and won it. Over two decades of research with the first generation born after independence, I have learned to make use of what is their characteristically generational thinking, rather than rely on their work skills and labor relations, or their homeland and culture to ground their shared concerns. I have reported on the preceding generation of nationalists who brought Papua New Guinea to independence, and subsequently have judged the post-independence generation as failing to act as adults and not furthering the cause of the nation. What has been lacking in accounts of the post-independence generation is their perspective on moral agency, which I report here through a set of case studies that resituates their lives in the context of the emerging modern extended households that they now make with spouses, parents, and siblings.

In order to understand the PNG perspective on adulthood as a condition of moral agency, rather than a form of political maturity, I found I needed to grind new lenses in order to see the post-independence generation's behavior in the round. One lens borrows Žižek's concern with political agency and how late capitalism exerts a particular kind of moral pressure on its citizens to accommodate to a liberal ideology of personal responsibility for individual action (Gershon 2010). A second lens is focused at a closer level and challenges his use of the concepts of moral agency and political maturity (see also MacIntyre and Patterson 2011; Sykes 2007). I came to see that Papua New Guineans demonstrate their moral agency and their political maturity in the way they form new households that connect people with commitment to making their lives work together. In so doing, I follow the vision outlined by Durham's introduction to this volume to reconsider adulthood as an intersubjective experience, and I thereby challenge the idea that rule breaking as political maturity is an ideal goal for the post-independence generation. In this chapter, I show that "inventing the rules" in order to create new ways of living together in new forms of the household is quite different from breaking the rules to achieve adult political maturity in the postcolonial nation. Asking "when," "why," and "whose" idea of adulthood was at stake pours doubt on the freighted meanings of adulthood and maturity, and clarifies the missing theoretical distinction between moral agency and political maturity. This chapter aims to outline, and thereby recognize, the moral agency of people who are unconcerned with the achievement of their political adulthood.

THE MORAL AGENCY OF THE FIRST GENERATION BORN IN AN INDEPENDENT PNG

The first generation of Papua New Guineans born into political independence are known among their peers and juniors as the "post-independence generation." They developed a critical perspective on the whole PNG nation and their place in it that sets them apart from their parents' generation, who founded the new government and style themselves as the fathers of PNG independence. Oddly, adulthood became problematic for the post-independence generation when some state officials and international aid agencies judged PNG's national independence to be a success because their state education system had fostered political maturity (see Foster [2005] and Weeks [1976] for different documentation of this moment). They then identified moral shortcomings in the next generation to benefit from the new nation's institutions (see Lipset [1988] and Robbins [1998] for different evaluations of the political and moral meanings of independence). Pre-independence ethnographies of political leadership and the life cycle in Melanesia deepen the puzzle, as they do not agree with the assumptions of developmental psychology (Strathern 1988). According to these accounts, Melanesians of all ages had lived as political adults, simply by inventing ways of living together and taking responsibility for each other.

Papua New Guinea's post-independence generation enact their moral agency by "inventing the rules," or more colloquially "giving it a try." Both are English translations for a neo-Melanesian idiom *triam tasol* (in Tok Pisin,[1] one of PNG's three major languages). Among Papua New Guineans, triam tasol is used to refer to new or innovative social action. It is uttered by people in everyday life for the pragmatic effect of helping others discern how they should react to each other. After the end of a contested claim to business ownership, a young Papua New Guinean will tell his family that he plans now to join those who first had contested his claim, in order make the new business arrangements work for a while, in order to give the new plan a try, which is to say, they will triam tasol. It is uttered modestly and good naturedly, protecting the speaker against the threat of the failure of important goals and perhaps grand plans. When setting up a new timber business with a "walkabout" saw mill, a man said that he was just giving it a try, with the hopes that the venture could prove to be lucrative in nontraditional ways. The words "triam tasol" are not uttered as if they were a rule, or a social norm that interprets otherwise unspoken conventional or customary behavior. Indeed, in the first example, by calling on his young nephews to triam tasol as business partners, the speaker knew that he was innovating upon social norms rather than breaking the rules, and thereby turned his obligations as an uncle of younger boys into a business arrangement.

I use the Tok Pisin phrase as a corrective lens to bring into focus the face of a generation that is by far the largest proportion of PNG's seven million citizens.[2] This generation's face is distorted by claims in the national and international press that they are politically immature because they lack the moral agency to shoulder the work of national development. The generation's character is often obscured because so much attention is given to the few who commit violent acts against political leaders and businessmen. The press describes the perpetrators as *raskols*, a word evoking the colonial past when the behavior of a "work boy" might be reprimanded good-naturedly as immature (Goddard 2005). The image of the raskol has come to define the whole generation as participants in a broadly felt culture of *raskolism* (Sykes 1999, 2000), even though they lack the means to organize as a group and to articulate a political vision. Even more effectively, metaphors of raskol activity erase the post-independence generation as a cohort from international records of economic growth and estimations of the nation's social capacity for it. From this external perspective on the (non)agency of the post-independence generation, they might be thought to be breaking the rules just by appearing in public, especially as unemployed men and women in town or the village, failing to develop the nation. However, once we can see the moral agency of this first generation born after PNG's independence through a different lens of their everyday life, then it becomes clear that their activity of "inventing the rules" is not evidence of their failure and that the reports of their violence do not extend to the entire cohort. A closer analysis of their moral agency shows something different than political maturity. Rather than breaking the rules to find a new social justice in the independent state, as Žižek calls for, this cohort invents rules, giving it a try, for living together in the household.

I also use the phrase "triam tasol" to challenge ethnocentric assumptions deeply embedded in Western social theory. Notably, the capacity to act as moral agents has been recognized in Melanesia for all people, including very young and elderly relatives. Quite simply, adulthood as a capacity for moral action is not a state isolated in the life cycle in PNG. Life cycle rituals (whether these are initiation or marriage rituals) do not produce adults by aiding the transition from childhood to adulthood. This critical point is made in the ethnographic record (Foster 1995; Lutkehaus 1995; Munn 1996; Robbins 1998; Weiner 1980), which gives a rich account of generation and gender, showing the Melanesian person exists in a composite condition and emerges as a male or female individual through participation in a gender ritual. Gender rituals works to divide androgynous beings into male and female, and thereby set up the conditions that make it necessary to reunite as spouses and parents. Gender rituals neither effect transition to a permanent condition nor a movement into a stage of life, and for this reason they are not comparable to life-cycle rituals. For example, at any point a man might decide to carry a basket on his head and work in his wife's father's garden, as if he were just like her. He might next transact yams from his wife's gardens with her brothers as if he were not the same person who had been weeding the land they (his wife's brothers) might also garden as the sons of his wife's father. I conclude that such inventive acts of social differentiation constitute moral agency in PNG today, leaving adulthood (as political maturity) neither a stage, nor a political problem, but something realized across and between people throughout their lives.

In this chapter I develop these critical theoretical points for twenty-first century late capitalism, and note three features of the post-independence cohort's moral agency that dislocate it from national ideologies of maturity, and instead relate it to the contemporary household as the most salient social and political form of everyday life. First, I show that this generation has a shared moral vision toward their future. Second, I relate how its members are also concerned largely with their relationships to other generations in the future, and, by way of this intergenerational moral agency, have been released from the burden of keeping Melanesian traditions or furthering the interests of the older generation in the present. Finally, I show how they prioritize their obligations to sustain and reproduce relationships in their households over their responsibilities to the clan, village, or nation. I conclude that the moral agency of the first generation born after independence is expressed by inventing the rules, and pertains largely to the household, by which I mean the household as a decision-making unit concerned for the future of its members who might not live under the same roof while they go about their everyday work of providing for each other. Such geographically extended, multi-sited households are composed of moral agents, who enable each other's social, economic and spiritual lives as spouses, parents, brothers and sisters in Papua New Guinea. Gudeman (2005; see also Gudeman and Hann 2015) and Gregory (1997, 2009) define the household as a jural, economic, and affective unit whose members are joined by primary concerns with everyday moral and political governance, with the provision for their shared needs and sustenance, and with mutual regard for the affective bonds between them. Gudeman and Hann (2015) turn to classical political theory (*oikos*) to better capture the meaning of household to the PNG independence generation, instead of to the popular rendering of household as those people who share the same physical residence.

Just as the post-independence generation's understanding of household as a political, economic, and affective unit escapes census takers' use of the term, so too does their understanding of political maturity and moral agency escape psychologists' theory of human development. Adulthood for Papua New Guineans, as noted, is less a life stage than a situated and intersubjective form of action. The post-independence cohort's understanding of their moral agency upends most external organizations' assumptions that this generation should support economic growth in the post-independence state, and at the same time asks us to critically engage with Žižek's challenge to think about maturity in the age of late capitalism.

(Not) Recognizing the Moral Agency of the First Papua New Guinean Generation

Unlike the generation that has been praised for bridging the colonial and post-colonial era and thereby fathering independence, the post-independence generation has been critiqued as subjects of rapid and frequent changes in national education policy simply because their actions are unrecognized as distinctive of an entire generation. They have been through a period of radical change, beginning with structural adjustment in 1991, and continuing with the Millennium Development Goals for 2015. In the course of these changes, this generation's contributions to the growth of the new nation do not fall into conventional categories of educational and economic analysis. Instead, national and international assessments tend to discuss their role in shaping the future of the nation in moral terms, rather than economic and social ones. The national press holds them responsible for the growth of the economy and the sustenance of the spirit and social life of this small Pacific Island nation, but they apparently fail at these challenges. PNG's major donor, AusAID, in its country report, states that they are a "mis"educated generation who pursue an immoral lifeway as raskols and thereby thwart the flourishing of the local economy and impede the progress of national infrastructural change. Accordingly, the entire generational cohort is known as the "greatest threat to the future social and economic development of the nation" (AusAID 2005: 30). Moral rhetoric focuses on the generation, but national and international measures focus on the success of educational institutions and also on individual employment records. It is hard to elicit the diverse features of an entire generation when it is not the primary unit of analysis. The largest reason for this generation's invisibility in the official record lies with the way the data is collected. In education, the school as an institution is the unit of record taking, and in economic reports, records of employment are not easily correlated meaningfully with age and educational achievement. The generation is not a unit about which official data is usually collected. Where it is collected, and analyzed, the data must first be extracted from other bases, such as the census, school enrollments, and some age-specific records of employment and taxation of eighteen- to thirty-five-year-olds. The records do not include an account of the livelihoods of the extended households, where the generations do count in the moral reckoning about their shared political future.

Most reports simply omit discussions of this generation's education and work, apparently giving it no moral value at all. At first glance, the Human Development Index (HDI) and the UNESCO country reports show they did not contribute to economic or social growth. In otherwise comprehensive accounts of national growth, such as the World Bank Reports (e.g., 2008), the first generation of Papua New Guineans are economically invisible. The majority of individuals of this age group have failed to find formal sector employment, and therefore have no place in the records of taxation, or of registration with government services, and do not constitute themselves as job seekers, as they might in other nations. The national records show that only five percent of those who paid income taxes were between twenty and thirty years old in 2000, although paying taxes is not a true measure for those who are working in unskilled labor or for those receiving the lowest wages in the country. It is as if they were dropped from the record of the country's economic development. In effect, while the press is concerned with the moral role of an entire generation in the development of the nation, the elision of most of the cohort from the education, employment, and work records creates its own moral picture, with implications for public rhetoric. National development agencies and their consultants come to see this generation as comprised of unproductive citizens, that is, as members of a nation who do not contribute to its growth.

Were the HDI concerned with the extended household, rather than the household as a single residence, then this generation's many innovations in making a livelihood might find an easier way into the record of social and economic development. Admittedly, the extended household is famously hard to define and to capture in statistics (Netting 1984; Yanagisako 1979; see also Bear et al. 2015). Its classical definition relies on the confluence of three features: provisioning of the necessities for its present and future members, moral governance of its members through demands on their obligations to their kin and other household members, and the bonds made by mutual affection as a source of emotional and social sustenance. The aggregates of national and international agencies cannot comprehend the scope of such knowledge and practices mobilized by households and used by them to foster their well-being into the future. Overall, it is perhaps unsurprising that this generation's moral agency has escaped notice in most political and economic reports on national growth.

A different approach to understanding the moral agency of this generation can illuminate more than the assumption of their immoral or amoral character and social contributions. Aid agencies, including those from the United Nations and the World Bank, provide suggestive details in their own records. There is evidence of the post-independence generation's burgeoning numbers in education despite their invisibility in records of employment and work. Since the 1990s, secondary school enrollments in PNG have increased, rising from roughly 25 percent of fifteen year olds in 1990, to 75 percent in 2005 (AusAID 2005). In addition, more students have been staying in school longer. For example, in New Ireland Province, secondary school enrollments totaled two thousand in five high schools in 1991, and the same number in 2010. However, in 2000 the enrollments spanned ages thirteen to fifteen, whereas in 1991 they spanned the ages of fifteen to eighteen, with village-based primary schools providing education up to the age of fifteen. The secondary school enrollments provide concrete evidence of both proportional and aggregate growth over a decade and a half.

Next, I draw on long-term fieldwork in Papua New Guinea during which I worked with a cohort of secondary school students and graduates who had been born in 1975, the year of PNG's independence. My work expanded over the years, to include their spouses, coworkers, and members of their generational cohort from other parts of the country. As they grew older they would habitually identify their generational cohort, not by face-to-face relations, but by inferred similarity based upon their personal knowledge of secondary education under the period of structural adjustment, when the school curriculum was rewritten and the arrangements for the payment of school fees became a matter of political debate, sometimes a fraught one. To them, their moral agency is demonstrated in experimental undertakings in which they triam tasol. And, rather than suggest that there is a shared key value, or a common moral norm, I will argue that the moral agency of this generation is immanent in social actions that aim only to invite a response, and are undertaken to see how others respond.

Recognizing Experiments in Inventing the Rules (Triam Tasol)

Triam tasol captures a sense of moral agency fitted to the era of late capitalism, yet escaping the mid-twentieth century assumption that theories of an individual's experience of personal moral development might converge smoothly with theories of national development as a pathway to modernity. These assumptions were embedded in many postcolonial education systems, just as they had been in the education systems of many early twentieth-century European nations that treated education as a moral institution for the creation of a secular society. Critical research on South Asia (Gellner 2015) has shown that national social studies curricula could shape neither students' nationalism nor their criticism of nationalist goals. The sentiments of nationalism have sprung from different wells than the nation. In PNG, villagers showed great enthusiasm for state-planned national education in the earlier period leading up to independence, and in the first decades following it by paying for primary and secondary education. Despite free tuition since 2006, education is no longer accepted as a given of family and village life. The shift of interest in education foreshadows a change in the possibilities open to the next generation of young Papua New Guineans.

As moral agents, members of the post-independence generation aim to open up possibilities within social relationships during this time of rapid growth. They triam tasol just to see what happens, and in so doing they invent the rules in each moral act. To say that someone is triam tasol suggests a morality that is implicit, or even immanent, in social action and creative of it (see also Das [2006] and Lambek [2015] who make this claim as a general theoretical argument). Alfred Gell (1999) considered moral agency to be implicit or immanent within a nexus of social relationships, and never an abstraction from them.[3] Gell's key point drew on Melanesian ethnography to show how a subject's agency is only realized by another's experience of it, which might or might not be the object of the actions of the subject, as when a gift is known as a gift only when it is received and acknowledged as such. From this point of view, refusing the gift denies the moral agency of both those who give and receive from each other by denying the relationship itself. Gell, like Das (2006) and Lambek (2015), also develops classical philosophy's argument that agency can be imagined *only* within a nexus of relations, and in dialectical relation to what those classical philosophers called a "patient." Somewhat different from Žižek's rule breaking as creative action, where moral agency must be informed by a decision to break the rules of the state for the abstract causes of wider humanity, Gell's study implies that moral agency might emerge within a nexus of social relations, wherein people try out new ideas of how to live together.

Perhaps it can be fairly said that most attempts to redefine moral agency pose larger moral questions for social science than to provide narrower definitions of the concept of agency. Among philosophers, debates arise around the measure of individual culpability for just or unjust acts, as when heroism is rewarded or vandalism is punished, or around the recognition of an individual's capacity to provide care for others (as when parents and guardians are honored or condemned). A different legacy can be found in the discipline of social psychology, where the theorist Kohlberg (1981) recognized three stages of moral development. The stages account for an individual's increasing sense of selfhood in relation to exacting justice for the family, the state, and, ultimately, the world. This theory of moral development has been reworked by Gilligan (1982), who argues that moral agency is a quality of personal relationships rather than the achievement of a sense of selfhood, and that some values such as caring rather than justice might orient participation in moral relationships. However, moral agency for philosophers and developmental psychologists alike presumes that morality is consciously enacted, and that moral action is focused toward singular outcomes. Anthropology shows that neither singular outcomes nor conscious choice can be assumed to be the conditions for any moral agent's acts.

An ethnographic focus on morality, by comparison to philosophical argument or social psychology's empirical studies of degrees and domains of social commitment, asks first how the researcher knows when, and for whom, it matters that political acts be examined as moral ones (Sykes 2009). In this case, that means asking what can be said about the primary importance of triam tasol to members of a generation who share a sense that the future could be different than the past, even if that future bears no resemblance to notably Western forms of modern life (Gewertz 1988; Gewertz and Errington 1991). Many accounts of intergenerational exchanges in Melanesia also parallel the belief, shared by English speakers, that "the child is the father of the man," something like the experiential wisdom that the passing of time is relational and perspectival, rather than unilineal and marking an absolute pathway with the unfolding of history.[4]

The notion triam tasol, so important to the independence generation, also captures how Papua New Guineans of the nationalist era think of their moral agency in bringing about political independence, rather than as an act to preserve their traditions. Reflecting on questions like these, Bernard Narokobi, who served as Minister for Justice in the independence era, wrote of how the experience of growing old peacefully cannot be transacted simply and directly across generations. His account of his consultations with elderly men from his home region reminded him that he, as the next generation, not they, as the past one, would enjoy the outcomes of his support for the new nation and the efforts in building it and so they shifted responsibility for independence onto the shoulders of those who sought it for themselves. However, his fathers' generation urged him to consider how his acts would change his life, and the lives of others, and used a vernacular analogy of generational time. Describing a lifetime as akin to the passing of the sun in the sky, they told him that they, as older men, "belonged to the evening": they had done their best and their day was done. They would not see the future now. However, they could sit on the banks of the river and think about their youthful days with pleasure. By comparison, as a member the younger generation, the young Narokobi "belonged to the morning," and this meant he would have to do what he thought was right in the day that stretched before him. He was charged with taking the only advice they had, an insight from their experience of growing old. Like them, Narokobi would have to live with the knowledge of what he had done when he was old. Their advice was not an answer, and it fell only somewhat short of an admonishment for asking the question, because independence had nothing to do with them, whose days were done.

In these stories, I explore the idea of triam tasol, and also the value of nationalist commitments to the relationships that theorists typically assume to confer cultural patrimony, as did Margaret Mead (1956) in *New Lives for Old*, when she analyzed Melanesian desires for full and radical change toward a dignified future. Narokobi finds the elders to be disinterested in national development and its incumbent notions of social modernity, but not because the older generations adhere to a Eurocentric idea that traditions are passed from one generation to the next, and bind men and women to repeat the past (in what has been called cold history, or even ahistorical politics). Instead, they rephrase changing times in the Melanesian idiom, honoring the inventiveness of that political act that resituates the passing of time in the dynamic unfolding of intergenerational relations that allows for the new generation to make their life as they wish, to "just give it a try" from their point of view.

The story is more than a personal remembrance and a morality tale told by Narokobi, a politician of the nationalist era, for politicians of the post-independence period. It shows how Narokobi's moral agency was made interactively for him by his clan elders, who attributed the capacity to act to him. They first urged him to find the process by which he could learn to live with who he is, a younger man with a future ahead of him. Then they reminded the young political candidate that he might need to invent the rules, not because the times are new, but because that is how his compatriots seek and have always sought their livelihoods. Once that was done, he would live out his old age in the company of others. Narokobi learned from his elders how nationalist categories of analysis simply privilege a nationalist and individualist point of view, rather than an intergenerational perspective from which to understand moral agency interactively. They raise key questions for a better understanding of inventing the rules, which is an interactive practice of moral agency in PNG.

MORAL AGENCY AS FULFILLING ONE'S RESPONSIBILITY TO OTHERS

In my fieldwork records there is a life history of a member of the post-independence generation that shows most clearly how this generation's experiments in moral agency are directed toward others, and away from adherence to state laws, even away from the criminal courts. The case is complex, but Sudo's story clarifies the moral agency of many members of this generation.

During my first fieldwork, I recorded how the twelve-year-old boy Sudo teased me about my fears in the field, suggesting that I feared there might be cannibals in Melanesia. He told me cannibalism stories, and taught me a song about Lasi, a loyal pet, that rescued a girl from the *tambaran* (an anthropophagic bush spirit or anthropophagic legend that is still told today in order to teach the limits of moral human behavior as taking responsibility for others' well-being). We made it part of a singing game that we played together on long walks through the bush, when it was not always possible to see each other clearly. By whistling one line at a time to each other, it was possible to stay connected as we walked. The spirited final line, *hun de, hun de, hun de* (which is translated as "come quickly"), kept the sense of the occasion as well as ended the story of the dog's rescue of the girl from the cannibals. He thought it was a great joke, and the game gave rise to hours of laughter about the absurdity of such fear. We both knew he was testing my ideas about his humanity by challenging me to see his cultural habits and beliefs as complexly related to either my fear of savages or his fear of the cannibals, named in tambaran.

Years later Sudo tested me again. Not just using the song as a trick to establish that we had a relationship in the village, this time Sudo used it to test my involvement in the drama that his life had become, which he then went on to tell me. Sudo's story described a course of events that had developed over several years. First, Sudo was jailed for an attempted rape, and released after three months when the trial determined there was not sufficient evidence to convict him. He recounted this story to me, highlighting his mistaken intentions and his attempt to escape the scene of the crime without his trousers. Without them, there was no way of hiding his identity as the perpetrator of the crime from the quickly assembling crowd, and the police arrested him to stop vigilante action that would surely have led to his death. Later, a second event marked Sudo out as a troubled figure yet again, when Sudo's younger clansman was expelled from school after trying to set the school generator ablaze. The headmaster made a few derisive comments about the younger boy's clan, which had already gained renown from Sudo's noted actions as a raskol man who had been acquitted of the crimes of rape and attempted rape. Something had to be done, and Sudo was warned by his older clansmen to protect his reputation and that of the clan, while his aunties belittled him with gossip about his deeds.

He shared these problems with me, and as we talked more, I failed to help him to forgive himself and put the two events behind him. To do that he first needed the forgiveness of his relatives, and that had not been forthcoming. Although he had opened the conversation about his problems by recalling and playing the game we once knew, he left abruptly in a downcast mood as the sun was setting on the hills. That night Sudo burned down his house and pulled up his crops in a spirit of abject despair.

Sudo's self-abasing response would normally have reconciled him with his clan; instead, his uncles, as his clansmen, battered him very badly. No relative came to his aid during the weeks of his recovery in the hospital. The member of Parliament took him to the hospital; I (the anthropologist) brought him back when he was better. All the while his kin withheld pity, as well as any indication of their readiness to allow him to return peacefully to the village to live with them. After a month, which he spent in my house, he was accepted finally in the village as the caregiver to his aging father. During that time I began to wonder what to make of the ethos of village relationships. Was his destruction of his house and crops a mature form of moral agency, or not?[5] But, I have learned that that was not the right question.

The decision to destroy one's wealth as a response to others' anger is not peculiar to Sudo or this story. The fear of jealousy that economically successful villagers feel might cause them to take a good quality truck off the road, and park it in the village as if it were broken and beyond repair. Such practices have a legacy in Melanesia more widely, where debasement of one's own wealth has been used to signal either a request for pity, or an apology for an inadvertent offence. By destroying his wealth, Sudo, like other Papua New Guineans before him established his moral agency, as he showed that he was thinking of others' well-being ahead of his own.

In this situation, Sudo's uncles went one step further than simply leaving him to the more usual cultural practice of publicly destroying his wealth. They challenged him to act, rather than remain a victim of their castigation. In this exercise of mortification, carried out by Sudo and his male clansmen, he put his livelihood into the hands of others and they made clear to him that his recovery depended on their help, should they choose to give it. The story of Sudo's fall from grace and his unhappy path to redemption in his father's house is far from unique. His experience follows a well-known narrative that ends when the hero finds his kin or old friends in a household they come to share.

MORAL AGENCY IN THE NEW EXTENDED HOUSEHOLD

Most people in this generation are making choices that prioritize their work to sustain large, extended households. Extended households are the central form of daily social association in contemporary PNG, even when their members live at great distance. The extended household is also the means by which people provide a livelihood for each other, by sharing what they have, combining their labor, and pooling their resources for larger, one-off undertakings. In this section, I recount Wilson's and Gerard's personal narratives as examples of the many members of this generation who do that.

Like others who do not appear in national records, and fail to contribute statistically to the GDP, Wilson makes a living by combining skills he acquired in school with those he found in his many different temporary and short-term jobs. Many, including Wilson, are also owners of impermanent yet surprisingly long-term businesses that open and shut, as their proprietors need. Reports on the forty thousand registered businesses in Papua New Guinea show that only four thousand submit tax returns, and of those that do, fewer than three hundred actually pay tax. The reasons for this vary, but it is thought that most business profits fall below the taxation line, and many are not stable over the year. Many businesses are "family groups" that are registered as companies for the economic advantage. Relatives share the investment in a small enterprise, such as haulage and cartage, trade stores, or in "work groups" that organize either for seasonal agricultural work or to produce a traditional art or craft for sale to tourism companies (personal communication, member of a Lae business association). Most businesses registered in Papua New Guinea are enterprises that are creatively organized, centered on family and friends who simply want to work together for a time, and are temporary.

For example, Wilson worked with his father and brothers in a family haulage and cartage business, and left that when he decided to try his luck in the world—much to their consternation. It had been an unhappy working relationship with his brothers. Despite his abilities in both truck driving and in accounts keeping, he was told to "*daunim laik bilong em yet*," or to "constrain his self-interest." Instead he should practice some humility about his good luck in finding an education, and take a secondary role in the family business as *boskru*—as a "sailor" who was part of a "boat's crew" in Tok Pisin, which in practice meant running errands for the brother who had been given the job of driving that day. After a few years in this role, he was entreated to show his bookkeeping skills to another brother, who was publicly reported as the business manager. Despite the fact that Wilson's brother never learned to keep the books, he carried the job title *bos* or "boss," and more often *kuskus* or "clerk" or "accountant."

Wilson took a job on a plantation, where he learned to manage a work crew, lining them up every morning in order to give them their day's work orders. His family enjoyed his stories of his new household, which included his *house meri* (housekeeper) and his gardener, and tales about his evenings spent learning the guitar. With that experience, he then sought a better salaried job in what he called "retail management." He became a store manager of a large shop on a mining site on Lihir Island and also owned and operated his own small delivery business from there. He provided deliveries of goods for the families of associated businesses on the island, and managed the transport for other small enterprises that had grown up around the principal operations of the mine. It was there he met his wife, and from there he made an attempt to settle a small sum of money on a house in his home village so that he could lay claim to gardens by routinely returning to work them in a traditional manner.

Wilson's experience of making a living in the last two decades is an example of the general habit by which people readily triam tasol in the course of making a living. His time in education was completed, and after ten years working on Lihir Island at the mining site he ended his employment working for the owner of a large store there. It was always his plan to go back to his home village where he could live well, and not live only off an employee's paycheck, which would entail that he must "eat money all his days." In 2005, at the age of thirty he bought and opened a trading store close to his home village. Sometimes it was closed for a month or two, while Wilson went about some work in horticulture, or prepared for a major traditional ritual, but for the most part, the large trade store is still his livelihood. This time he both managed and owned the business, which meant he lived on the business profits and not a staff salary. However, because of its yearly closings, Wilson never needed to pay tax for the registered business, and he is officially an unemployed worker, living by subsistence in the village. Nonetheless, his business has operated for over ten years as a supplier of household goods for local villagers, and has offered sales of drinks and snacks to bus passengers who stop at his store, partway on their journey between Kavieng, the provincial capital, and Namatanai, the second most important administrative center on the island.

Wilson's obligations to his household, which included his clansmen as well as his wife and children, have been a priority in all of his business decisions, even while he seeks to limit his obligations to some of his cousins and even some siblings who fail to recognize their obligations to him. Because he married a woman who is not from his home village, Wilson has found that the responsibilities that he keeps to her natal family have been subject to ongoing negotiation. One of his wife's brothers is a matter of special concern, and while Wilson has given bridewealth to him and her other brothers, many discussions continue about the duration of that debt. In this, Wilson is not alone, as many Papua New Guineans who live in cities that are distant from their home villages also report their desire to restrict the number of affinal obligations that they meet (Sykes 2013). Keir Martin (2007) has shown that some Papua New Guineans who have retired to their home villages now also seek to limit their debts to relatives there with stricter household rules on how to ask and receive gifts from relatives. My own research shows that the post-independence generation leads in forming such households as an emergent social form, within which the members meet various forms of obligations and responsibilities to each other, and thereby come to define the terms of a good life.

Another life history shows how men and women in good jobs or with successful businesses create an extended household of new relationships, over the observance of traditional relations. I consolidated my understanding of this feature of the lives of the post-independence generation when a member of the cohort of people who graduated from secondary school in 1991 contacted me by email. No longer a schoolboy, he was by then working as an accountant for an international coffee company operating in Lae. Gerard wanted to show me his success, but first made an overture to me that highlighted our common concern for his clansmen. I had known his sisters, as well as his parents. He reported on their current situation, reminding me that I too had called his grandmother *pupu* ("our grandmother"), and he effectively called on me to stay part of their household. In so doing, Gerard showed me that the extended household could stretch across time and space, perhaps in ways that the nuclear household could not.

Gerard's email addressed me as his sister, and told of the death of "our" grandmother. Gerard's use of kin terms to address me is indicative of a widely known habit in Papua New Guinea of calling out to someone as a relative or as a friend as a way of creating a closer relationship with another person and reminding each other what they share. For example, in our email exchange, Gerard addressed me as a respected sister, and then reminded me that we have common interest in the well-being of many of the same people. He wanted to know if I would help him with a small loan to care for his sister's needs for her new baby's first year. Gerard, like others living in town for work or advanced education, calls on relatives and close friends from the same village for support. Like other urban residents, he calls on those who are ambiguously related as if they were his relatives, and thereby calls on them to find common ground with him. In general, as a spoken term of address, the use of kin names such as "aunty" or "grandmother" can be understood as ways of recognizing kinship between people, and also as the very making of kin, as when a person effectively becomes a brother of the family after years of being addressed as our brother. This latter practice is common in contemporary Papua New Guinea, and Gerard was using it with me to assert the continuing importance of our relationship to each other and my place in his extended household. My experience underlined that triam tasol features in kin and household relations, as much as in new friendships forged through education and work.

Wilson and Gerard came from similar kinds of extended households, a kind that became increasingly familiar among the rest of this generation as they confronted the moral choices ahead of them. Wilson and Gerard had each met his future wife while employed at work undertaken after graduation from secondary education. As Papua New Guineans whose closest relatives were spread across several provinces, they expressed their anxiety about keeping up the many commitments created by marriages that were not made according to the traditions of their home village. It is common in this generation to marry and constitute new households that effectively cross provinces, language groups, and cultural groups, and also remain geographically dispersed. By contrast, their parents' generation married within the language group into which they were born, and largely remained in their home region.

Both Wilson and Gerard usually resolved their problems by coming up with new living arrangements, yet they often called on their relatives in more traditional ways. Although Gerard had continued to post-secondary education and gained several accounting certificates before entering his employer's staff training program, the dilemmas that he faced every day in his household were not so different from those that Wilson confronted as a graduate of secondary school in his various work and employment sites. Both Wilson and Gerard were responsible for selecting which relationships they would keep up from the many they each had, with many relatives through marriage (their affinal relations), and with clansmen (their consanguine relations). As was also the case for Wilson, the frequency of contact demanded as much of Gerard personally as the actual financial commitments demanded from his paycheck. Recurrent visits from members of the extended household, most often from kin who were less well-off and in need of financial and emotional support, are a constant source of stress for members of the post-independence generation. They say they are challenged to sustain so many relationships at one time. They are less concerned with how much of the household budget goes to relatives, and more worried about how long the relatives will stay. The principal tension experienced by both men lies in their struggle to reconcile their commitments to kin from their home village and their wife's village, managing the demands these commitments make on the everyday budget of their household and the social life of its members.

The post-independence generation of Papua New Guineans describe themselves as moral agents when their actions are directed toward facilitating the achievement of a better future for other people. They do this by prioritizing care for known others, rather than working toward economic and political justice in the abstract, or toward specific political ideals and values that are perceived to serve the nation directly. While international agencies judge them a failure for not contributing to a greater national good, theirs is a moral economy, focused on the present well-being of the members of the extended household, a group that is described in a traditional idiom, but made up of people who would not traditionally be considered "kin" or "clansmen."

Inventing the Rules

In elaborating the point of view of the first generation born after independence in PNG, I have focused on those deliberations about social relations that external agencies and international organization find hard to recognize. This generation is economically and statistically invisible in international measures of political agency simply because the analysis of their contributions to national development does not measure their work and relationships as economically productive. This generation neither created their own account of an ideal form of social life, nor the value of the kin relationships by which they live. Instead, they are labeled raskols by others. For them, social relationships are experiments in living with others in creatively formed extended households that might produce nothing except the immediate care that they provide to each other. Their morality is implied; it exists intersubjectively in social actions directed at testing the other for a response, an exercise in giving it a try *together*, as when "*mipela* triam tasol."

Perhaps it helps to recall that other critiques of productivity in Melanesian societies have raised questions about agency and political economy, as I have here. Gell (2000) revisited an earlier inquiry by Malinowski (1935) into the nature of yam gardens, their magic, and the collective work they involved, and in doing so illuminated the aesthetics and ethics of human creativity in economic production. A yam garden for Gell, and for Malinowski before him, is a work of art, one in which the nature of moral agency is as clear as the nature of creative agency. Gell reminds readers that Malinowski presents the case for Trobriand gardening as a function of wide networks of people involved in exchange relations, rather than as a simple set of individuals engaged in horticulture or subsistence farming. The technologies of enchantment that matter are not magical spells used to bring wealth to humans in return for their work. They are those that have the pragmatic effect of making the yam garden visible to all, so that they might share their lives. Gell reminds us that for Malinowski, yam gardens are grown neither magically nor by Trobriand agricultural science: they are experiments in making a livelihood with others and caring for them.

As part of the post-independence generation, the Papua New Guineans I have described are not alone in redefining moral agency. In addition to anthropologists who have theorized moral agency as an intersubjective relationship, as did Gell (1999), twenty-first-century continental social theorists also challenge the assumption that political maturity captures the definition of moral agency. In asking about the nature of moral agency and political maturity in post-industrial developed nations, Žižek (2010) joins a long line of continental political philosophers who have argued against the assumption that morality, moral relationships, shared values, and the good life all can be the outcome of productive activity.[6] The problem is that production is a highly elaborated form of social activity (Baudrilliard 1981), which is obscured by an ideology of the heroic individual as moral agent. Some scholars argue that the emphasis on the rational economic actor debases knowledge of social life (see, e.g., Debord 1995). This feature of moral agency pre-determines what can be desired and hoped for in the contemporary political economy of the post-industrialist state (Lyotard 1984). Much of the work of these continental political philosophers is concerned with a critique of human agency as a key concept of political economy more broadly. However, in an intellectual departure from this vast literature on political agency, Žižek (2010) outlines the parameters of moral agency in a lawless, perhaps stateless, economy wherein a restless collective consciousness of social difference shares no one sense of the good.[7] While he advances a theoretical debate that posits that a stateless economy is the desired moral outcome for late capitalist developed nations, this chapter proposes that moral agency of people living in the late capitalist postcolonial nation is deeply intersubjective and aims to invent the rules.

Without a corrective lens to see the post-independence generation in their own terms, some scholars fall into the same trap as those who explained the economic irrationality of cargo cultists as breaking the rules of colonial control, when they were better understood as long-term projects in social transformation (Worsley 1957). Refinements of those analyses showed that examples of how Pacific Island people invent the rules together are timeless. Marshall Sahlins (1964) acknowledged the long history of social innovations by Oceanic societies as an inspiration to rethink comparative political histories of the Pacific. A decade later, Roy Wagner (1974, 1981) focused on Melanesian creativity and warned against studying ossified culture by searching for culture as a thing. Later, Andrew Lattas (1998) and Holger Jebens (2004) warned anthropologists of the risks entailed in making the same errors as their predecessors who mistook cargo cults as failures of immediate economic aims.[8] They thereby replicate the very knowledge practices that James Scott (2004) once defined as "seeing like a state." In this chapter, I have shown that when an entire generation does not produce livelihoods in terms that the state can see, the nationalists' terms of evaluation fail, and therefore the nationalists cannot even see the very generation they sought to produce. Scholars who seek to understand adulthood as a mature life-stage by mistaking it for an effective form of political activity blinker themselves to recognizing the interactive forms of moral agency in late capitalism. However, their scholarship improves with corrective lenses, ground to accommodate the point of view of the independence generation.

Most people in PNG speak of their moral decisions, and elicit distinctive models for living together in the present, as members of emerging extended households. In them, they meet their obligations to each other with care and think of their generation as intersubjectively related to the generations that begat them. Although external evaluations find failure with adulthood as a stage of life on the stage of national political life, the elusiveness of their individual moral agency is not a current concern to the post-independence generation in PNG because they know and experience it interactively. Neither has this been a matter of angst in the past. In this chapter, I account for the moral agency of the post-independence generation in its own terms. My ethnography of moral agency as inventing the rules aims to bring into view a cohort that has been largely invisible to nationalists' accounts of them as failures, but can be known otherwise, even in the terms of the households they are making as the first post-independence generation.

Karen Sykes is Professor of Anthropology at the University of Manchester. Since 2011, she has been researching the livelihoods of Papua New Guineans living in Australia.

NOTES

1. Contemporary Tok Pisin spelling is no longer standardized as it was in the colonial era.

2. The 1990 census records 50 percent of the population of five million people as born after 1975, and then under the age of sixteen. With a population of seven million in 2010, the proportion born after independence has grown to 68 percent, and four million and five hundred thousand people are as of 2010 under the age of forty.

3. As regards moral agency (which admittedly Gell's [1999] study of creativity in art does not explicitly address), we can say that for Gell the agent knows how to act because he or she imagines what it means to be a patient of the earlier actions of other agents.

4. My heart leaps up when I behold
    A rainbow in the sky:
    So was it when my life began;
    So is it now I am a man;
    So be it when I shall grow old,
    Or let me die!
    The Child is father of the Man;
    And I could wish my days to be
    Bound each to each by natural piety. (William Wordsworth, "The Rainbow," 1807)

5. Žižek's writings do not extend to the ambiguities raised in such concrete situations.

6. Recent scholarly attention has turned to discuss the dispersal of agency through social relations, rather than to presume the outcomes of the intentional agent's actions are meaningful products of his or her consciousness (see Candea 2010, and for comparison, see also Thrift 2010).

7. Notable earlier anthropological research into noncapitalist societies had similar goals (see especially Godelier, 1996; see also Evans-Pritchard 1937 [1974], 1940; Malinowski 1922).

8. There is a scene in the award-winning ethnographic documentary, *Koriam's Law and the Dead Who Govern* (dir. Kildea and Simon 2005) that exposes the hopes shared by Papua New Guineans to create different relations with others, as they invent the rules for a cargo cult that will change their lives, or at least give it a try. Residents of rural West New Britain hope that the custodianship of money will bring them equality with white men, and a roadway to the kind of wealth and lifestyles that only international company executives hold. Late in the film, an elderly woman asks the ethnographer, Lattas, "when will the wealth come, what is the secret?"—although she knows well enough that she has participated in a village-wide experiment by inventing the laws for bringing white man's wealth to West New Britain and he has not. Lattas, who has contributed significant works in the study of cargo cults in Melanesia, walks away without a word, and we do not know if his character feels shame because he knows and cannot say that they never will hold the secret of white man's wealth.

REFERENCES

AusAID. 2005. *Country Report, Papua New Guinea*. Canberra: Government Printers.

Baudrilliard, Jean. 1981. *For a Critique of the Political Economy of the Sign*. London: Telos.

Bear, Laura, Karen Ho, Anna Tsing, and Sylvia Yanagisako. 2015. "Gens: A Feminist Manifesto for the Study of Capitalism." *Fieldsights—Theorizing the Contemporary, Cultural Anthropology Online*, March 30. http://www.culanth.org/fieldsights/652 -gens-a-feminist-manifesto-for-the-study-of-capitalism.

Candea, Matei. 2010. *The Social after Gabriel Tarde: Debates and Assessments*. London: Routledge.

Das, Veena. 2006. *Life and Words: Violence and the Descent into the Ordinary*. Chicago: Chicago University Press.

Debord, Guy. 1995. *The Society of the Spectacle*. New York: Zone Books.

Deleuze, Gilles. 1977. *Anti-Oedipus: Capitalism and Schizophrenia*. London: Viking Penguin.

Evans-Pritchard, E. E. [1937] 1974. *Witchcraft, Magic and Oracles amongst the Azande*. Oxford: Oxford University Press.

———. 1940. *The Nuer*. Oxford: Clarendon Press.

Foster, Robert. 1995. *History and Social Reproduction in a Melanesian Society*. Cambridge: Cambridge University Press.

———. 2005. *Making Nations*. Ann Arbor: University of Michigan Press.

Gell, Alfred. 1999. *Art and Agency*. Cambridge: Cambridge University Press.

———. 2000. *The Art of Anthropology*. London: Berg.

Gellner, David. 2015. "Schools as Organizations: On the Question of Value Consensus." *Anthropology of This Century* 12. http://aotcpress.com/articles/schools -organizations-question-consensus/.

Gershon, Ilana. 2011. "Neoliberal Agency." *Current Anthropology* 52(4): 537–55.

Gewertz, Deborah. 1988. *Cultural Alternatives and a Feminist Anthropology: An Analysis of Culturally Constructed Gender Interests in Papua New Guinea*. Cambridge: Cambridge University Press.

Gewertz, Deborah, and Fred Errington. 1991. *Twisted Histories, Altered Contexts: Representing the Chambri in the World System*. Cambridge: Cambridge University Press.

Gilligan, Carol. 1982. *In a Different Voice*. Cambridge: Harvard University Press

Goddard, Michael. 2005. *Unseen City: Anthropological Perspectives on Port Moresby*. Honolulu: University of Hawai'i Press.

Godelier, Maurice. 1996. *The Mental and the Material: Thought, Economy, and Society*. London: Verso.

Gregory, Chris. 1997. *Savage Money: The Politics of Commodity Exchange*. Amsterdam: Harwood.

———. 2009. "What Ever Happened to Householding?" In *Market and Society: The Great Transformation Today*, edited by Keith Hart and Chris Hann, 133–159. Cambridge: Cambridge University Press

Gudeman, Stephen. 2005. *Economy's Tension*. Oxford: Berghahn Books.

Gudeman, Stephen, and Chris Hann, eds. 2015. *Oikos and the Market: Explorations in Self-Sufficiency after Socialism*. Oxford: Berghahn Books.

Jebens, Holger, ed. 2004. *Cargo, Cult, and Culture Critique*. Honolulu: University of Hawai'i Press.

Kildea, Gary, and Andrea Simon. 2005. *Koriam's Law and the Dead Who Govern*. DVD. London: Royal Anthropological Institute.

Kohlberg, Lawrence. 1981. *Essays on Moral Development*. Vol. 1: *The Philosophy of Moral Development*. San Francisco: Harper & Row.

Lambek, Michael. 2015. "On the Immanence of the Ethical." *Anthropological Theory* 15(2): 128–32.

Lattas, Andrew. 1998. *Cultures of Secrecy: Reinventing Race in Bush Kaliai Cargo Cults*. Madison: University of Wisconsin Press.

Lipset, David. 1988. "Papua New Guinea: The Melanesian Ethic and the Spirit of Capitalism, 1975–1986." In *Democracy in Developing Countries: Asia*, edited by Larry Diamond, Juan Linz, and Seymour Lipset, 409–19. Boulder: Lynne Rienner.

Lutkehaus, Nancy. 1995. *Gender Rituals.* Berkeley: University of California Press.

Lyotard, Francois. 1984. *The Postmodern Condition: A Report on Knowledge.* Minneapolis: University of Minnesota Press.

MacIntyre, Martha, and Mary Patterson. 2011. *Managing Modernity in the Western Pacific.* Brisbane: University of Queensland Press.

Macpherson, C. B. 1962. *The Political Theory of Possessive Individualism: From Hobbes to Locke.* Oxford: Oxford University Press.

Malinowski, Bronislaw. 1922. *Argonauts of the Western Pacific.* London: Routledge.

———. 1935. *Coral Gardens and Their Magic: A Study of the Methods of Tilling the Soil and of Agricultural Rites in the Trobriand Islands.* London: Routledge.

Martin, Keir. 2007. "Your Own *Buai* You Must Buy: The Ideology of Possessive Individualism in Papua New Guinea." *Anthropological Forum* 17(3): 285–98.

Mead, Margaret. 1956. *New Lives for Old: Cultural Transformation–Manus.* New York: William Morrow.

Munn, Nancy. 1996. *The Fame of Gawa.* Durham: Duke University Press.

Narakobi, Bernard. 1983. *Life and Leadership.* Suva: University of the South Pacific.

Netting, Robert, R. Wilk, and E. J. Arnould. 1984. *Households: Comparative and Historical Studies of the Domestic Group.* Berkeley: University of California Press.

Robbins, Joel. 1998. "On Reading 'World News': Apocalyptic Narrative, Negative Nationalism and Transnational Christianity in a Papua New Guinea Society." *Social Analysis: The International Journal of Social and Cultural Practice* 42(2): 103–30.

Sahlins, Marshall. 1964. "Poor Man, Rich Man, Big Man, Chief: Political Types in Melanesia." *Comparative Studies in Society and History* 5(3): 285–303.

Scott, James. 2004. *Seeing Like a State.* New Haven: Yale University Press.

Strathern, Marilyn. 1988. *The Gender of the Gift.* Berkeley: University of California Press.

Sykes, Karen. 1999. "After the Raskol Feast: Youths' Alienation in Papua New Guinea." *Critique of Anthropology* 19(2): 57–74.

———. 2000. "Raskolling: Papua New Guinean Sociality as Contested Political Order." In Cyndi Banks, *Cultural Criminology in Papua New Guinea.* Sydney: Sydney Institute of Criminology.

———. 2001. "Paying a School Fee Is a Father's Duty: Reciprocity, Bribes and Citizenship in Papua New Guinea." *American Ethnologist* 21(1): 5–31.

———. 2007. "Interrogating Individuals: The Critique of Possessive Individualism in the Western Pacific." *Anthropological Forum* 17(3): 213–308.

———. 2009. *Ethnographies of Moral Reasoning: Living Paradoxes of a Global Age.* New York: Palgrave Macmillan.

———. 2013. "Mortgaging the Marriage: Problems with Value and Problems with Brothers." *HAU: Journal of Ethnographic Theory* 3(2): 97–117.

———. 2014. "Adopting an Obligation: Innovative Forms of Democracy in Papua New Guinea." *Classical Sociology* (14): 110–21.

Thompson, Edward P. 1963. *The Making of the English Working Class.* London: Vintage Books.

———. 1978. *The Poverty of Theory and Other Essays*. London: Merlin Press.
Thrift, Nigel. 2010. "Pass It On: Towards a Political Economy of Propensity." *Emotion, Space and Society* 1: 83–96.
UNESCO. 2008. *Country Report: Papua New Guinea*. http://en.unesco.org/countries/papua-new-guinea.
Wagner, Roy. 1974. "Are There Groups in the New Guinea Highlands?" In *Frontiers of Anthropology*, edited by M. Leaf, 95–121. New York: D. Van Norstrand.
———. 1981. *The Invention of Culture*. Chicago: University of Chicago Press.
Weeks, Sheldon. 1974. *Education for Independence*. Port Moresby: Institute of Papua New Guinea Studies.
Wiener, Annette. 1980. "Reproduction, a Replacement for Reciprocity." *American Ethnologist* 7(1): 71–85.
Worsley, Peter. 1957. *The Trumpet Shall Sound: A Study of Cargo Cults in Melanesia*. London: Magibbon and Kee.
Yanagisako, Sylvia. 1979. "Family and Household: The Analysis of Domestic Groups." *Annual Review of Anthropology* 8: 161–205.
Žižek, Slavoj. 2010. *Living in the End Times*. London: Verso Books.

CHAPTER SIX

"JUST SITTING," BUT NOT SITTING STILL

Delayed Adulthood and Changing Gender Dynamics in Northern Sudan

Janice Boddy

THIS CHAPTER EXPLORES how economic growth and new information technologies are stimulating changes in sociality, kindling aspirations, and reshaping normality in peri-urban Khartoum, Sudan.[1] It is based on ethnographic research conducted over six winters between 2008 and 2016 with a group of related families who originate from or currently live in Hofriyat, the pseudonymous village on the Nile where I began ethnographic research in 1976.[2] The economic status of Hofriyati ranges from working to middle class; while not the poorest of the Sudanese poor, most lead lives of considerable precarity.[3] In what follows I describe how some Hofriyati born between the 1970s and 1990s also find themselves in collective limbo, chronologically adult but still regarded as youth because they are not yet able or willing to wed. In contrast to some societies in sub-Saharan Africa (e.g., Rice 2015) where having children regardless of one's marital circumstance offers a route to adult or quasi-adult status, in strongly patrilineal Muslim Arabic-speaking Sudan where the only legitimate way to reproduce is in the context of contractual (that is, Islamic) marriage, mature never-married persons are regarded as less than fully adult. Adulthood means having, or being positioned to have, children who carry one's own (if male) or one's husband's name and, to complete the process, to have established an independent household. But while many are caught in between, in what Singerman (2007) has called "waithood" (see also Malmström 2015; Schielke 2015), others are finding ways to sidestep convention and in the process are challenging, perhaps transforming, what being a social adult entails. In tandem, personhood, once thoroughly relational, is becoming ever so gradually individuated. Here new information technologies, in particular cell phones, are deeply implicated in social change.

Mise en Scène

In December 2008 I returned to Sudan after an absence of fifteen years and found the place transformed.[4] The makeover has continued since. In Khartoum dun colonial facades crumble next to glass-fronted shops, car dealerships, and brave cigar-shaped office towers and hotels. The city extends for miles in all directions connected by four new bridges over the Nile built in part with Chinese aid. Road maps are always out of date: the topography shifts quick as a desert dune.[5] Despite continuing US sanctions, oil wealth plus Gulf and Chinese investment have revolutionized the country. There are millions of cell phones in use, three satellite TV companies with hundreds of foreign stations and at least a dozen local ones, and an appalling crush of cars.

Sudan's economy began to pick up with the development of oil and gas reserves in 1997 and ensuing exports of crude in 1999. By 2003 neoliberalization was in full sway: negotiations with the International Monetary Fund had produced a reformed banking system, restructured taxes and tariffs, and privatized social services, including health care. Then, in 2005, the Comprehensive Peace Agreement officially ended twenty-two years of civil war between the Islamist government and southern Sudan, allowing international access to the country's oilfields at least until South Sudan's independence in July 2011. Between those years the economy soared; in 2006, 2007, and the first part of 2008, Sudan's GDP grew at over 8 percent per year.[6] With the global monetary crisis of 2008, expansion waned yet did not immediately stall.[7] But in 2012, secession and the attendant loss of petro-revenue spun the north's economy into decline. A modest recovery began the following year but the petroleum rush did not resume.

Despite the slump, inflation surged.[8] Informants say that the costs of necessary foodstuffs such as flour, sugar, and cooking oil rose faster than those of other items, by 40 or 50 percent per year. Price controls are illusory or nonexistent and wages have not risen to keep pace for the working poor. By the United Nations Population Fund (UNFPA) estimates around one-third of the labor force is jobless and over half of those are youth between the ages of fifteen and twenty-four; those who work are often underemployed.[9] Poverty and prosperity are close companions, especially in greater Khartoum. Sudan's economic revolution is a mixed blessing indeed.

During the boom a new mega-dam was built at Merowe on the main Nile to provide electricity to regions north of Khartoum while flooding a further swath of historically significant land. As the government released its hold on the market private capital, imported foods, electronic equipment, and all manner of Chinese goods rushed in. Automobiles—once closely regulated— became widely available for purchase by bank loan at favorable rates. With improved access to credit, commercial enterprises sprang up all over—poultry farms, dairies, market gardens. Paint stores and home renovation shops opened on every suburban block. Cell phones became ubiquitous, and each remotely middle-class house acquired a satellite dish; the world once kept at bay by courtyard walls was now bidden to enter domestic space. On November 23, 2008, the sleepy village of Hofriyat was electrified and villagers were prepared. The next day they tuned in to Al Jazeera and CNN.

QARABA AND MARRIAGE: CHANGING
DIMENSIONS OF RELATEDNESS

While relative peace, growing prosperity, and the relaxation of government controls led to greater possibilities for some and hopes of positive change for most, they also brought uncertainty, owing in part to shifting consumption patterns and new ideas about what constitutes "normality." Such shifts are noticeable in contestations over the shape of domestic life, and exploring these in turn requires an elucidation of *qaraba* (closeness). Qaraba refers to proximal family ties traced through any combination of male and female links with a preference—in practice slight, in theory strong—for patrilineal kin. Closeness implies embodied moral obligation and mutual responsibility, a sense of shared identity or personhood. It is, however, a relative concept and graduated: because siblings share paternal and/or maternal bodily substance they are deemed too close to wed, but their children are ideal mates.[10] In the past, close (*qarīb*, ideally first cousin) marriage was prevalent and families focused on strengthening bonds over the generations, with each new marriage arranged to build on previous ones, though the definition of qaraba could certainly expand when it suited people's needs (Boddy 1989).[11]

While anthropologists have generally focused on the historical or retrospective dimensions of patrilineality, among Hofriyati (and perhaps others who practice endogamy), kin calculation is also oriented *prospectively*: parents contract their children's (close) marriages with an eye to future close marriages that might result among those children's offspring. The dynamic is one of enclosure. At the same time, marriageability as an embodied relational trait is manipulable: unrelated women seeking to strengthen ties between their families may nurse one another's infants. Despite the absence of past genealogical connection, children who ingest one woman's maternal bodily substance become *awlad laban* (milk kin) and are thereby deemed siblings, hence unmarriageable. Thus, nursing creates marriageable closeness between the biological mother's and the nursing woman's future descendants (including milk children's maternal siblings). Unmarriageability in one generation produces preferred marriageability in the next.

Closeness inheres in bodily substance and is material in other senses too. In the village, it signifies spatial as well as genealogical contiguity: kin are neighbors. Equally, however, neighbors may become kin. Especially in the city, spatial or social proximity can serve as the prior connection that enables non-kin to become maritally, hence genealogically, entwined.[12] As such, the children of long-standing urban neighbors or coworkers may be deemed potential mates. Yet in 2015, female university students were proudly matchmaking their brothers and male cousins with classmates, thereby stretching the limits of both proximity and parental control. This brings us to the issue of age.

Arranged marriages may involve the very young, something the law in Sudan permits. According to the Muslim Personal Law Act declared by the Islamist government in 1991, Muslim children (girls or boys) can be legally married at the age of ten.[13] As long as I have known them, however, Hofriyati have considered it shameful to let a daughter marry before she has completed high school, generally at age eighteen. Men typically marry much later, given the lengthy wedding preparations they are tasked to perform, discussed within. Yet for pre-millennial Hofriyati of either sex the average age at marriage has risen sharply, and some may never wed. Subsequent sections explore the social dynamics that contextualize this claim.

It would, however, be disingenuous to ignore an emerging trend that may challenge those observations. Several young women I know have recently become cowives, fresh out of high school, to men far older than they. From concern for their welfare in an ever more perilous world, they and their parents agreed to proposals from well-established men—work colleagues of the women's fathers or brothers—even though a polygynous first marriage is hardly ideal. According to Sudanese colleagues and informants, polygyny is on the rise, evidence of growing disparities of wealth within the middle class.

Moreover, some parents now seek early marriages for their daughters lest they end up like older sisters and aunts and remain unwed. The incidence of child marriage—of girls under the age of eighteen—is said to be escalating in Sudan, particularly among the poorest and most vulnerable groups.[14] Local non-governmental organizations (NGOs) such as SEEMA (Centre for Training and Protection of Women and Child's Rights), and international NGOs such as the UNFPA have recently launched campaigns to halt the practice as a violation of the girls' human rights and rights to health (e.g., given the prevalence of obstetric fistula caused by pelvic disproportion in girls who give birth before they are fully grown).[15] While I have seen no examples of early marriage among contemporary Hofriyati, it could well be that daughters in the future do not find adulthood elusive but thrust upon them all too soon. So while this chapter focuses on Hofriyati in seemingly perpetual "waithood" it may be wise to consider the potential evanescence of that status as a structural form.

Another point: in urban Sudan those who are delayed are not only youth unable or unwilling to establish adult lives, but also the parents who support them. Much as Solway (this volume) describes for Botswana, parents seek to advance their status too, by becoming grandparents and venerable elders able to relinquish the torch of social and financial responsibility before they become infirm. One of my urban friends remarked that for over a decade she and her husband had put off building a modest retirement house in the village because they have daughters in their thirties who are not yet wed. Focusing on youth as stymied adults risks disembedding them from their familial context, endowing them with unnuanced individualism and over-estimated agency, however much we acknowledge their enveloping local constraints. Lots of folks are waiting, it seems.

With these caveats in mind, I explore some novel gender and generational tensions that have surfaced in the wake of Sudan's economic transformation to inhibit the transition of youth to full adulthood. Information technology is subtly implicated in them all.

MOBILE PHONES

Sudan has leapt from the mid-twentieth century into the twenty-first where communications technology is concerned.[16] Robust evidence comes from figures on telephone use: between 2006 and 2009 the number of landlines increased from 1.5 to 3.6 million, while the number of cellular lines rose from five to over fifteen million, growing at a rate of 500 percent per year (Zain Group 2010: 4). After the separation of South Sudan and the loss of one-third of Sudan's population, that rate did not dip in the Muslim north; in 2012 over twenty-seven million cell lines were in use among some thirty to thirty-five million people, indicating a rough saturation rate of 78 percent, remarkable for one of the poorest countries in the world.[17] Since 2004 when cell phones became widely available in Sudan, three, sometimes four, wireless companies have been in fierce competition, offering extremely low rates and family plans that include text and photo messaging; range is exceptionally good and blind spots are rare. Herd boys, camel drivers in the desert, and street-corner tea ladies all can be seen using mobile phones. Until recently, when handsets that can hold up to three SIM cards came on the market, successful businessmen would have late model phones from each company on the go; carrying a particularly expensive handset—or two or three—had become a public assertion of prestige. Having different cellular lines allows a user to distinguish among contacts and group them for different purposes; incidentally or intentionally this increases personal privacy and the potential for secrecy in one's interpersonal affairs (see also Brinkman et al. 2009: 87).[18]

For political and economic reasons kin are widely dispersed these days and every Hofriyati family has members living abroad, in Doha, Dubai, Saudi Arabia, Libya, Egypt, the UK, Canada, or the United States. Cheap phone cards and low long distance rates enable scattered kin and friends to remain even more intimately connected than when they lived in adjacent neighborhoods. Hofriyat and its sister villages have several branch settlements in Greater Khartoum; people "from the village" meet regularly in the city and rural areas at engagements, weddings, funerals and other events, and maintain a vast network of immediate yet physically distant relations every day. When someone has an accident or falls sick, family members find out within seconds and begin to converge en masse at the person's home or hospital bed. It is far easier for rural and urban Hofriyati to visit, thanks to a paved road that, given a surfeit of automobiles and the launch of regular bus service, has reduced the trip between village and metropole to around four hours one way (from eight to ten hours as recently as 1994). In the village and in the city, everyone always has family and neighbors as guests.

Ingenious new forms of entrepreneurial activity have arisen, such as the brisk trade in cell phone minutes made possible because credits can be readily transferred from line to line: one can buy a phone card for, say, one hundred Sudanese pounds, load it into a mobile phone, then sell the time in small quantities to others at a small profit (*ribḥa*)—somewhere between 4 and 10 percent. Moreover, an urban woman may buy inexpensive clothing, sandals, cosmetics, and costume jewelry from city suqs, send the items to the village with returning kin, and ask a relative there to resell the items in the countryside where they are less readily available or more expensive to buy from local shops. When the agent has managed to sell the lot, she uses the cash to buy a scratch card, loads the minutes into her phone and sends them to the original purchaser, minus a fee (in cell-time) for her services. The recipient reaps the proceeds when she resells the transferred credit for cash. Indeed, cell-time has become a surrogate currency in Sudan, allowing people to bypass the bank: remittances to kin and support for university students living away from home can be sent as cell phone credits convertible to cash. Here time is literally money, as is the sociality that this "time" represents.

Education

For decades Hofriyati and other Arab Sudanese have placed a high value on educating girls. This concern declined during the first years of Islamist rule, but revived after 2005 when the state relaxed enforcement of women's deportment rules. There are more universities and colleges in Sudan than ever before—over sixty in 2015, I was told—and women are attending in droves. I do not suggest that the institutions are all first-rate or significant barriers to female education have disappeared; women's reproductive roles are still valued over their productive ones, and in poorer families a daughter's education may be sacrificed for a son's if resources are tight. Since the late 1980s, the costs of pursuing the civil war, and the economic sanctions and structural adjustment programs that ensued, have led to reductions in government funding for education (despite a growing number of universities) and an attendant decline in quality. The fees for books, uniforms, school breakfasts, and the like that must be privately borne are prohibitive to many (Bedri 2009). Moreover, given the very high dependency ratio in Sudan—four persons of dependent age (under fifteen or over sixty-five years of age) per Sudanese of working age (between the ages of fifteen and sixty-four years), and an employment rate of only 68 percent among the latter—a daughter's post-secondary education may be impossible to afford, and even a polygynous first marriage may seem the better option.[19]

That said, the economic boom produced an emergent bimodal attendance rate at universities and colleges, echoed in other parts of the world. According to the United Nations (CRIN 2011) and Sudan government (2010) figures, female enrollment in post-secondary education now greatly exceeds that of males.[20] With increased access to university places and a growing economy, it is the rare Hofriyati family that does not have a daughter engaged in post-secondary studies or recently graduated, even among those of the working class.[21] And the cell phone is a contributing factor: with it, relatives feel they can monitor a young woman and ensure she is safe even while attending a public coed school such as the University of Khartoum. Moreover, so few men now enroll in university that coeducation has become a moot point. If the graduation ceremony I attended in January 2010 is any indication, only 10 to 20 percent of today's university students are male. Students at the University of Khartoum confirmed that guess in 2015. Indeed, female domination of post-secondary education is a familiar topic among Hofriyati. By educating themselves girls are making it harder to find husbands, they say.[22]

I was told that fewer young men continue to "read" because they need to make money to contribute to household expenses (most live with parents or extended kin), help fund their sisters' educations, and accumulate savings toward their own future marriages. Several of those I spoke to hope to start some enterprise—collectively buy a car for use as an unofficial taxi, or form a musical ensemble to entertain at weddings (wedding businesses are numerous and lucrative in Sudan). Some young men work at several jobs in order to make ends meet. Thus more twenty- and thirty-something Hofriyati daughters than sons have college educations, but few of either are permanently employed.[23] Many remain with their natal families well into their twenties and thirties, studying, working, "just sitting" (*qaʿidīn bus*), or participating in the gray economy through which goods and services are distributed via the domestic market. Unmarried women typically live with their parents or, if the latter are deceased, with other responsible kin; not to do so would court disgrace. Sons, married or not, typically live with their parents as well. Newlyweds usually reside with the bride's mother for the first year, and often until after several children have been born, then move into their own or the husband's family home. Uxorilocal residence may be prolonged if the husband is a labor migrant and only able to visit from time to time. In such cases marriage and childbirth do not definitively end a couple's waithood, merely bring its horizon in sight.

Weddings and Marriage

Men must typically work many years before they can afford to marry, at least in a conventional, proper, legally binding way by Islamic contract, the form known as *zawāj nikāḥ*. The expense of a modern wedding is high: unless a prospective couple are very close kin, the groom's parents are wealthy, or the bride-to-be is particularly religious and agrees to modest proceedings, it can cost tens of thousands of pounds. I attended six weddings and three engagement parties during nine weeks of research between 2009 and 2010; weddings are not rare. However, in each case the groom was between thirty-three and fifty years of age, and the bride fifteen to thirty-two years younger. When I first began doing fieldwork the age differential was not as great, ten or twelve years at most. Singerman (2007) notes that in Egypt, where comparable conditions prevail, a man's wedding may cost the equivalent of his entire earnings and those of his father for a period of five to seven years (see also Malmström 2015). Yet in Cairo the bride's family can be expected to pay about one-third of the wedding costs (Singerman 2007), far more than is the norm among Hofriyati in Khartoum. Moreover, not only has the time it takes to accumulate the requisite funds increased, so too have notions of what a proper wedding should entail.

In the 1970s and 1980s the groom's opening gift to the bride consisted of a *towb* (three meters of fine cloth used as a modesty wrap), a gold ring, and a new pair of sandals. This would later be followed by a nominal cash payment—the *mahr* (surety) for the bride in case of divorce—and a *shaylah* (trousseau) containing several matched sets of underwear, dresses, shoes, handbags, and towbs, plus a watch, gold jewelry, perfumes, sweets, and food enough for the wedding feast. It was expensive to amass, and often meant having to go abroad to work for several years (Boddy 1989). But given the growing availability of consumer goods and the escalating expectations of how a proper wedding should be staged, the time spent working away has only increased.

Now when a man has been accepted by a woman and her family, he heads to a wedding shop to buy a specially designed metal tray containing crisp new paper money in ten, twenty and fifty pound denominations. The bills are shaped into funnels and artfully arranged on the tray in fans or overlapping circular tiers as petals of a currency "flower," in the center of which are piled gold jewelry, a watch, an ornately decorated cell phone, imported cosmetics (often including the latest skin-lightening cream), and expensive perfumes. Once filled, the tray is wrapped in decorative transparent cellophane and tied with a bow. Its cost may exceed twenty thousand SDG.[24] In addition, the bride, her mother, and her sisters receive towbs and other clothing, sweets, cases of soft drinks, and quantities of food. The transfer is called the *sadd-al-mal*, the discharge of wealth, the gift that ends negotiations. It is delivered to the bride's home with considerable fanfare, and received with piercing ululations followed by refreshments all around. In preparation, the groom pays for the bride to have her hair coiffed with flowing extensions, her nails polished, face made up (false eyelashes have become de rigueur), and hands and feet hennaed in intricate designs. He will repeat this just before the wedding proper, plus buy or rent her a frothy white wedding gown, hijab and/or Western-style veil. He is also responsible for making several subsequent deliveries of foodstuffs for meals, paying the mahr, plus organizing rental cars (always white), official photographs and videos, musicians, DJ, sound system, and venue rental. All are his and his family's expense, though the amounts may be included in the sadd-al-mal should the bride's family prefer to make arrangements on their own.

In addition to the sadd-al-mal and the wedding bash there may be several other festivities with many guests, depending on the status of the families involved. Typically, the night before the wedding proper there is a "henna party" for the bride at which she appears in the red dress and gold jewelry associated with brides of Sudanese Arab descent; the party may be paid for by her parents, or its costs shared with the groom and his kin. At the same time, or in succession, comes the *jirtiq* celebration for the groom, when he is vested by his female kin with traditional life crisis ornaments: the gold *hilāl* (a new moon shape pinned on suit lapel or turban) plus beads, and red silk tassels worn on the wrist or arm. His hands and feet are hennaed, his head smeared with oil and powdered sandalwood. Finally, the *ṣubḥiya* (breakfast fete) follows the wedding night. All such parties demand outlays for clothing, venue, band, videographer, soft drinks, bottled water, and individual plastic-wrapped plates containing an assortment of prepared foods and fruit. Invitations to any and all such events are no longer delivered by mail or word of mouth, but mass messaged by cell phone to those within the bride's and/or groom's families, their friends, and WhatsApp circles. As the hosts do not always know in advance who plans to attend, accommodations must always be made for extra guests: family and friends may invite others to join in. For second marriages the fanfare may be more subdued, but costly all the same.

Celebrations are only a part of the expense, for it is expected that the couple will go on a honeymoon and, upon their return, furnish a room in the bride's or groom's parents' house, or if particularly well-off, rent or build their own home. But as local wages have not kept up with inflation, the purchasing power of each pound earned (and spent) has fallen dramatically since 2011: the annual inflation rate hit 47 percent in November 2012, moderated to 35 percent in 2014, and at the outset of 2015 was still extremely high at almost 26 percent.[25] To help accumulate funds for a large purchase (such as a refrigerator or TV), many people participate in rotating savings associations called *ṣandūg* (sing., for *ṣandūq,* box) or *jamī'ah* (sing., association): each member contributes a set amount monthly or weekly and once every so many months collects the whole sum in turn. However, inflation works against those receiving the pot later in the year and has eroded the savings of some prospective grooms. Friends report that men about to marry may buy on credit (*raṣīd* [sometimes *qaṣīd*, lit. "intent," as in "intent to pay"]), which makes items pricier than if they were bought for cash. Wedding debts can prove difficult to manage and lead to marital conflict, perhaps even divorce—becoming more common now that conjugal bonds are not always bonds between kin. For those without access to credit, establishing even a modest household may be impossible at first. If so, the bride will remain temporarily in her mother's home while her husband continues to work abroad. The long chain of outlays and support could be considered a form of bride service, where a man must prove his worth to the family of the bride in order to cement the deal. The less "close" the groom to the bride, the higher the costs are likely to be.

Prevailing conditions have modified women's expectations of marriage more, it seems, than men's. I know a number of Hofriyati women with post-secondary education who do not want to live with their parents or their husbands' kin after marriage, but look forward to having a car and a nicely furnished house of their own. Some have refused suitors who were unable to include such items in the sadd-al-mal, which would surely try a man's confidence in proposing a match to an educated woman's kin. I once discussed the situation with two doctoral students who teach courses at a local university. They agreed this had become a problem, but went on to say that for them even a wealthy Sudanese suitor would not be enough. As single working women they have good lives: they can travel abroad, own and drive a car, do what they like (both were living with their natal families). A husband would be too disruptive, able to restrict his wife's mobility, require her to be home to fix meals at regular times and serve him and his friends, have too many children, do housework. Neither wished to marry, even as a prelude to having a family, for reasons I discuss below. These students have a no-nonsense view of the entailments of marriage and in-laws in Sudan, and prefer the liberty they currently enjoy. For them, Sudanese men are not yet sufficiently "evolved"—they used the English word—to be desirable mates. Other bachelor women, however, were hoping for companionate marriages to well-off men of their choice and, as a sign of waning parental authority, several had successfully eluded matches arranged by kin.

As Jennifer Hirsch and Holly Wardlow (2006) have shown, the desire for companionate marriage is growing in various parts of the world where interfamily alliance or, as in Sudan, the intensification of preexisting kin ties were once the norm. In peri-urban Sudan TV broadcasts from abroad have clearly fueled aspirations: programs such as "Grey's Anatomy," American films, and popular serials from Egypt, India, and Turkey are avidly watched and their characters have become role models for local girls. New terms have entered everyday speech: "love story" (from the 1970 film) and *jikies* from the English slang word, "chicks." Both refer to boy-girl romantic liaisons based on mutual attraction and care, and apply to either sex. In the heady days following the Comprehensive Peace Agreement, couples could be seen walking side by side in city streets or sitting together in cafés. Short years before such acts were punishable by imprisonment or the lash; now the authorities seldom pay close mind. Although the influx of foreign images is significant here, the recent easing of cross-sex relations may have something to do with the protocols of television viewing as well.

NEW MEDIA AND GENDER

Satellite TV has reshaped domestic space. Televisions are communal objects; only better-off households boast more than one set. Hofriyati women and men of all generations often watch programs together, in the same room, even if they are not immediate kin (a degree of gender segregation was previously the norm). Viewing preferences vary, of course, with younger women and men favoring foreign films, talk shows, fashion channels, music videos, soccer, wrestling, and intriguingly, programs on medicine and science. Because most Hofriyati under the age of forty are at least partially literate they can follow subtitled foreign shows, and many understand some English even if they hesitate to speak it. When left on their own, older women and men tend to watch religious programming in Arabic, or local programs featuring some aspect of village life. Yet during the Israeli bombardment of Gaza in 2008–9 everyone was glued to Arabic news stations, especially Al Jazeera. The inauguration of US president Barack Obama was more popular still.

An intriguing upshot of satellite access is that modern standard Arabic spoken throughout the Middle East has been slowly displacing colloquial forms, drawing even those with little education into the broader Arabic speaking world. The marked differences between women's and men's speech that I'd noted on earlier field trips are fast disappearing. With educated daughters quick to correct their mothers' folksy (*dariji*) words, the colorful malapropisms that had provided me a window onto Hofriyati women's lives some thirty years ago surface less frequently, too. The spread of international Arabic is drawing the genders and the generations more closely together, and integrating them into global information space.

These trends owe just as much to the ubiquity of the mobile phone as to satellite TV. As noted earlier, cellular technology has been liberating for young women, who are no longer out of earshot when attending university, going to the suq, reading in the library, or riding crowded buses from place to place.[26] Family members speak by phone several times a day, in essence performing surveillance, policing each other's whereabouts, and giving parents a sense of security about their daughters' behavior that is not consistently justified. Even if girls do not linger outside the home, their friends can reach them through its now porous defensive walls.

Significantly, cell phones are personal, individual means of communication. In any spontaneous gathering of neighbors and kin, a phone is bound to ring every few minutes, whereupon the owner may get up to answer it in private. *Privacy* is a relatively new phenomenon, especially for women and girls. Once when my research assistant received a call in my presence she turned aside saying her jikies was on the line. When I asked if her parents knew she had a boyfriend she said no, they'd been discreet, carrying on their relationship over the phone, texting, sending photos, and arranging places to meet. Another woman in her mid-thirties had, to her mother's intense chagrin, refused offers of marriage from three men, each of whom had a house and a car, because she hoped to marry her "love story" with whom she carried on an active cellular (and perhaps less virtual) relationship but who was still too poor to ask for her hand. So as to maintain privacy should a parent find one's cell phone lying around, daughters regularly delete records of incoming and outgoing calls and use the phonebook function solely for family-approved contacts. Cell phone use has helped foster newly ascendant sensibilities of intimacy and privacy among youthful Sudanese.

I would venture more. The cell phone, together with satellite TV, have provided support for a subtle realignment of personhood in northern Sudan, away from its once highly collective relational form (in which it was impossible to think of oneself without reference to kin), toward a more individualized and interiorized sense of self and agency, though given the continuing salience of kinship this is hardly the bounded individualism of Euro-American repute, at least not yet.[27] Contemporary media have also nurtured aspirations for companionate marriage, nuclear family investment, and financial independence, especially among educated women and men.

SOCIAL REPRODUCTION AND FULL ADULTHOOD

Under these conditions, it may not be surprising to learn that unwed pregnancy is on the rise and a matter of considerable public concern. An unmarried girl who gets pregnant has few resources; she can search for an illegal abortionist or try to disguise her condition under voluminous wraps, but if she's discovered she risks a shotgun marriage (apparently becoming more common), being disowned and forced to live on the street (also becoming more common), or being beaten or killed for dishonoring her kin (extremely rare in Sudan but not unknown). Since most young women have undergone genital cutting, she would likely need assistance to deliver, preferably enlisting a trustworthy midwife, parent, or friend. Hospitals require a husband's name and address for childbirth admission, but it's not difficult to give false information and the hospital is bound to help regardless. I was told by nurses and medical residents that single and very poor married women who present for emergency delivery often sneak out of the hospital afterward, leaving their babies behind. Newborns are also being abandoned in the backs of three-wheeled taxis, at the sides of busy roads, or in cardboard boxes on the steps of mosques at an average rate of 110–120 per month in Khartoum alone (Al Jazeera 2010; Goddard 2007; UNICEF Sudan 2007; WUNRN 2007). So prevalent has the problem become that the main foundling orphanage in Khartoum—an Islamic charity—is always full to overflowing.[28] The growing number of *awlad ḥarām* (morally illicit children) is widely talked about and, I was told, one of the main differences between the Sudan of the mid-1990s and today. It surely reflects the diminishing supremacy of communal concerns.

Coincidentally, the high costs of getting married and creating a conjugal home mean that marriage (hence full adulthood) is often delayed until early middle age or even beyond, especially for men. According to Hofriyati, the failure of recently married couples to conceive is a growing problem and late marriage may be contributing to that distress; though how one determines "failure" is by no means clear, as newlyweds are expected to have a child within the first year of marriage. Lest all blame be cast on the prevalent but slowly declining practice of female genital cutting (FGC), there is ample evidence that the procedure does not lower fertility in the population as a whole, which is why fertility impairment is no longer cited by NGOs working for the custom's demise. While FGC may well contribute to individual fertility problems, Sudan has about the same infertility rates as other countries and a healthy growth rate of 2.5 percent, reflecting the large segment of the population currently in their reproductive years; on average a Sudanese woman bears five to six children in her lifetime.[29] Yet statistics provide no solace to the afflicted. Because identity in Muslim Sudan, as in other Islamic societies, is based on descent defined by shared bodily substance, surrogacy and gamete donation are taboo. But in vitro fertilization (IVF) techniques using husband's semen and wife's ova offer religiously approved redress (Clarke 2009; Inhorn 2004, 2006a, 2006b), and several IVF clinics have sprung up in Khartoum over the past half decade. IVF attempts are expensive, at least US$5,000 per treatment. Families often contribute to the cost, and may use savings associations to amass the funds required. Yet failure rates are high. Researchers at Ahfad University noted that women undergoing IVF or failing to conceive in a timely way may hedge their bets by consulting Islamic folk healers, some of whom appeal to *zār* spirits (ethereal entities that may possess women and seize their reproductive blood [Boddy 1989, 2007, 2013]), even though zār rites have been proscribed by the Islamist regime.

For both women and men, having a child, and ideally one who carries the family patronym, is the sine qua non of full adulthood. Given the acute pressures to reproduce, along with the state's pronatal stance toward the northern Muslim population (Caesarean sections are now free to any in need) and the growing number of abandoned infants, one would think that non-kin adoption might be seriously entertained. That it is, however, comes as a surprise. Adoption in Islamic societies is not an uncomplicated resort; it is possible to raise an orphaned child whose father's name is known, and several families of my acquaintance have fostered children in this way. Under Islam, caring for someone else's child is a charitable act and the legal obligation of an orphan's male kin. But "closed" (confidential) non-kin adoption where the father's name is not known or not reported is forbidden, considered a legal fiction (Bardagh 2002; Inhorn 2006a; Mattson 2008; Sonbol 1995; Women's Shura

Council 2011; see also Fioole 2014). Social as distinct from biological parentage is oxymoronic: all children are expected to carry evidence of their paternal bloodline (*nisab*) in their names, which provide guides to both domestic modesty protocols (i.e., who veils for whom) and future patrimony, for a step-or foster-child cannot inherit equally with a natural child even if they were raised as siblings. As Marcia Inhorn (2006a: 95) notes, Islam "privileges—even mandates—biological descent and inheritance. Preserving the 'origins' of each child, meaning his or her relationships to a known biological mother and father, is considered not only ideal in Islam, but a moral imperative."

Fostering a child of known parentage is fairly common in Muslim Sudan, but the raising of foundlings has, until recently, been abjured. Indeed, foundlings (sing., *laqīṭ*) were not considered orphans (sing., *yatīm*) at all, but awlad ḥarām and routinely shunned and despised. Yet the state has recently made it feasible to adopt them in the Islamic way: in 2006 following investigations by a coalition of Sudanese government officials, religious organizations, international NGOs, and UN agencies, and as the numbers of abandoned infants rose, Sudan's supreme religious body, the Fatwa Council, opined that foundlings should be considered orphans too, and society has a religious duty to care for them. They further declared that children born out of wedlock should not be made to suffer for their parents' sins (Polgreen 2008) and should be raised by their birth mothers, who should not necessarily be punished for getting pregnant. If the birth mother cannot be found or is unable to care for her child, then the state must pay for an "alternative family" to raise him or her (Goddard 2007; Sudan Government 2010), and provide the child with a fictional Islamic name. Ads touting adoption now regularly appear on local TV.

Recall the two PhD students I spoke about earlier, the ones who were loath to wed. Although they did not want husbands to tie them down, they did want children, and one had investigated the possibility of adopting a little girl. She learned that it is now legal for a single woman to adopt so long as she is financially secure and her brother or father agrees to stand as guarantor. My recent investigations (Boddy 2016) suggest a key correction: according to the National Policy on Welfare and Protection of Children Deprived of Parental Care (2011), this option is available only to a single woman *who has been married* (i.e., is divorced or widowed), though a marriage and divorce of convenience may be possible to procure. Motherhood without an existing marriage, social motherhood that is not coincident with biological motherhood, all of this is new and, needless to say, reconfiguring kinship in intriguing ways. Adoption appears to be unavailable to single men, who still need biological offspring to become full adults.

UNCONVENTIONAL LIAISONS

Not all unmarried women want to stay that way. Very few once-married women have the resources to adopt a child, and the stigma of adoption is not easily overcome. Further, while young women are earning university degrees, they do not necessarily find better, or indeed any employment after graduation. I know several well-educated Hofriyati daughters in Khartoum who describe themselves as "just sitting," waiting for their adult lives to begin. They may never wed, or if they do, will become second or third wives to prosperous elderly men. Few are likely to fulfill their dreams of companionate marriage or financial independence from kin.

Some young men attend university, of course, and their job prospects may be better than their sisters' in the long run. But many withdraw from school so as to earn in order to marry; the escalating costs of a wedding and setting up house may mean they must postpone full adulthood until their forties or fifties. Then, when they can afford to wed, they seek brides younger than themselves, leaving their sisters' cohort behind in their fraught quest for sons.

In Sudan's last census, completed in 2008, women outnumber men in every population cohort twenty years and over, an artifact of the high rate of male emigration for work.[30] Yet even though a reduced portion of the male population was available to count, government nuptiality figures show that 30 percent of men and fifteen per cent of women between the ages of twenty and fifty-four have never been married, with the lower percentage for women reflecting not just age differences at marriage but also the rising practice of polygyny as disparities in wealth increase.[31]

Still, economic, social, and cultural factors do not tell the whole story here: demography is also at play. Singerman (2007: 7) notes that countries of the Middle East and North Africa are undergoing a demographic transition owing to declining mortality rates, rising life spans, improvements to child and maternal health, and an attendant late conclusion to childbearing. These changes have produced a new age structure and a "youth bulge" where 60 percent of the population is below the age of twenty-five. The figure for Sudan is slightly higher, at 62 percent.[32] This suggests that more and more young people will be competing over ever-scarcer means to enable them to formally wed.

The economic challenge of conventional marriage coupled with new sensibilities and desires are beginning to shift how people think about gender and sociality. As Singerman (2007:29) notes, referring to the Middle East and North Africa region as a whole: "Whatever the reasons that young people are delaying marriage—the financial burdens . . . lack of a suitable spouse, or a preference to remain single, and new forms of desire—they are creating new approaches to long- and short-term intimate life and sexuality." In Sudan, as in Egypt (Schielke 2015), 'urfi or common-law, secret, temporary, and unregistered marriages that do not involve cohabitation are becoming more frequent, I was told, especially among university students.[33] Such arrangements are legitimate under Sunni Islam; the parties pledge that they are wed before two witnesses who may sign a document to that effect. The marriage is not financially binding on the man. Hofriyati friends say such unions are shameful as they deny family oversight and are bound to come out should pregnancy occur; none of their kin (to their knowledge) had married this way. Moreover, the child of an 'urfi marriage may be considered illegitimate (hence abandonable) if there is no documentation and the father does not step forward to acknowledge the birth. I do not have figures on how often such marriages occur, as even the families of those involved may never know that one took place; however, faculty and researchers in Sudan affirmed that 'urfi had become commonplace among university students.

According to Sudanese colleagues, government officials recently took a startling move—perhaps designed to curb such liaisons and infant abandonment—by approving a form of temporary or transient marriage analogous to that available in Shi'i Iran (where it is called *mut'a*; see Haeri 1989, 2005, 2014) but previously anathema in Sunni regions such as Sudan. Referred to as *zawaj misyār* (ambulatory marriage), it first emerged in Saudi Arabia (Singerman 2007: 29) where it received religious approval in 2006.[34] From there it spread to the Gulf, Egypt, and Sudan. As it requires a contractual arrangement between the parties involved, two witnesses, an agreed mahr paid to the woman, and no fixed time frame (unlike mut'a), it fits within the general rules for legitimate Sunni marriage. Singerman (2007) notes that the husband of a *misyār* marriage is not automatically obliged to provide housing and maintenance for his wife, who is expected to live with her parents; he visits periodically. Anthropologist Margaret Otto reports that in some neighborhoods of Greater Khartoum female university students have found "sugar daddies" who support their studies and desires for fashionable clothes in return for sex.[35] It may be that some of these are misyār marriages, which are typically entered into by married men. Importantly, children born of a misyār union are legitimate and eligible to inherit as kin. My Hofriyati friends had not heard of misyār, though a few had heard of what they called *muda* (durational) marriage, which may be an interpretation of the Shi'a form. Despite government approval, it seems that such marriages are currently rare in Sudan. However, should it be widely taken up misyār will enable the state to collect information about and responsibilize couples whose unconventional relationships lead to birth, a classic biopolitical move (see Campbell and Sitze 2013; Foucault 1978; Rose 2007). Its recognition, though controversial, may also be a concession to the high cost of conventional marriage and the rising number of stuck and disaffected youth; indeed, a step to deter civic unrest.[36]

CONCLUSION

Issues surrounding late marriage and delayed adulthood in Sudan are complex, not easily teased apart. "Waithood" is hardly an unusual life stage for men but has certainly lengthened with economic growth, rising expectations, shifting patterns of consumption, increased opportunities for women's education, and the altered gender dynamics such strains entail. Waithood has long been experienced by women, too, though present circumstances have exacerbated the condition for some. Even the newest form of "visiting" or ambulatory marriage does not mean that a wife will move out of her parents' home or receive full financial support from her spouse. It is crucial to realize that youth, however defined, are not the only generation in waiting. Their parents may also find themselves in status limbo, thwarted on the path to becoming elders or retire.[37]

In Sudan the problems of stymied youth are dilemmas for family and state alike, and have elicited varied forms of response. Parents and their aging progeny must attend to a host of contextual cues, such as those leading some to encourage daughters into polygynous contractual marriages with wealthy older men lest they wait too long to wed. Conversely, the Islamist state has enabled couples and once-married single women to adopt abandoned children, the obvious victims of their parents' plight, enabling some who are well off to avoid remaining wed. The state also allows transient marriages with an eye to ensuring that the parentage and entitlements of their offspring are known. All such moves are inexorably governed by the "biological clock" in a cultural order where identity and social support critically depend on being able to demonstrate genealogical ties.

Janice Boddy is Professor of Anthropology at the University of Toronto, Canada. She is author of *Wombs and Alien Spirits: Women, Men and the Zar Cult in Northern Sudan*; *Aman: The Story of a Somali Girl* (with Virginia Lee Barnes and Aman); and *Civilizing Women: British Crusades in Colonial Sudan*.

NOTES

1. I am grateful to the SSHRC of Canada, the University of Toronto's Research Completion Grant and Chair's Research Fund for funding my research and am deeply indebted to Ahfad University for Women, Omdurman, for ongoing affiliation and assistance between 2008 and 2016. As ever I am profoundly obliged to "Hofriyati" for their kindness, hospitality, assistance, interest, and care.

2. The number of people on whose experiences I base these observations is difficult to estimate with any accuracy, as constant visiting is customary, one never knows when someone you drop in on will have other guests, and planned or unforeseen events involving several hundred people regularly occur (e.g., illnesses, accidents, deaths). Conversations with people I know are supplemented by conversations about others whose families belong to the community. In 1977 and 1984 the village was home to some eight to nine hundred individuals; even with normal attrition that number has grown, though not all of them have remained in Hofriyat. Since resuming fieldwork in 2008 I have been in contact with at least four hundred Hofriyati from a cluster of related families.

3. The people of the rural north between Khartoum and Atbara belong to the general Arabic speaking population that has long held political and economic sway in Sudan, though Hofriyati themselves are not close to the present regime. Expectations of prosperity raised during the oil-boom are now being assailed. In September 2013 the government removed subsidies on gasoline; this had the effect of raising prices on all basic commodities and, together with other grievances plus the hopes of the Arab Spring, sent "youth" into the streets. The government responded with a heavy hand, which seems to have staved off further demonstrations as people scramble to survive. Government deregistration and abolition of several prominent NGOs has further fragmented dissent, even as a host of new NGOs arise to work around the constraints.

4. Some of what follows is based on Boddy (2013), updated to 2016.

5. I had no luck explaining to Hofriyati friends what a "street map" is when I asked them where I might buy one, though I eventually found an outdated English version of one in an upscale bookshop in Khartoum.

6. See http://www.economywatch.com/economic-statistics/country/Sudan.

7. *The World Factbook: Sudan,* https://www.cia.gov/library/publications/the-world -factbook/geos/su.html; http://www.economywatch.com/world_economy/sudan/.

8. Trading Economics, http://www.tradingeconomics.com/sudan/inflation-cpi, based on figures supplied by the Sudan Central Bureau of Statistics. The Khartoum-based newspaper *Sudan Vision* (February 17, 2015) suggests that inflation dropped in response to government programs aimed at boosting production.

9. UNFPA: Population Dynamics of Sudan, n.d., http://countryoffice.unfpa.org/file manager/files/sudan/facts/population_fact_sheet_final1.pdf.

10. Polygyny is permissible in Muslim Sudan, and remarriage after divorce or death of a spouse is common.

11. In 1976–77 some 70 percent of marriages that I documented over four generations were between first (40%) or second (30%) cousins.

12. See Malmström 2015 on similar patterns among working-class families in Cairo.

13. This is the lowest legal age of marriage in Africa, and a subject of current national and international feminist activism and debate (see http://www.ipsnews.net/2013/07/time-to-let-sudans-girls-be-girls-not-brides). The law states that the age of marriage for Muslim girls is puberty, or age 10 with the consent of a judge (The African Child Policy Forum, http://www .africanchild forum.org).

14. Katy Migiro, "Sudan Worst in Africa with Legal Marriage at Age 10," Thompson Reuters Foundation, November 18, 2013, http://www.trust.org/item/20131118080551-ikgwx/.

15. See, for instance, "Africa Launches Historic Campaign to End Child Marriage," June 9, 2014, http://www.unfpa.org/news/africa-launches-historic-campaign-end-child-marriage.

16. Some material in this section appears in different form in Boddy 2016.

17. See http://www.economywatch.com/economic-statistics/Sudan/Telephone_Statistics/. The population of Sudan was estimated to be 35.5 million in mid-2014.

18. Having several accounts may make economic sense, given that calls within a company network are more likely to "land" and are less expensive than calls placed between them.

19. UNFPA: Population Dynamics of Sudan.

20. See also http://www.uis.unesco.org/DataCentre/Pages/country-profile.aspx?code=
SDN. For a somewhat less rosy picture that nonetheless shows higher female university attendance than male, see Nour (2011).

21. While there are now two universities within twenty miles of Hofriyat, children of families who remain in the village and farm are less likely to attend university, and are apt to marry far younger and genealogically "closer" than their urban cousins do (see Singerman 2007: 13ff., on Egypt).

22. For an alternative view of education as a contradictory resource, see Hughes, this volume, on Sri Lanka.

23. The plight of the well-educated unemployed is also discussed in the chapters by Hughes and by Dungey and Meinert, this volume.

24. The official exchange rate in 2012 ranged from 2.70 SDG to 4.40 SDG to US$1.00; in early 2015 the rate rose from 6.00 SDG to 7.00 SDG or more.

25. For 2012, see https://www.cia.gov/library/publications/the-world-factbook/geos/su
.html. For subsequent years, see www.tradingeconomics.com/sudan/inflation-cpi. Inflation was a hot topic in local newspapers during my visit in the winter of 2015.

26. Portions of the following section appear in a different form in Boddy (2016).

27. Nonetheless, it is intriguing and ironic that such contemporary redefinitions of personhood are those that British colonial agents claimed to be "normal" decades ago and desperately tried to inspire in Sudanese without great success (Boddy 2007).

28. See Bargach (2002) on such a system in Morocco.

29. Balghis Bedri personal communication; UNFPA: Population Dynamics of Sudan; *The World Factbook: Sudan.*

30. UNFPA: Population Dynamics of Sudan.

31. Republic of Sudan Central Bureau of Statistics, Censuses, Nuptiality (23/10/2010): http://www.cbs.gov.sd/en/files.php?id=7#&panel1-1. Retrieved May 7, 2015.

32. This is the 2013 UNFPA figure for Sudan. UNFPA: Population Dynamics of Sudan.

33. Singerman (2007) notes that a study in Egypt found six percent of university students in 'urfi marriages.

34. Miriam Hakeem, "Misyar Marriages Gaining Popularity among Saudis," *Gulf News,* May 25, 2006, http://gulfnews.com/news/gulf/saudi-arabia/misyar-marriages-gain-popularity -among-saudis-1.238221. This form of marriage was approved by fatwa from Saudi's Islamic Fiqh Academy.

35. Margaret Otto, personal communication, February 2015; see also Bledsoe and Cohen (1993) for secondary school students elsewhere in Africa.

36. See also Dungey and Meinert, this volume, on how state interventions in Uganda, namely the 1996 defilement law, may have unintended consequences for men's status and be seen to thrust responsibility on them for the children that they sire.

37. See also Solway, this volume, for a similar instance of multigenerational limbo.

REFERENCES

Al Jazeera (English). 2010. *Witness: Orphans of Maygoma.* https://archive.org/details
/linktv_al-jazeera-english-orphans-of-magoma2010026.

Bargach, Jamila. 2002. *Orphans of Islam: Family, Abandonment, and Secret Adoption in Morocco.* Lanham, MD: Rowman & Littlefield.

Bedri, Balghis. 2009. *Sudanese Women Profile: Pathways to Empowerment.* Omdurman: Ahfad University Press.

Bledsoe, Caroline, and Barney Cohen, eds. 1993. *Social Dynamics of Adolescent Fertility in Sub-Saharan Africa*. Washington, DC: National Academy Press.

Boddy, Janice. 1989. *Wombs and Alien Spirits: Women, Men, and the Zar Cult in Northern Sudan*. Madison: University of Wisconsin Press.

———. 2007. *Civilizing Women: British Crusades in Colonial Sudan*. Princeton: Princeton University Press.

———. 2013. "Spirits and Selves Revisited: *Zar* and Islam in Northern Sudan." In *A Companion to the Anthropology of Religion*, edited by Janice Boddy and Michael Lambek, 444–67. Oxford: Wiley Blackwell.

———. 2016. "Engendering Change: New Information Technologies and the Dynamics of Gender in Northern Sudan." In *Networks of Knowledge Production in Sudan*, edited by Sondra Hale and Gada Kadoda, 187–200. Lanham, MD: Lexington Books.

Brinkman, Inge, Mirjam de Bruijn, and Hisham Bilal. 2009. "The Mobile Phone, 'Modernity' and Change in Khartoum Sudan." In *Mobile Phones: The New Talking Drums of Everyday Africa*, 69–91. Leiden and Bamenda: Langaa and African Studies Centre.

Campbell, Timothy, and Adam Sitze, eds. 2013. *Biopolitics*. Durham: Duke University Press.

Clarke, Morgan. 2009. *Islam and New Kinship: Reproductive Technology and the Shariah in Lebanon*. New York: Berghahn Books.

CRIN (Child Rights International Network). 2011. "Sudan." https://www.crin.org/en/library/publications/sudan-child-rights-references-universal-periodic-review.

Fioole, J. C. C. M. 2014. "Give Me Your Child: Adoption Practices in a Small Moroccan Town." *Journal of North African Studies* (May). doi:10.1080/13629387.2014.917587.

Foucault, Michel. 1978. *The History of Sexuality*. Volume 1: *An Introduction*. Translated by Robert Hurley. New York: Vintage Books.

Goddard, John. 2007. "Saving Khartoum's Abandoned Babies." *Toronto Star*, April 15.

Haeri, Shahla. 1989. *Law of Desire: Temporary Marriage in Shi'i Iran*. Syracuse, NY: Syracuse University Press.

———. 2005. "Mot'a." In *Encyclopaedia Iranica*. Edited by Ehsan Yar-Shater. http://www.iranicaonline.org/articles/mota.

———. 2014. *Law of Desire: Temporary Marriage in Shi'i Iran*. Revised edition. Syracuse, NY: Syracuse University Press.

Hirsch, Jennifer S., and Holly Wardlow, eds. 2006. *Modern Loves: The Anthropology of Romantic Courtship and Companionate Marriage*. Ann Arbor: University of Michigan Press.

Inhorn, Marcia. 2004. "Middle Eastern Masculinities in the Age of New Reproductive Technologies: Male Infertility and Stigma in Egypt and Lebanon." *Medical Anthropology Quarterly* 18(2): 162–82.

———. 2006a. "'He won't be my son': Middle Eastern Muslim Men's Discourses of Adoption and Gamete Donation." *Medical Anthropology Quarterly* 20: 94–120.

———. 2006b. "Making Muslim Babies: IVF and Gamete Donation in Sunni and Shi'a Islam". *Culture, Medicine, and Psychiatry* 30: 427–50.

Malmström, Maria F. 2015. *The Politics of Female Circumcision in Egypt: Gender, Sexuality and the Construction of Identity*. London: I. B. Tauris.

Mattson, Ingrid. 2008. "Adopting Children: What Are the Islamic Guidelines for Muslim Americans Who Wish to Adopt and Foster Children?" *Islamic Horizons* (January–February): 23–28.

Nour, Samia Satti Osman Mohamed. 2011. "Assessment of Gender Gap in Sudan." UNU-MERIT Working Paper No. 2011-004, Maastricht, Netherlands.

Polgreen, Lydia. 2008. "Overcoming Customs and Stigma, Sudan Gives Orphans a Lifeline." *New York Times*, April 4.

Rice, Kathleen. 2015. " 'Most of them, they just want someone to under them': Gender, Generation, and Personhood among the Xhosa." PhD diss., University of Toronto.

Rose, Nikolas. 2007. *The Politics of Life Itself.* Princeton: Princeton University Press.

Schielke, Samuli. 2015. *Egypt in the Future Tense: Hope, Frustration and Ambivalence before and after 2011.* Bloomington: Indiana University Press.

Singerman, Diane. 2007. "The Economic Imperatives of Marriage: Emerging Practices and Identities among Youth in the Middle East." The Middle East Youth Initiative Working Paper No. 6, Wolfensohn Center for Development, Dubai School of Government.

Sonbol, Amira al-Azhary. 1995. "Adoption in Islamic Society: A Historical Survey." In *Children in the Muslim Middle East,* edited by E. Warnock-Fernea, 45–67. Austin: University of Texas Press.

Sudan Government. 2010. "Sudan's Initial Report on the Implementation of the African Charter on the Rights and Welfare of the Child." National Council for Child Welfare, Secretariat General, October. http://www.acerwc.org/wp-content/uploads/2011/03/English-ACERWC-Initial-State-report-Sudan.pdf.

UNICEF Sudan. 2007. "Technical Briefing Paper 1: Alternative Family Care." http://www.unicef.org/sudan/UNICEF_Sudan_Technical_Briefing_Paper_1_-_Alternative_family_care.pdf.

Women's Shura Council. 2011. "Adoption and Care of Orphan Children: Islam and the Best Interests of the Child. American Society for Muslim Advancement." http://www.wisemuslimwomen.org/images/activism/Adoption_%28August_2011%29_Final.pdf.

WUNRN (Women's United Nations Report Network). 2007. "Alternative Family-Based Care for Abandoned and Orphaned Children Launched in North of Sudan." http://www.wurn.com/news/2007/07_02_07/070807.

Zain Group and Telefonaktiebolaget LM Ericsson. 2010. "Economic Impact of Mobile Communications in Sudan." http://www.ericsson.com/res/thecompany/docs/sudan_economic_report.pdf.

CHAPTER SEVEN

BETWEEN "TOO YOUNG" AND "ALREADY OLD"

The Fleeting Adulthood of Russia's Split Generation

Anna Kruglova

Here, to the young all roads are open;
Here, respect is paid to the elders.
—"A Song about Motherland" by Isaak Dunaevskiĭ
and Vasiliĭ Lebedev-Kumach (1936)

PEOPLE WHO WERE born in the USSR in the 1970s and were in their thirties at the time of my fieldwork in 2009–11 questioned their adulthood in ways that are different from other parts of the world. Whereas many others are finding adulthood "unattainable" or "elusive" (see Durham's introduction to this volume), perestroika teens wonder whether adulthood had somehow passed them by. Given the intersection of culture, history, and personal experiences, many find their adulthood fleeting, squeezed between being "too young" and "already old." First, accepting one's adulthood was in general problematic because late-Soviet ideals glamorized childhood and youth as the locus of moral agency, contrasted with the "unmarked" world of adults (see introduction) that was vaguely traumatic and morally compromised by routine. For the perestroika teenagers, however, growing up was further aggravated by the disappointments of the 1990s when none of the various social and moral strategies helped them build a good foundation for a professional career. In 2010, they often felt they belonged "neither here nor there"; in other words, split between Soviet and post-Soviet moral orders, and between their glamorized childhood and questionable adulthood. A growing realization that being just a few years older or younger would have changed their life opportunities and the way they experienced adulthood has reinforced this structure of feeling. Finally, pronatalist policies and discourses that dominated the public sphere in Russia in the 2000s helped to seal the "has-been, already old" sentiment among these men and women.

Perestroika Teens: "The Last Soviet Idealists"

There is a growing awareness about the theoretical purchase of seeing Russia—a country that underwent a century of rapid and substantial social change—through the lens of age cohorts, or generations.[1] This chapter looks at people born in the Soviet Union in the 1970s. They do not have an established label used by scholars or the media (such as the greatest generation, baby boomers, or millennials in the United States, or "children of perestroika" in Russia[2]). Interruptions in personal maturation and socialization taking place alongside (post)-Soviet transformations are a key feature of this age cohort's experience. Born Soviet children, they were teenagers during perestroika (1986–91), young adults looking for jobs in the "chronic crisis" (Shevchenko 2009) of the 1990s, and mature in the uneasy stability of the 2000s. If adulthood indicates normalcy, as Durham notes in the introduction to this volume, then the perestroika teens have witnessed at least three different ways of being "normal" before they turned forty—Soviet, post-Soviet, and what could be called (arguably) the post-post-Soviet regime.

They were also the last age cohort whose primary and secondary education was framed by the Marxist-Leninist tenets of social and historical teleology. This is important to realize in order to understand the sensibilities described below. As followers of an everyday, "vernacular" Marxism (Kruglova 2016, forthcoming), people in the USSR were encouraged to be conscious of the mutual articulation between their life and personal identity, on the one hand, and social/historical forces, on the other. Social historian Mikhail Rozhanskiy (2010) identified one type of this articulation as "Soviet idealism." Specific meanings of "Soviet idealism" differed from person to person, and changed over time. But in general terms, it was a desire to live not just "better" but somehow "truer" or more authentically (*nastoyashchii*) within some equally authentic collective life (although not necessarily a Soviet type of collectivity). This desire often transpired in the way my informants talked about their lives.

Idealism, Rozhanskiy points out, is a fertile ground for disappointment. Like many people living in Russia, perestroika teens were often doubtful about the wild growth of Russian capitalism after perestroika that transformed one of the most egalitarian countries in the world, especially in terms of wealth, to one of the least egalitarian. Nonetheless, perestroika teens were born in the time of late socialism when a private sphere had developed within the collective and public life of the country. When new paths of social and personal alignment appeared within an accelerating capitalism in the 1990s, many perestroika teens sincerely attempted to take them. At that time, a rise of the middle class was highly celebrated: a new group of small- and medium-level business owners, highly credentialed management, law, medicine, IT, and media professionals, and academic science experts with better access to international scholarly arenas appeared. There is no consensus in sociological literature on whether the rise was real, or was just an ideological construct employed by the elites to justify perestroika. But for the perestroika teens, the rise was real enough, if not real for themselves.

Conversations on which I draw for this chapter happened mostly as kitchen "Russian talk" about life (see Ries 1997). Because I was a native coming home to catch up with friendships I had made in childhood and youth, the talk naturally included many biographical reflections and accounts. People in my study do not have elite Soviet professional backgrounds, and the rise to the middle class, especially the stability and surety of the future associated with it, did not happen for them. A small number of them moved to Moscow and Saint Petersburg, but the majority continue to live in Perm, a provincial medium-size city and the place of their childhoods. Their income, at the time of my fieldwork, ranged between 15,000 and 50,000 rubles a month, approximately US$500–1,600. Most of them led a lifestyle much the same as it would have been at the time of their birth: routinely divided between work, home, children's school, and mutual visits. They, however, consumed more than would have been possible in the Soviet Union. Many had cars, often on high-interest credit.[3] For those in the upper range of the income spread, pools, cinema, or even an occasional nightclub outing was within reach. Every household had a computer. Many had been abroad at least once, mostly to the Turkish or Egyptian seaside. They did not, however, have savings to last several months if they found themselves without work. They may therefore be placed into that uncomfortable position, lower middle class, from which they could imagine what a better fortune could buy, but also in which they lived with the realization of their precarious proximity to poverty.

Growing Up In and After the USSR: Agency, Memory, and Historical Consciousness

The meaning of adulthood (*vzroslost'*) in the USSR in the 1970s and 1980s had been, in many respects, the same as in other modernities and nonmodernities (see Durham's introduction). Financial independence, skills, a separate household, marriage and children, greater responsibility, taking care of parents and younger siblings, all contributed to the subjective experience and public acknowledgment of adulthood. There were, however, important differences. Growing up was "unremarkable" in the same sense that Margaret Mead (1928) calls Samoan coming of age unremarkable (see also Oushakine 2008). Growing up was hardly a "project," a "rite," or even a "time period."[4] Adolescents did not have a variety of competing models of adulthood to choose from. One exception was the decision of which professional occupation they would take up (I describe the significance of this choice below). In public discourse, coming of age and generational succession highlighted the sameness of groups of people who carried on the same utopic communist project (Oushakine 2008: 21), rather than regeneration or renewal (Cole and Durham 2007). Membership in countrywide organizations started in primary school and marked growth in a rather perfunctory manner, commencing and ceasing for each individual according to age, and sometimes professional affiliation. Sexual maturation, and sex at large, were not represented in any way, and sexual education or rites of passage, if any, were largely undertaken informally by family or peers.

This formally unproblematic coming of age was, in many ways, conditioned and sustained by the planned economic structure of the late socialist welfare state. A notably comfortable life was difficult to achieve, but basic sustenance was guaranteed. Upon finishing their education in the mandatory school system, graduates were expected to work, and university graduates often were assigned to specific positions; unemployment was a punishable offense. Pensions and health care were universal, and officially, at least, there was free housing, although in fact there was both an official waiting list and many other unofficial factors affecting its distribution. Pronatalist state policy and propaganda made being married and childless subject to stigma, and also subject to a fine of six per cent of one's wages or school stipend.[5] Under these conditions, plunging into adulthood by means of an early marriage did not make much practical sense. Neither were there reasons to delay childbirth, because no significant detriment to one's material or professional circumstances was anticipated. The average age of marriage in Russia increased only slightly in the twentieth century, from eighteen to twenty-two for women, and from twenty to twenty-four for men (Chernova and Shpakovskaya 2010).

This unremarkable move into adulthood also conditioned, and reflected, the specificity of moral agency for a population living in a paternalistic state. On the one hand, the state demanded the utmost compliance to norms and orders; on the other, it required sincere emotional engagement, one aspect of which was the "authentic life" sensibility mentioned above, to give a foundation to its political enterprise. This contradiction between compliance and emotional engagement was resolved partially by a model of moral agency that disconnected happiness and freedom from responsibility, political initiative, or self-sufficiency. Happiness and moral goodness, especially in the 1970s, was associated with the authenticity of experiences and emotions, a concern often translated in terms of a contrast between good spontaneity and bad routine. Unlike today's consumer capitalism with its emphasis on constant reinvention of oneself through changes of lifestyle and accumulation of new goods and new experiences (see Durham's introduction), Soviet spontaneity was associated more with creative freedoms and rich social interactions. Cultured professionalism and (often very low-budget) travel afforded creativity, publicity and mobility, which stood opposed to the private and static routines of domesticity. But spontaneity was not always cheerful: late socialism in particular saw a relative proliferation of existentialist concern and black humor centered on the trope of "anything can happen" (Kruglova 2016), especially a sudden and unmotivated loss, accident, or violence, for which one had to be always prepared (Oushakine 2008). The ideals of spontaneous and authentic emotional engagement were embodied especially in childhood and youth, which were associated with talent, purposefulness, potential, and enthusiasm, and yet stood apart from decision making and political agency. Inhabiting a world that was separate, joyful, sociocentric, and purposefully active (Kelly 2007), children were exalted in public and popular culture discourse for the immediacy and the authenticity of their emotions and desires, afforded precisely because the state/adults provided the material and moral foundations of life. When contrasted to childhood, becoming a *vzroslyĭ* (grownup) was problematic because of an inevitable loss of authenticity and the introduction of routine that adults experienced in building and maintaining their world. (This model of adulthood, which must be common in modernities of Christian origins, is mentioned in the introduction to this volume.) The end of childhood indexed a necessary departure from a happy world to either an uncertain future, or a life that lost its freshness in the habitual comforts of marriage and occupational stability (Oushakine 2008).

Chris Hann (2011) has explained how, paradoxically, both those who benefitted and those who suffered from the post-socialist transformations tend to view socialism as *morally* superior to its subsequent regimes. Hann points out that this sensibility may be traced to the prominent role that moral superiority played in the USSR's claim of the superiority of socialism to capitalism. Thus, the connections and oppositions between moral and economic successes that Karen Sykes (this volume) describes as part of her theoretical discussion, in the Soviet Union were central to official ideology, governmentality, and the techniques of self.[6] Perestroika teens, however, have an additional reason to believe in the morality of the Soviet order. They were not old enough to actually experience the order's real shortcomings: the economic shortages, the censorship of personal expressions. In conversations, they invariably fondly remembered their childhood as a time of freedom and spontaneity, flourishing in the security guaranteed by parental and social protection. The cultural scenario of a happy child, distinguished from that of a burdened, anxious adult, took form for them especially against the historical experience of the postsocialist transition. It is not surprising that for them the appreciation of their childhoods often took a form of defiance—"You can bash me for that, but I will tell you, we had a happy childhood! We were lucky to have the childhood we had"; "Those who came after us, they had a much worse childhood"; "I am, honestly, downright nostalgic about that time, our childhood"; "If we can still be optimistic, it is because we were taught to be optimistic then, to believe in a happier tomorrow."

Their youthful idealism persisted later in life in the form of a powerful affect, and a kind of historical determinism. It could take the form of a conscious reflection on the mutual articulation of identity and history. According to Roman[7] (a married medical university dropout, hi-tech factory worker),

To understand anything in how life is *now*, you have to talk to younger people. I am a man of an epoch that passed, from the socialist epoch. Honestly, I want to say that our generation, born 1975, is a complicated generation. It was very hard for us to adapt. We lived through that, when everything changed so fast around us . . . and we were so, so young . . . It is hard for us to find ourselves in life. Because our ideals were destroyed.

Yet if people like Roman felt historically dislocated, the ideals of their childhood also persisted in the form of a claim to moral personhood, often connected to growing up in the Soviet Union. "Growing up in the Soviet Union gave us *moral'nyi sterzhen'* [moral backbone]." "It gave us *moral'nye ustoi* [moral foundations]; those who came later, especially those born in the 1990s—poor kids, their parents had no time to spend on their upbringing, none at all! They are empty inside."[8] "Their roofs are sliding off all the time [they are psychologically or mentally disturbed], with the drugs and alcohol . . . they don't see beer as an alcoholic drink!" "There is so much *zloba* [anger, grudge, cruel indifference] in kids these days. It is because they only think of what they wear, who owns more expensive shit." The moral identity claimed was sometimes (but not always) presented as "Soviet," "socialist," or "leftist," and is formulated in terms of humanism, contempt for self-centeredness, and a focus on sincerity and especially sociality. Two women reflected that they regret the collapse of the Soviet Union because their "natural characters" (*po nature*) fitted better with what they remembered to be the Soviet forms of sociality. Sofiya, a university graduate with a diploma in French language and now a manager at an alcohol beverages wholesale company, declared: "I am very social, you know. In the USSR, I would have been an *obshchestvennitsa.*" A derivative from the word *obshchestvo* (society), obshchestvennitsa is Soviet-speak for a public life enthusiast and an organizer of social activities. For Sofiya, being an obschestvennitsa was an idealistic life-choice she was unable to realize in the 2010s, where, it appeared, society was no more.

From Boldness to Fear: Mid-Life Crisis at Thirty-Five

Understanding childhood as a time of security complemented views of child-hood and youth as a time when certain resources are at a maximum. "Young-ness," *molodost'*, was seen as a *limited* resource of vital energy and idealistic enthusiasm, indispensable for laying the foundations for status and stability in life. Through the experience of grown-up life one loses energy and becomes fearful, whether by the "harsh teachings of life" (*zhizn' nauchit*), its "natural" deprivations and limitations, or because "anything can happen." "In Russia, you know, so much happens to one's life; if one survives to be twenty, one learns to deal with everything." "I am no longer young, I have fear now." "I can-not imagine how we went to visit strangers' apartments when we were young . . . and we did not think at all about what could have happened to us. . . . I cannot think of doing something like this now!" "When we were young, we used to go walk on the 'wilder' side of the Kama River . . . me and my wife, we had so little fear. We went fishing! Now, such a thought would never cross my mind."[9] By the time of my fieldwork, these perestroika teens, afraid to go fishing on the wilder side, felt something akin to a mid-life crisis.

Pavel, who had worked in sales, oil extraction, fire prevention, but mostly in electrical engineering (for which he finally obtained official university cre-dentials in 2013), and who had been married twice, admitted his anxiety about becoming old. Feeling that they were entering the time of life when youthful energies are no longer abundant, others accentuated the continuous work of the self they had to carry out to stay young. Elena, who lived alone with her only child and supported her household by working as a tour sales operator and manager, "felt young" because she was a "night person," "played poker," and "visited nightclubs." Evgenii, a married academic, praised himself for keeping his youthful appearance, unlike "all Russian men who inevitably get fat by their forties, especially if married." Others declared: "I had checked it in the hospital, and they told me that my biological age is that of a twenty-seven-year-old girl"; "I am terrified when my peers talk, with zeal, about their dream to become pensioners"; or, somewhat more desperately, "I try and have all possible sensations before forty, because after that, it is over."

Feeling over the hill in one's late thirties was overwhelming for this group, and yet it was especially normalized by the discussion about Russia's demographic crisis. High mortality and short life spans of Russian citizens loom large in popular imagination. The dwindling of the population on account of both a decrease in birthrates and an increase in mortality rates was in the public spotlight in the 2000s. State biopolitical rhetoric and policies made it the responsibility of citizens to fulfill their nationalist conviction through their reproductive capacity (Rivkin-Fish 2005). Some material incentives were also introduced. Many of my interlocutors qualified for state-sponsored "maternal capital," introduced in 2007, through which they received the equivalent of approximately US$10,000, an amount sufficient to get an extra room outside Perm's city center, for a second or third child in the family. Other incentives, however, were restricted to "young families" only, specifically those under thirty-five (Chernova and Shpakovskaya 2010). This new mandate implicitly identified those born after 1975 to be already "not young," and capable only of contributing to the mortality side of the Russian demographic equation. Those young enough to still qualify sometimes had to scramble to collect the required paperwork within days.

At thirty-something, mortality entered the lives of perestroika teens in ways other than losing peers to drugs, wars, and the rise in violent crimes that came to define the 1990s, and traffic accidents that accompanied the burgeoning car culture of the 2000s. Their parents, reaching their 60s, started to die, which could have contributed to a sense of being adult, as they became the heads of their "clans." But parents' deaths often reminded them of their own mortality, their passage into an old age where they were "next." Representations of the elderly as having valuable experience, labor value or fulfilling lives, are largely absent in the everyday Russian milieu (Smol'kin 2010). In popular imagination, growing old is widely seen as falling into social irrelevance and insecurity—a perception confirmed when the state was seen to be treating pensioners as a largely expendable part of the population.[10] My interlocutors worried about their security in old age, or, in a version of the "anything can happen" rhetoric, they were brazenly not worried, not thinking or planning about it at all. "What is the point of forming and reforming these pensions? They are legal at the age of sixty for men, and the average lifespan of a man is, like, fifty-five?" "I am not going to quit smoking, because I will not live long enough to get cancer from it. I will die much earlier from something else, like from a heart attack, because of all the stress."[11]

Losing One's Profession: Morality, Mobility, and Opportunity

This historically interrupted, or split, generation started their first jobs and often married for the first time in the 1990s, activities associated with adult-hood. It was the decade when new dimensions of agency—self-sufficiency, self-responsibilization, taking initiative—were touted as the spirit of the time. Stories of a self-sufficient meritocracy, and the rise of a (new) middle class, circulated. Pavel recalled a story about the meteoric rise of an "ordinary pro-grammer" who, after having been fired from his job in Perm, moved to Moscow where he got a job with an astronomical wage of US$10,000 a month.

What Pavel's story reflected was not just admiration for the programmer's rise, but the hesitation of transitioning from an agency of adaptation to an agency of taking initiative: the programmer, whose skills, it turned out, were worth so much, had to be jolted into action by being fired. Was this taking initiative or adaptation? Should one act or react? The following stories of maturing during the 1990s also reflect this hesitation. Coming from the lower middle class, from the rank-and-file intelligentsia of teachers and doctors, or from the working class (blue collars, factory hands) and sales, some of my in-formants followed an ethics of adaptation to the system, associated with the Soviet period, self-consciously sacrificing idealism to meet circumstances into which they were put:

I was born in a *rabochiĭ* [working-class] family. My parents were those hardworking types, at a factory, there is a metallurgical factory in Chusovoĭ [town near Perm]. What did parents usually think? That if they did not get a higher education, they should give it to their children. My brother went to study to *pribaltika* [one of the Baltic republics; a sophisticated "European" environment]. And to me, my dad suggested that I become a chemical technologist, at the polytechnic university, so after graduation I could work [at a factory] one year for two [in counting towards pension eligibility] because chemicals, it was [designated] a harmful working environment. So I could have retired at forty-five ... So he *kak by* [in a way] was caring about me. ... [He thought] it was not bad for a woman to retire at forty-five.[12] Or maybe work later as an engineer. I applied to a polytechnic university, with a classmate of mine ... But myself, I always wanted to work in aviation. At an airport. (Mariya, university graduate in chemistry, factory chemist, single)

Mariya yielded to parental pressure, but for many it was rather obvious that in the turbulent times of the industrial collapse Mariya's parents' choice to exploit the older social structures was not a good strategy. A more idealistic and ambitious goal of pursuing highly educated professions made more sense. A few universities had only just started to charge money for education, and though entrance to the elite universities was limited to the well connected or exceptionally talented, a five-year specialist diploma in economics, law, or medicine was within the reach of the majority. Such a diploma was supposed to translate, through hard work and education, into dividends in terms of social status, economic stability, and an authentic life.

But ordinary programmers who made it big were rare. As one of my interlocutors put it, "in those years the whole country produced nothing, so there were no jobs but in the resale of foreign goods. All that mattered was to sell another Snickers bar." Pursuing self-sufficient opportunism associated with commerce, especially the resale of foreign goods, was one more alternative to adapting within one's parents' class and lifestyle, or an attempt at educated professionalism. In 1992–95, the period of the fastest private business development, stories about (and, for some, the reality of) easy money to be got distributing goods made investment in education doubtful:

A friend and I, we went to medical university together, and dropped out together in the third year. And N now works at a factory. And [another friend], he also dropped out of the law department in the third year, but now is a police captain! [laughs] I went to work in sales . . . a so-called distributor . . . there was not a thing I did not "distribute" . . . I avoided the army, I managed to fake an ulcer . . . after three years at a medical school, it was easy! So I went from office to office, with a bag of goods on my shoulder, in a suit and tie. I could sell anything! When I was unemployed afterward and needed money, I already knew the drill, I went to a wholesale warehouse, bought something and sold it at three times the price. (Roman)

Oksana, a married college graduate, also had dreams of educated middle-classness. Her first dream was to become a musician, but the hardships associated with her lower middle-class background and the collapse of the Soviet musical education system cut short her piano training. Next, she tried driving a bus, realizing a romantic and somewhat childish dream that she was a bit embarrassed, a bit proud to reveal to me. But bus driving proved to be "hazardous for female health," and she quit. With her mother working in sales, she did not have the Soviet moral compunction about associating with commerce, and she got a college degree in purchase management. First, she took a job selling jackets and fur coats in a local market. Earnings were good, but the job was soul-killing with boredom—and therefore alcoholism. She "escaped just in time," because "so many people drank themselves to ruin in these marketplace jobs." She tried to open her own trade stall at the same market, but was cheated out of her business. Somewhere in between, her husband became addicted to drugs; she divorced him. A single mother, she sought refuge in the church and found, to her surprise and satisfaction, an application for her talents in managing the church bookstore, and the fulfillment of her first musical dream in playing the church pipe organ. Content with her place, she saw herself, however, as "no longer young" or "pretty" (at roughly thirty-five years old) or able to "start anything new." Recently remarried, she felt grateful to a man "who took her as wife," despite "having a kid in tow to burden him."

For those who graduated in a profession they had chosen, the pain of not working according to one's profession lingered almost two decades after. For Anastasia, a wife to a wealthy businessman (in terms of income and social background, she was an exception in my study), the pain became somatic: "doctors tell me that I got ill from not realizing myself." Becoming a professional in other fields, especially in sales management, did not seem to count for many of them. Sofiya described the collapse of her idealistic belief in a beautiful, respected middle-class professionalism:

You know how I always loved French. How I loved the language, how I read all the books at university, all these beautiful novels! I graduated with a "red diploma" [with a perfect GPA], of course. Then it was the time—only money started to matter, nothing else. The good jobs disappeared. I thought—I will wait, with my red diploma, I will sit at home a while . . . nothing happened, and I went to what I could find. I went to work on the shop floor, selling liquor. Got use out of my knowledge of languages—reading the labels on the bottles! [laughs bitterly]. But I was lucky [it could have been worse]. I worked as a "consultant" at this high-end liquor shop. My wages were 6,000 rubles when any ordinary shop girl got just 2,000. Three times more! So I am still at this company, kind of grown up [*vyrosla*] within it . . . Then I married a coworker. He started a business, of his own, a small dumpling-making line . . . but he got framed by his partners, you know, it was the times. They demanded that we hand over our apartment to them in payment, or else. We of course did not even think to resist, you know, *bratki* [mafia], you don't kid around with those people . . . we were left with several suitcases [of belongings] to our name, and a small kid on our hands. I still regret it did not work out . . . We might have been well off now. I wish we had something to do with the head office, some sort of brand management, it might have been interesting. . . . Do I know wines? Of course not, Anya. Knowing wines requires time and money to study, being able to travel a lot, worldwide, where these vines are growing. I never had such an opportunity. And anyways, I myself prefer *prostoĭ* [morally good, for its unpretentious simplicity] *vodochka* [endearing for vodka]!

Sofiya's life took shape in the context of major social transformations. Her marriage, motherhood, unsuccessful attempt to take part in the brutally accelerating economy of the 1990s, an encounter with the notoriously murderous mafia of that time, her father's death, her brother's alcoholism and banishment from the family and his early death, all left her, at roughly thirty-five years of age, with a feeling that so much happened. And yet, her life had not really progressed—a lack of progress that started with the collapse of her dream of self-realization in educated professionalism.

Conversely, perestroika teens often contemplated, in the same hesitant style, that maybe now was the time "to really start something." This dream often took the form of (re)turning to "real" professionalism, through either work or education. "I have a feeling I need to change everything, maybe go to school, to work as a teacher, according to my profession" (Tat'yana, university graduate in philology and pedagogy, distributor at a wholesale company). "I wish I could go and study something, maybe English . . . or psychology" (Elena). "I work at the factory, and I cannot pay for education now, with two kids and all . . . but I do not give up on the idea of getting a real education in economics . . . I don't give up, not yet!" (Roman).

Their subjectively perceived lack of professionalism was objectively confirmed for them by employers who interpreted their age and their employability along the lines of history and old/young value regimes. Employers may have been doubtful about them for many reasons: because their history of employment often looked haphazard; because their diplomas, if any, were obtained in the murky 1990s; because they were still "Soviet" in their minds. Such doubts, combined with the common ageism of hiring practices in Russia, contributed to feeling no longer young:

I don't know why, but employers always think people past thirty-five are useless. Like, their brain has rotted or something! And they still want 'experience'! How can someone be under thirty-five and yet very experienced? I don't even mention that because our children are mostly grown, we are more stable as a workforce, taking fewer sick leaves. I do not understand." (Mariya)

Several people in the study realized their dream of educated professionalism, but never achieved the independence and self-sufficiency that the rising middle class was supposed to enjoy. Evgeniĭ, for example, built an academic career; however, academic salaries are notoriously low in Russia. Furthermore, realizing how much he depended on the inertial institution of science in Russia, he had consciously—albeit bitterly—used adaptive strategies: "My whole life, I was very good at pretending to fit in this terrible system." At the time of my fieldwork, he saw himself as proactive: dreaming about emigrating abroad. Another almost middle-class person, Elena, who was once self-employed and one of the few people to have saved enough money from earnings to buy a small apartment, had never felt secure in her middle-classness because of the considerable precariousness of business in Russia:

I was—I still am!—considered a professional, one of the best professional tourism managers in the city. But I will never—never! invest in anything other than a computer. Because anything can happen. Because there are high seasons, and there are low seasons, and the [office] rent is to be paid all the time. And I don't want to work under other people, either, because those who have a business, who have money, are fickle and build their business around their personal lives. Like, the boss who made his lover a director and once they quarreled, the whole business collapsed.[13]

Pavel reached almost middle-classness only recently. First, he attempted to study at a university, but dropped out to join his brother who made "good money" doing manual work in Russia's newly privatized oil industry. After several years he quit his job in oil extraction to move back to Perm because his then wife insisted on "cultured" life in the city. After working a few years as an electrician, he quit because it earned him little money, and also divorced. He got a job at a market reselling automobile parts and, because his knowledge of mechanics was considerable, was good at it. His income at least doubled, but he "escaped just in time" because the work at the market, much as Oksana would have concurred, plus spending the day among mostly male coworkers, led to "crazy boredom" and to drink. Having once binged for seventy-two days straight, he left the market and returned to work as an electrician. Working hard and never passing up on an opportunity to learn on the job, he again progressed to good earnings. Completing a long-distance university course in 2013 allowed him a supervisory position, the status of officially working according to his profession, and the social and cultural capital associated with the middle class. Yet "now, I am tired of working, I only want a job where I can do nothing but supervise what other people do. And . . . I feel comfortable in my life. So comfortable, so adapted . . . It scares me! When, please do tell me, when did it happen that I lost . . . I don't know . . . my connection to the *cosmos* [universe; something larger or more significant]?"

To sum up, perestroika teens tried three different strategies to build professional and material foundations in life. First was an unambitious adaptation to the lower middle-class life of their parents, a choice that seemed to some of them more predictable and stable. Others attempted to reach a higher-class educated professionalism, a choice promising a more emotionally fulfilling and "authentic" life. The third choice was to venture opportunities in the fledgling market economy. The latter two strategies may seem to us, and appeared to some of them, to be more advantageous in the light of the social transformations of 1990s Russia. But real opportunities were scarce for perestroika teens, and the stories about all three strategies reflected disappointment.

Partial successes were hardly more satisfactory. Anastasia, the wife of a wealthy businessman, enjoyed money but had not reached idealistic professionalism, and she became depressed. Evgeniï enjoyed his academic pursuits but his position provided him no money and no freedom of initiative, and (as he saw it) he had no hope unless he moved out of the country. And if both money and educated professionalism in the career of choice were achieved after almost two decades of tribulations, as happened for Pavel, exhaustion put creativity or initiative out of question.

First Comes Love, Then Comes Marriage, Then Comes Another Marriage: Family as Necessity and Contingency

The replacement of Soviet morality and state determinism with post-Soviet anomie and neoliberal precariousness left the perestroika teens with the certainty of uncertainty, the feeling that anything can happen, but nothing really changes. In their work lives, even when their lives seem to have followed a path of improvement, they remember their decisions as contingent rather than consistent or coherent. The presupposition of spontaneous unplanned actions and fateful accidental meetings are even more alive in amorous relationships. Love is associated with youth; youth is associated with the spontaneous flow of desire; and spontaneous desire is the authentic basis for truly moral agency.[14] Marriage, by contrast, is a not-so-joyful necessity expected from an adult. Marriage has a disciplinary connotation, opposed to the emotional freedom and immediacy of desires and actions associated with being (young and) in love (see Patico 2009). Nevertheless, marriages are represented as accidental and unthinking, brought into existence by chance, but also by the forces of circumstance, boredom, custom, parental pressure, youthful inexperience, and the turbulence of the times. The same inadvertent forces ended marriages, too. Decisions about marriage were represented as taken but not really taken, in the sense of considering such decisions to lead to serious responsibility, have life-long consequences, or even to be parts of a technology of happiness:

I married at twenty-two. Well, if I knew it would be that bad, I would not have married at all. Every time I am drunk, my wife files for a divorce. And then takes her application back [chuckles]. [AK: So why did you?] Well, it was kind of time to do so. That age has come to marry. It also felt like it was time to try [something new]. (Batyr, security specialist and entrepreneur)

I was only nineteen and I did not want to marry, but I really, really wanted a child. So me and my boyfriend, we "worked" on having a kid. And I got pregnant, and both he and my mother were so surprised, silly people! But mother insisted that I marry him. She said, "The child needs a father," "people marry, live together, if you

don't like it, you can always divorce." So I married him. So stupid! This is how I
married at nineteen years of age, and I have not had any of the fun that I should
have had. (Tatiana)

The discourse of the precariousness and contingency of love and family
life was shared by different classes within the split generation. Anastasia remembered "madness" rather than decisions, and a spontaneity that was exter-
nalized instead of located in herself. Instead of growing up Soviet-style, "unre-
markably" as many remembered, she grew up "unthinkingly":

At university, I wrote a thesis, you know, on the history of Estonia. Graduated
with a "red diploma." We assumed that after graduation I would work in the city
administration [because of her parents' connections]. And then everything
collapsed . . . my parents divorced, I was so bewildered that my family, my *tyl*
[rear-guard and supply-lines, a military term] collapsed . . . I went mad, and I
married in that state, unthinking.

Evgeniĭ, in particular, presented himself as a rational actor ("I don't like
doing things Russian style, I usually plan my day in advance"). A man from an
intelligentsia background, he had purposefully delayed his marriage for professional reasons until the age of twenty-eight. And yet he also described his
marriage as poorly thought through. He married his long-term girlfriend
because: "I thought about marriage like some people think about drinking.
You know, you drink a glass and it feels good. You think: why not drink more?
If one feels so good, would not ten glasses be even better? I thought marriage
will be like more glasses, more happiness. And instead, it was like drinking
ten glasses, when you vomit and feel sick."

The majority of my respondents were divorced, or in their second or
third marriage. Few resolutely continued with their first marriage. The
vague transcendentalism of old Russian beliefs in *sud'ba* (fate, destiny, pre-
destination) came into play in marriage.[15] Sud'ba is accepting that something that seemed accidental or discontinuous really was not. Families, being a twist of fate, were often appreciated also precisely in terms of fate, as
being God-given (and -taken) gifts. The power of sud'ba is seen in the ves-
tiges of an ideology that conditioned people to accept that life/history/col-
lectivity (a portmanteau phenomenon) should be accepted as bigger than
any self-centered calculation:

The biggest *udacha* [fortune/luck] of my life is the birth of my children. I mean, I
was lucky . . . though [hesitantly] luck and fortune have a sense of some [superficial]
game . . . but in general, all my life, is a streak of luck. All that happened in my life,
all was for the better. If I wanted it, if I didn't want it, it happened how I wanted it/
needed it in the end. I was kicked out of university. If I were not, I would not have

met my [current] wife . . . I would have met another woman, of course . . . but who knows how it would have turned out with another woman? I would not have my children. Or they would be different, and I love them as they are! So I am who I am, that I was born that way, and it is big luck for me. (Roman)

After all, as we started this section, "anything can happen." Even good fortune.

Missing Out by Just a Few Years: Between "Communist Leaders" and "Naglyĭ Puppies"

The short span between 1991 and 1995 was the crucial period when various kinds of capital were fast accumulated. Perestroika teens were not old enough to take advantage of that time. Just a few years made the difference:

It is easier for those younger and those older—those already having experience, wiser, they knew what to grab and where to grab when grabbing started! All that mattered in our country, was grabbing, always been this way. And youngsters, they are free from that *sovdepovskiy mentalitet* [derisively, Soviet mentality]. From this *pioneriya* [derisively, Young Pioneer League] . . . from this *ravneniye* [saluting that symbolically represented alignment to collectivist ideals]—what we were taught when we were young. We became cynical. And this is what the Americans wanted. Our values are constantly shifting. And too many drank themselves to death. And perished in Chechnya. . . . We were too young . . . we were not Young Communist League [YCL] leaders. Who are the state *chinovniki* [state officials] nowadays? The former YCL leaders. They were just a bit older, and they are now chinovniki. (Roman)

One of my interlocutors, a human resources manager (herself born in 1977) who routinely did job interviews, claimed that she could instantly identify the representatives of the split generation precisely because they displayed tension between "diametrically opposed values" (*diametral'no protivopolozhnye tsennosti*). The snippets above—pronounced by Roman within an hour—showcase just that. One moment, Roman firmly believed that to survive, to be agentic—relevant to the larger social world of "business" and "success" (which, one could hesitantly assume, became the new society)—one needed to "grab," to be "a schemer," a "distributor," *torgash* or *delets* [derisively, entrepreneur], an assertive person in "a suit and tie." At another moment, he referred to the "Soviet ideals" that were lost through grief and cynicism (and "American influence"). Yet he sometimes referred to these values using derisive perestroika-speak: the "Soviet mentality," "that pioneriya."

The YCL leaders mentioned by Roman came of age in the 1970s and early 1980s, in times with no inspiring historical events, and with public life filled with ossified rituals. In his influential work on "the last Soviet generation,"

Alexei Yurchak (2006) focuses on the complex strategies of disengagement and irony employed by people born in the 1950s and 1960s. An "ironist" born in 1965 was a twenty-five-year-old "young specialist" in 1990, and well positioned to participate in business. But the reference to the YCL leaders has another dimension, beyond simply being old enough to benefit from the early 1990s opportunities. Pragmatic careerism was a worldview associated with membership in the YCL. Powerful and cynical opportunists, they knew how to act situatedly, grabbing when "all that mattered, was grabbing," playing the new system that they were creating through their own actions, when the conditions of grabbing had changed from "business" to state capitalism.

Noticeably, and also self-consciously, when members of the split generation talked about youth, they talked about people who were just a few years younger than themselves. These new youth, so close in age, seemed to them to be very different, and to be at an advantage. They had not spent the limited resources of their youthful energy:

Is there a difference between being twenty-nine and thirty-five? It is not just a difference, it is an abyss! In actuality, we are capable of accomplishing anything we want. But the desires, the motivations, they leave us . . . what comes, is the realization, do you really want to take this risk? Is it worth the danger? Your fate may have such a bad blow for you! And you know, good fortune always changes to bad. But in the end, anyway, fuck-all. So here I am . . . especially after my parents' death. It was a blow. I had more than I could handle. So in actuality, we are always capable of everything, but . . . we do not want to anymore. (Pavel)

Just six years of difference in age marked the transition from being young and having potential, to being old, fearful, and passively preparing for the worst. Perestroika teens wondered, self-consciously, how the character and the spirit of those just five to ten years younger can be so profoundly child-like, lighter and unworried, than their own. Marina said, "We got those packaged gifts for the New Year at work [corporate presents], the bags with candy and whatnot, and there were some Chupa Chups [lollipops] in them. I don't eat Chupa Chups. My colleague saw that and she was, like, drooling—can I have yours? It is really weird—she was just, like, five years younger. But I look at *them* often and think to myself—puppies [*shchenki*], jeez, but young pups!" Svetlana—a university graduate in engineering, sporadically employed, single—stated: "I quit my job; part of this was because I could not bear the *kollektiv* [collective, a working unit]. I mean, hardly anyone my age, young girls, well, how young, maybe twenty-seven . . . and they . . . they chatter loudly, in those high-pitched voices, all the time, my head was spinning!" Both remarks were half-derisive, half-envious. "Puppies" can be spontaneously transfixed by small joys, like candies; they still have energy to "chatter"; they were not "hit by fate." By contrast, experience and worry go hand in hand, and perestroika teens felt exceptionally experienced, if not professionally credentialed.

In the eyes of the people of my study, these nonhesitant, often cynical twenty-five-year-olds represented a problematic kind of pragmatism, a (post?) post-Soviet model of agency. They did not develop a "moral backbone" in their upbringing, and as a result, they were often naglyĭ/naglost'—aggressive, impudent, and self-entitled in unjustified ways. Batyr recalled, "She called me asking for a job. I asked—what can you do? She said—I *want* to be an administrator. I asked again—but what can you do? Those youngsters, this is how they behave—no experience, and she wants to be an administrator!"

What was the difference between Batyr's own entrepreneurial assertiveness, and the naglost' of his younger (not) to-be employee? Like all small-scale businessmen without high-placed connections who persevered through the 1990s, Batyr saw his success relying exclusively on his grit. If needed, he distributed in a suit and tie, and endured the boredom of working in sales. Filling fleeting business niches and adjusting to opportunities, going bankrupt several times, he carried out ever larger and more complex resale schemes, all the while being careful not to tread on bigger businesses' territory. He mostly owed money at the time of my fieldwork, but was on stable ground after realizing a couple of successful deals in 2012–14. He developed a fair share of cynicism himself, especially toward any help that may come his way from the state.[16] But, as Batyr noticed, nagliĭ puppies had no respect for any meritocratic rhetoric. They expected to be given a secure and idle position within the newly arisen systems.

The naglost' of puppies, ironically, may be the result of developments aimed to remedy a Soviet lack of creative initiative that was deemed unproductive in the market economy. A new thriving market in self-help and coaching embraced positive psychology and the development of *uverennost' v sebe* (self-assuredness; see Lerner 2011; Matza 2009) as primary targets to be developed among the post-Soviet populations. Svetlana mused self-consciously about her lack of self-assuredness, and she half-seriously, half-ironically called it naglost':

To work in this capacity, little is needed—just internet and naglost' . . . But, there is this eternal inferiority complex, that I do not have enough skills and knowledge . . . and I know that this is bullshit, that I have all that. Besides, anything can be learned on the job. So, maybe I simply do not really want it that much. I got a bit calmer these days . . . and I never had that desire for expensive things. But maybe it is because I undervalue myself . . . or I am simply a *raspizdyaika* [a crude slang for a lazy, unfocused person]!

So the twenty-five-year-olds, the children of perestroika and (perhaps) the first truly post-Soviet generation, had embraced self-assuredness as the sine qua non of social success. But they did not confuse the value of self-assuredness with creative initiative, or merit. The opportunities of the 1990s were slowing to a stop, and new ones increasingly depended on proximity to the state-economic neoliberal conglomerate. Gambling on bare naglost' ("she just wants to be an administrator!"), as "puppies" did, may have been a more effective strategy than trying to merit success.

Ironically, in their unquestioning compliance with the world, the naglyĭ puppies exemplify, to some extent, the Soviet ideals of (youthful) agency. And yet the satisfaction and the lack of worry that the split generation sees in the puppies may be an illusion, because the worry and the rhetoric of fleeting adulthood perpetuated itself down the generational line. The 1980s-born "children of perestroika" discussed how "weird" they felt that "yesterday's infants," the issue of the 1990s, suddenly "open their own companies, take mortgages, bear children."[17] Twenty-year-olds, born in the 1990s, made thirty-year-olds feel obsolete. Anyone over the age of eighteen feels the pressure. One of my interlocutor's daughters declared proudly on her eighteenth birthday that "I am no longer a *maloletka* (a child, also with an implication of being sexually underage), now I am *maksimal'no moloda* (maximally young)." She thus publicly acknowledged that the clock, the short race of opportunity between being too young and already old, had started for her.

Conclusion: Eighteen Going on Thirty-Five

If we are to believe, after Mannheim ([1925] 1952), that the uniqueness and the novelty of historical experience at the moment of one's youth are pivotal to the formation of a generational consciousness, then the tumultuous twentieth century in Russia gave rise to a rapid succession of generations. For perestroika teens, the very rapidity of change in social, economic, and especially moral order was the generational experience. I have outlined three forms of moral agency and of successful adulthood from which they had to choose in the times of their socialization. Viewed as incompatible, these models were the self-sufficient opportunism of commerce, the educated professionalism, or the patient work and accumulation of benefits within the leftover structures of welfare state.

Regardless of what they chose, they were not sure if the choice was right, and were increasingly not sure if there was a right choice altogether. The disappointment was deeper for the belief, coming from perestroika teens' childhood education, that personal progress and societal progress should be conjoined in order for self-direction to be "authentic," and they did not see progress in either field. Successes appeared to have come at too high a price, and there was a growing understanding that the 1990s reshuffling of Russian social hierarchy was not as deep or promising as it appeared. Perestroika teens were aware of the fourth model of agency, an automatic, idle rise through a state/corporate ladder. They dismissed this model as morally unacceptable, and ascribed it either to their generational predecessors, who aspired to be the YCL leaders; or to their successors, the naglyĭ puppies who aspire to be capitalistic state officials. Yet the new reality of the 2000s saw this latter strategy rising in prominence and promise, adding to the already bewildering social equation that dis/connected morality and agency, Soviet and post-Soviet orders, work and initiative, merit and social success.

Anna Kruglova is a Research Fellow at the National Research University Higher School of Economics, Moscow. Her research interests include anthropology of ethics and morality, risk and security studies, and the anthropology of the state.

NOTES

This paper is based on research conducted with generous support from the University of Toronto, the Social Sciences and Humanities Research Council of Canada, an Ontario Graduate Scholarship, and the Wenner-Gren Foundation for Anthropological Research. I also thank the Centre for Independent Social Research in Saint Petersburg for intellectual and logistical support, and the editors of this volume for the inspiration, comments, corrections, and other contributions. Michael Lambek, Ivan Kalmar, Bruce Grant, Donna Young, Mikhail Rozhanskiy, and Nikolay Ssorin-Chaikov made this chapter better through their thoughtful comments. My biggest debt is to my friends in the field, who made it all possible by agreeing to share their lives and their stories with me.

1. For example, Pilkington 1996 and 2005; Levada and Shanin 2005; Shanin 2005; Polukhina 2006; Yurchak 2006; Lovell 2007; Pedersen and Hojer 2008; Baiford 2009; Semenova 2009.

2. In some of the newest literature, those born between 1970 and 1985 are called "a disappointed generation" (Pastukhov 2015).

3. Changes in consumption reveal the influence of global imaginaries on what constitutes "normal." Postsocialist Romanians assumed that the luxurious bathrooms and kitchens shown in American commercials were "normal" in the "West," and felt compelled to find the means to follow the utopian representations in order to live "normally" (Fehérváry 2009). Among my informants, the normality of car ownership was similar.

4. Although parenthood has always been a stepping stone to adulthood, especially for women. Mandatory two-year military service, once a rite of passage for eighteen-year-old men, had been discredited in the 1980s and 1990s when media started covering the reality of Russian wars and especially the debilitating hazing practices in the army.

5. Applicable to men between the ages of twenty and fifty and women between twenty and forty-five, the so-called tax on childlessness was introduced in 1941, and existed with

modifications until it was annulled in 1992. The size of the tax should be viewed against an understanding that money did not play as significant a role in a socialist economy. Currently families with children are eligible for tax deductions, which may be seen as an equivalent of the childlessness tax.

6. This is a particular problem of "theorizing" post-Soviet space. Often, the ideas that anthropologists would count as social-theoretical are central to local discourses, although contextualised in a very different way. It is not surprising considering the rootedness of Soviet ideology in the nineteenth-century political economy and sociology, and Marxian ideas in particular (see Kruglova forthcoming).

7. All names are pseudonyms. Some personal details have been altered to ensure anonymity.

8. The latter remark came from a childless person; many of my interlocutors were parents to those kids referred to in the quote.

9. Although some research suggests that comparing the security of life in the USSR and the precariousness of postsocialist life is among the top three narratives of "nostalgia for the Soviet" for all age groups (Polukhina 2006).

10. Pensioners were most affected by a 2005 scandalous reform when multiple in-kind social welfare programs were replaced by insufficient and erratically paid cash payments.

11. In 2010 the average age of death for a man was sixty-three, but strong public focus on demographic woes made speculating about the life-span a mythology in its own right. Lower figures may have been reported in the media, and people were often unaware of the importance of adjusting longevity rates for the year of birth.

12. Early retirement was/is usually a privilege of the military—male—professions. These stories have a significant gender component.

13. Always precarious, the tourism industry was the first to collapse in the 2014 economic crisis.

14. I use the word "desire" in a broader psychoanalytical sense that covers all drive or motivation.

15. For an overview of the concept, see Baiburin 2015.

16. See Anoshkin (2012) on the expectations of small-scale businessmen in Perm.

17. A discussion started on August 25, 2013, at http://www.yaplakal.com/forum6/topic637382.html that collected about 49,000 views and eighteen pages of comments.

REFERENCES

Anoshkin, Artem. 2012. "O chom molchit 'srednii klass'" [What the "middle class" does not speak about]. *Otechestvennye Zapiski* 1(46). http://www.strana-oz.ru/2012/1/o-chem-molchit-sredniy-klass.

Baiburin, Albert. 2015. "Kategoriya sud'by: Proshloe i nastoyashchee" [A category of "fate": The past and the present]. Lecture delivered at the European University in Saint Petersburg. http://albertbaiburin.ru/cntnt/lekcii/kurs_lekcii/lekciya_5_.html.

Baiford, Andy. 2009. "'Poslednee sovetskoe pokolenie' v Velikobritanii" ["The last Soviet generation" in Great Britain]. *Neprikosnovennii Zapas* 2 (64): 96–116.

Chernova, Janna, and Larisa Shpakovskaya. 2010. "Molodye vzroslye: Supruzhestvo, partnerstvo i roditel'stvo. Diskursivnye predpisaniya i praktiki v sovremennoi Rossii" [Young adults: Marriage, partnership and parenthood. Discursive norms and practices in contemporary Russia]. *Laboratorium* 3: 19–43.

Cole, Jennifer, and Deborah Durham. 2007. "Age, Regeneration, and the Intimate Politics of Globalization." In *Generations and Globalization: Youth, Age, and Family in the New World Economy,* edited by Jennifer Cole and Deborah Durham, 1–28. Bloomington: Indiana University Press.

Fehérváry, Krizstina. 2009. "Goods and States: The Political Logic of State-Socialist Material Culture." *Comparative Studies of Society and History* 51(2): 426–59.

Hann, Chris. 2011. "Moral Dispossession." *InterDisciplines: Journal of History and Sociology* 2(2): 11–38.

Kelly, Catriona. 2007. *Children's World: Growing Up in Russia, 1890–1991.* New Haven: Yale University Press.

Kruglova, Anna. 2016. "'Anything Can Happen': Everyday Morality and Social Theory in Russia." PhD diss., University of Toronto.

———. Forthcoming. "Social Theory and Everyday Marxists: Russian Perspectives on Epistemology and Ethics." *Comparative Studies in Society and History.*

Lerner, Julia. 2011. "TV Therapy without Psychology: Adapting the Self in Post-Soviet Media." *Laboratorium* 3(1): 178–80.

Levada, Yuri, and Teodor Shanin, eds. 2005. *Ottzy i deti: Pokolencheskiĭ analiz sovremennoĭ Rossii* [Fathers and children: Generational analysis of contemporary Russia]. Moscow: Novoe Literaturnoe Obozrenie.

Lovell, Stephen, ed. 2007. *Generations in Twentieth-Century Europe.* New York: Palgrave Macmillan.

Mannheim, Karl. [1925] 1952. "The Sociological Problem of Generations." In *Essays on the Sociology of Knowledge,* 276–322. New York: Routledge.

Matza, Tomas. 2009. "Moscow's Echo: Technologies of the Self, Publics and Politics on the Russian Talk Show." *Cultural Anthropology* 24(3): 489–522.

Mead, Margaret. 1928. *Coming of Age in Samoa: A Psychological Study of Primitive Youth for Western Civilization.* New York: W. Morrow and Company.

Oushakine, Sergei. 2008. "My v gorod izumrudniĭ idem dorogoĭ trudnoĭ: Malen'kie radosti vesolykh chelovechkov" [We walk a difficult path to the Emerald City: Small joys of merry little people]. In *Vesolye chelovechki: Kul'turnye geroi Sovetsk-ogo detstva* [Merry little people: Popular culture characters of Soviet childhood] edited by Ilya Kukulin, Mark Lipovetsky, and Mariya Mayofis, 9–60. Moscow: Novoe Literaturnoe Obozrenie.

Pastukhov, Vladimir. 2015. "Teoriya o pokoleniyakh v Rossii: Ot frontovikov—k 'pokoleniyu bez buduschego' i dal'she" [Theory of generations in Russia: From "frontoviks"—to "the futureless generation" and beyond]. *Novaya Gazeta,* July 18. http://www.novayagazeta.ru/comments/69250.html.

Patico, Jennifer. 2009. "For Love, Money, or Normalcy: Meanings of Strategy and Sentiment in the Russian-American Matchmaking Industry." *Ethnos* 74(3): 307–30.

Pedersen, Morten Axel, and Lars Hojer. 2008. "Lost in Transition: Fuzzy Property and Leaky Selves in Ulaanbaatar." *Ethnos* 73(1): 73–96.

Pilkington, Hilary, ed. 1996. *Gender, Generation and Identity in Contemporary Russia.* New York: Routledge.

———. 2005. " Chem bol'she eto obsuzhdaetsya, tem bol'she k étomu vlechet': Raz-myshleniya o diskursivnom porozhdenii pokolencheskogo opyta" [The more it is discussed, the more attractive it is: Some thoughts about the discursive production of generational experience]. *Forum for the Anthropology and Culture* 5: 379–407.

Polukhina, Anna. 2006. "Delat' kar'eru v postsovetskoi Rossii: Iz lichnogo opyta" [To build a career in post-Soviet Russia: From personal experience]. *Vestnik Evrazii* 3: 132–162.

Ries, Nancy. 1997. *Russian Talk: Culture and Conversation during Perestroika*. Ithaca: Cornell University Press.

Rivkin-Fish, Michele. 2005. *Women's Health in Post-Soviet Russia: The Politics of Intervention*. Bloomington: Indiana University Press.

Rozhanskiy, Mikhail. 2010. "Raznomyslie v dobrovol'noi nesvobode. Raznomyslie v SSSR i Rossii (1945–2008)" [Differences of opinion in voluntary unfreedom. Raznomyslie in the USSR and in Russia], in Proceeding of the conference "Raznomyslie v SSSR i Rossii," Saint Petersburg, May 15–16, 2009, edited by Boris Firsov. Saint Petersburg: European University Press.

Semenova, Mariya. 2009. "Pokolenie X, pokolenie perestroiki ili 'poteryannoe pokolenie.'" [The generation X, the perestroika generation, or the "lost generation"]. *Smena,* October.

Shanin, Teodor. 2005. "Istoriya pokolenii i pokolencheskaya istoriya Rossii" [The history of generations and the generational history of Russia]. Polit.ru, March 17. http://polit.ru/article/2005/08/09/shanin/.

Shevchenko, Olga. 2009. *Crisis and the Everyday in Post-Socialist Moscow*. Bloomington: Indiana University Press.

Smol'kin, Anton. 2010. "Bednost' i sotsial'nii status pozhilykh lyudei v sovremennoi Rossii" [Poverty and social status of older people in Russia today]. *Monitoring Obshchestvennogo Mneniya* 3(97): 186–99.

Yurchak, Alexei. 2006. *Everything Was Forever Until It Was No More: The Last Soviet Generation*. Princeton: Princeton University Press.

INDEX

DEBORAH DURHAM is Professor of Anthropology at Sweet Briar College. She is coeditor, with Jennifer Cole, of *Generations and Globalization: Youth, Age, and Family in the New World Economy* and *Figuring the Future: Globalization and the Temporalities of Children and Youth.*

JACQUELINE SOLWAY is Professor Emeritus of the International Development Studies and Anthropology Departments of Trent University of Canada. She is editor of *The Politics of Egalitarianism: Anthropological Theory and Practice.*

www.ingramcontent.com/pod-product-compliance
Lightning Source LLC
Chambersburg PA
CBHW030329270326
41926CB00010B/1557